List of figures

1   Charter school timetable for summer months,
    1 March–1 October 1809.   12

2   Daily timetable, St Joseph's Reformatory School,
    Ballinasloe, 1878.   23

3   Daily timetable, Lancasterian Industrial National
    School for Females, Belfast, 1852.   27

4   Alternative scheme for girls of sixth class, 1889.   58

List of tables

1   Parental information on imprisoned juveniles, 1851   22

2   Expansion of the industrial schools' system, 1880–1900   28

3   Number of males and females attending National
    Schools in 1868   39

FEMALE EDUCATION IN IRELAND
1700–1900

FEMALE EDUCATION IN IRELAND
1700–1900

Minerva or Madonna

DEIRDRE RAFTERY

AND

SUSAN M. PARKES

IRISH ACADEMIC PRESS
DUBLIN • PORTLAND, OR

First published in 2007 by
IRISH ACADEMIC PRESS
44, Northumberland Road, Dublin 4, Ireland

and in the United States of America by
IRISH ACADEMIC PRESS
c/o ISBS, Suite 300, 920 NE 58th Avenue
Portland, Oregon 97213–3786

WEBSITE: www.iap.ie

British Library Cataloguing in Publication Data
A catalogue entry is available on request

ISBN 978 0 7165 2650 6 (cloth)
ISBN 978 0 7165 2777 0 (paper)

Library of Congress Cataloging-in-Publication Data
A entry can be found on request

Typeset by Carrigboy Typesetting Services, County Cork.
Printed in Great Britain by Antony Rowe Ltd., Chippenham, Wiltshire.

Me tutore tutus eris.

For

Catherine KilBride
Scoil Íosa, Malahide, 1972–83
&
Beatrice L. White
Alexandra School, 1929–70

Contents

List of illustrations   viii

List of figures   ix

List of tables   x

List of abbreviations   xi

Foreword   xiii

Acknowledgements   xvii

Introduction   1

1   Industry, Piety and Servitude: Schooling
for the Female Poor, 1700–1900   5

2   The Education of Girls Within the National System   33

3   Intermediate Education for Girls   69

4   Women and Higher Education in Ireland   105

Appendix   145

Bibliography   163

Index   177

List of illustrations

1   Linen production by girls at the Mercy Convent, Queenstown, County Cork, 1900. Courtesy of The National Library of Ireland.

2   A National School classroom, Clash, County Limerick, c.1910. Source: Folklore Department, University College Dublin.

3   National School girls, Roscommon, c.1890. Source: D. Raftery, Irish Education Visual History Collection, UCD.

4   Directions for measurement, in the *Manual for Needlework*, CNEI, 1869. Source: D. Raftery, Personal Collection.

5   Directions for making wrist-bands and collars, in the *Manual for Needlework*, CNEI, 1869. Source: D. Raftery, Personal Collection.

6   Inspector's Report on Grange National School, County Wicklow, commenting on the teaching of needlework to girls. Source: Mary Munro, Personal Papers, Dublin.

7   Gymnastics lesson at the Ursuline Convent, Waterford, 1908. Courtesy of The National Library of Ireland.

8   The Nine Graces: the first women graduates of the Royal University of Ireland, 1884. Source: Susan M. Parkes, Personal Collection, Dublin.

List of abbreviations

ALS	Autograph letter signed
CNEI	Commissioners of National Education in Ireland
IBVM	Institute of the Blessed Virgin Mary (Loreto Order)
IRIS	Inspectors of the Industrial and Reformatory Schools
KPS	Kildare Place Society
MS	Manuscript
n.d.	No date
n.n.	No name
n.p.	No publisher
SJ	Society of Jesus (Jesuit Order)
SPCK	Society for Promoting Christian Knowledge

Foreword

Until the late twentieth century, histories of Irish education made little specific reference to the education of women. They tended to be written from the perspective of the policy-makers of their eras, and the primary sources used were more often official documents than personal or local records. However some schools and colleges, including girls' schools, ensured that the history of their institutions was committed to print, and such histories provide an invaluable insight into the education of women at various periods of the eighteenth, nineteenth and twentieth centuries in Ireland. One of the more significant such histories is *Gladly Learn and Gladly Teach: a History of Alexandra School and College*, co-authored in 1983 by Anne O'Connor and Susan M. Parkes. Parkes' more recently published history of women in Trinity College – *A Danger to the Men? (2004)* has also made an invaluable contribution to our understanding of the issues surrounding the inclusion of women in education in Ireland in the late nineteenth and early twentieth centuries. This new book, co-authored by Deirdre Raftery and Susan M. Parkes, provides a very welcome addition to the growing list of publications which address issues relating to women's education in Ireland.

While the book does not purport to be a comprehensive history of women's education, it covers a wide range of topics spanning the period from 1700 to 1900. It includes chapters on the schooling of the female poor; the education of girls within the National School system; girls and Intermediate Education and Irish women and higher education. Deirdre Raftery's work on the schooling of the female poor in the eighteenth and nineteenth centuries expands the reader's understanding of the social and economic history of Ireland during that period. It includes a discussion of the Dublin Foundling Hospital and workhouse schools; charter schools; hedge and pay schools; orphanages for girls, reformatories and industrial schools. It is sobering to be reminded of the bleak circumstances in which the education of these poor girls occurred. As a consequence of hard labour and poor diet in the charter schools, the girls had 'a very mean and pauper-like appearance'. They were also susceptible to infectious diseases, such as ophthalmia, that spread through insanitary institutions at that time, and many died from measles and tuberculosis.

The role of religious women is referred to in various chapters of the book. Following the repeal of the penal laws at the end of the eighteenth century, religious orders and congregations established primary and secondary schools throughout Ireland and their role in providing education for girls throughout the country should not be underestimated. Congregations such as the Presentation Sisters, the Mercy Sisters and the Irish Sisters of Charity played an important role in providing primary education for the poor girls of Ireland through the National School system, and religious orders such as the Ursulines, Dominicans, and the Loreto order complemented these congregations in providing intermediate education for girls from the second half of the nineteenth century onwards. As Susan M. Parkes shows, these latter religious orders were also pioneers in the provision of higher education for women and their pro-active role in preparing women for the examinations of the Royal University at the end of the nineteenth century paved the way for university access for women.

Ending as it does at the beginning of the twentieth century, when a major victory in relation to university education for women in Ireland had been achieved, this book might lead an uninformed reader to assume that the battle for equality for women in education in Ireland was over and that there would be no looking back. Alas, this was not the case, and the story of women's education in Ireland in twentieth century Ireland, especially in the Irish Free State after 1921, is a depressing one. The recognition in Article 41 (2) of Bunreacht na hEireann in 1937 that 'the life of the woman was within the home' and that 'mothers should not be obliged by economic necessity to engage in labour to the neglect of their duties in the home' contributed to the imposition of a ban on married women in the public service. Many parents felt that if their daughters were not to be permitted to remain in the workforce after marriage, there was no point in educating them at secondary or university level, and the proportion of women attending universities showed little increase in Ireland until the 1970s when the marriage ban was removed after Ireland joined the EEC. However, in the same way as Irish women in the late nineteenth century proved that they could succeed in higher education, women in recent years have proven that they can compete more than successfully with their male counterparts. Today over 60 per cent of students in Irish universities are women and a significant majority of students on highly competitive courses such as Medicine, Dentistry and Law are women. In spite of this, the unequal place of women is still reflected in the proportion of women holding senior positions in Irish universities – only about 10 per cent of Professorships are currently held by women and no woman has ever been President or Provost of an Irish university.

Inevitably, given the limitations of any one book, there are aspects of women's education which are only touched on here. The vocational and technical education of women gets little attention as does the professional training of women for a profession in which they have always dominated, i.e. primary teaching. The education and conditioning of women in teacher training colleges in the nineteenth and twentieth centuries made an important contribution to ensuring that women and girls accepted their subservient position in Irish society and this aspect of women's education is worthy of further research.

For readers who wish to carry out further research on the history of women's education in Ireland during the period in question, the bibliography in this book is an invaluable source. It provides references to primary archival sources such as papers in the Dominican Archives, Dublin; the Ursuline Convent Archives, Cork; and Victoria College Archives, Belfast. There is a significant list of relevant articles, reports and books which would provide an excellent starting point for extending the research which led to the publication of this book.

This book is a very important addition to women's studies' literature and will appeal to a wide audience including historians, educationists, and all those who are interested in understanding the origins of our current social and gender structures. The authors are to be commended on producing a fascinating and readable book.

Professor Aine Hyland
Vice-President
University College, Cork

Acknowledgements

The cooperation of a number of archives and libraries is gratefully acknowledged: Alexandra College Archives; Dominican Convent Archives, Cabra; the Dominican Convent Generalate Archives; the Dublin Diocesan Archives; the National Library of Ireland; the Ursuline Convent Archives; Trinity College Dublin Library and Archives, and University College Dublin Library. Special thanks to Mary Munro, who provided material from her personal collection.

It is with gratitude that Dr Deirdre Raftery acknowledges the Mistress and Fellows of Girton College, Cambridge, at whose invitation she became Research Associate in 2005. Chapter 1 of this book was written whilst at Girton College, Cambridge.

Our deepest gratitude to Catherine KilBride for the care with which she read drafts of each chapter, and for giving generously of her expertise during the preparation of the final manuscript.

Finally, our sincere thanks to: Dr Judith Harford for contributing to this book; Professor Sheelagh Drudy (University College, Dublin) and Dr Maryann Valiulis (Trinity College, Dublin) for their ongoing interest and encouragement; our students in the history of education, whose enthusiasm for our subject makes both teaching and research a pleasure; and our friends and families, who are constant sources of support and affection.

This book was supported by a University College, Dublin Research Publication Grant.

Introduction

DEIRDRE RAFTERY

The distinguished historian Maria Luddy (1992) drew attention to the fact that there were many areas of Irish women's lives that demanded research and analysis by historians. Female education in nineteenth-century Ireland was one such area, and at that time one of the few published works that included an analysis of educational change for women and girls was Mary Cullen's volume *Girls Don't Do Honours: Irish Women in Education in the 19th and 20th Centuries.*[1] Cullen's book contained two chapters that supported an argument that there had been a distinct 'female education movement' in Ireland, which gained impetus in the second half of the nineteenth century and which was influenced by a similar movement taking place in England at that time. Anne V. O'Connor's chapter, titled 'The revolution in girls' secondary education, 1860–1910', argued that 'by the beginning of the twentieth century, *the* fundamental revolution had already taken place in the education of girls in Ireland'.[2] O'Connor argued that this revolution took the form of radical change in the provision, content and assessment of female education. The passing of the Intermediate Education (Ireland) Act, 1878, had a direct impact on female education, as girls were thereafter able to compete in public examinations. Such examinations enabled women to obtain well-paid jobs and, in some cases, to continue on to university education. O'Connor recognised that this was very much a middle-class movement, and that the benefits of change accrued to the daughters of wealthy merchants, prosperous farmers and professional men. O'Connor drew attention to the network of Protestant women in Dublin and Belfast who energised this movement, and also noted the particular role that Catholic religious orders played. In noting the involvement of Catholic religious orders, including the Dominican, Loreto and Ursuline Sisters, Anne O'Connor signalled areas for further research. The argument that Catholic religious orders brought a different dimension to the debate about 'appropriate' education for Irish women was developed by Breathnach (1987), Peckham Magray (1998) and Raftery (1995; 2004).

The second chapter in Cullen's book that was to provoke interest was that of Eibhlín Breathnach. Titled 'Charting new waters: women's experience in higher education, 1879–1908', Breathnach's chapter illustrated how the passing of the Intermediate Education (Ireland) Act, 1878, had a direct influence on the growth in the demand for higher education for women. When, in 1879, legislation was passed which allowed women and men to compete for the degrees of the newly formed Royal University of Ireland, new opportunites were opened to women. While this did not bring about immediate change in the working lives of women, it ensured that women's higher education was not relegated to second-rate status.

While both O'Connor and Breathneach have acknowledged the middle-class character of the female education 'movement', scholarship has widened to embrace other areas in the history of female education. In some cases, female education has been located within studies of education change, such as Barnes's study of industrial schools (1987), while the work of Clear on nuns in nineteenth-century Ireland (1987), Luddy (1995) on philanthropy and Walsh (2005) on Anglican women in Dublin has pointed to other developments in female education.

It is the object of this book to bring together some of the findings of such scholarship, and to add additional material that provides the reader with some understanding of how girls and women 'experienced' education. Chapter 1 looks at an area that has received little attention: the education provided to girls via charitable institutions and voluntary societies. It also attempts to establish that both girls and women were involved in the hedge schools of Ireland. Chapter 2 examines female education within the 'official' National School System, which was established in 1831. The gendered nature of the curriculum is explored, and the schoolbooks used by girls are examined. The particular experience of girls in workhouse national schools and convent national schools is also scrutinised. Chapter 3 develops a study of the impact of intermediate education on girls, and looks at the involvement of different schools and activists. Chapter 4 gives an overview of the higher education movement, developing a discussion of key moments in the 'revolution' identified by O'Connor (1987), and assessing the contribution of individual Protestant laywomen and Catholic Sisters to changes in education and in the contemporary ideology of femininity.

The book has been written to introduce readers to this field of research, and to indicate some of the areas in which much work remains to be done. It has not been possible to include every type of education, and every agency involved in providing schooling. For example, while work on the role of the governess has been done elsewhere (Raftery, 1997), home education and the education provided by governesses has not been examined here, as these were forms of education that left few records and they were experienced by a minority of pupils. Neither has it been possible to include women's involvement in manual and technical instruction, or their education in nursing, although the latter area has recently been the subject of two substantial studies by Fealy (2005, 2006). However, in bringing together a variety of material relating to other aspects of female education, it is hoped that this book will make some contribution towards developing the reader's interest in one of the most significant aspects of Irish social history: the education of Irish girls and women.

NOTES

1 Mary Cullen (ed.), *Girls Don't Do Honours: Irish Women in Education in the 19th and 20th Centuries* (Dublin: WEB, 1987).
2 Anne V. O'Connor, 'The revolution in girls' secondary education, 1860–1910', in Cullen (ed.), *Girls Don't Do Honours*.

Chapter 1
Industry, Piety and Servitude: Schooling for the Female Poor, 1700–1900

DEIRDRE RAFTERY

BACKGROUND

Primary education in Ireland in the early nineteenth century was characterised by the involvement of a variety of voluntary educational societies, charitable institutions and individuals. As a consequence, the interests of such societies and individuals, and particularly their missionary zeal, played a significant role in defining the aims and the educational content of the schooling of the poor. While official support of education was administered through some of these voluntary societies, it was not until the National Board was established in 1831 that the government discontinued the practice of supporting education through voluntary agencies. Research has examined some of these agents of education.[1] But little focus has been placed on the schooling of girl pupils, and this has resulted in creating the impression that Irish girls did not participate significantly in education before the second half of the nineteenth century. This chapter looks at educational provision for pauper girls within some voluntary and official systems, and attempts to develop an understanding of their experiences.

The involvement of so many societies and individuals in education, prior to the establishment of the National Board in 1831, resulted in a confusion of types of school, sources of funds and ideological influences. This is evident from even a cursory examination of the Reports of the Commissioners of Irish Education Inquiry (1825, 1826–27).[2] Schooling was supported by Protestant organisations such as the Association for Discountenancing Vice, the London Hibernian Society, the Baptist Society, the Kildare Place Society, and the London Irish Society. In addition, schools were established by the Incorporated Society for Promoting English Protestant Schools in Ireland (better known as the Charter School Society). There were also hedge schools (or pay schools) run by Roman Catholic schoolmasters and mistresses, Erasmus Smith schools, Royal schools, Diocesan Free schools, Parish schools, landlord schools, orphanages, and Catholic schools regulated by religious orders. The Religious Society of Friends (Quakers) ran schools, as did a significant number of individuals. Some of these individuals were teachers, while others were wealthy persons who sponsored schools.

Within the 'formal' National system of education established in 1831, there were also different types of schools providing education and training for girls. The more commonplace day-schools run by the National Board are examined in Chapter 2. But in this chapter schools supported by the Board that were established specifically for vagrant and mendicant girls are included. The aim, therefore, is to provide in one chapter an overview of the many types of schooling catering for the female poor. It is not possible to do this in a rigidly chronological sequence, as the 'lifespan' of different systems overlapped. This chapter, therefore, is ordered by theme and not by an analysis of developments and change over time.

THE DUBLIN FOUNDLING HOSPITAL AND THE WORKHOUSE SCHOOLS

The establishment of the Dublin Workhouse at James's Gate, in 1704, had marked the first provision by the government for the poor of Ireland. In providing for unwanted children, it was at that time 'the only important government provision for any category of charity child'.[3] It was not until the passing of the Irish Poor Relief Act of 1838 that workhouses became the main official sources of care for charity children. Conditions were harsh, particularly during the famine years of 1845–49, and children often experienced callous indifference. Indeed Robins (1980) suggests that the Dublin Workhouse was established to relieve prosperous citizens of the nuisance of beggar children, rather than to provide charity. It was not until the end of the nineteenth century that such institutions showed sustained concern for the welfare of children. The governors of the Dublin Workhouse had the power to take in children between the ages of five and sixteen, who were without support. Typically, these were abandoned children and orphans. They were retained until the age of sixteen, and then apprenticed out to Protestant housekeepers and tradesmen. Governors were also empowered to seize destitute children from the streets, retaining them at the Workhouse until they could be apprenticed out.

From 1727, the law obliged all Dublin parishes to appoint overseers who would arrange the care of destitute children under the age of six. The overseers were to pay nurses to care for the children and to inspect the situation four times each year. After the age of six, the children would then be admitted to the Workhouse, where they would be taught to read and write, and to learn the principles of the Protestant religion. By 1730 it was found that the system was not working. Foundlings were 'lifted' from parish to parish by night, in an attempt to transfer the financial burden. Others died in the care of nurses who were overburdened with their work. Legislation enacted in 1730 stipulated that all foundling children, no matter the age, should be sent to the Workhouse. The Dublin Workhouse at that time became the Foundling Hospital and Workhouse. It adopted a device common to foundling hospitals: a revolving basket placed on the gate into which unwanted children could be placed. When a bell was rung the porter would revolve the basket and take the infant inside. Foundlings under the age of two were put out to nurse with rural women who were paid a wage of two pounds per annum, and 3s 4d for the expenses of the child. The children were branded on the flesh of one arm, in an attempt at easy identification. The fate of the children varied. Nurses, for example, murdered some children once they had received their payments.[4] Those who remained in the Workhouse, or who were returned to it later, lived in appalling circumstances. And mortality rates were high. For example, by 1759, of the 7,382 children who had been admitted since 1750, only 837 were still alive. The situation was equally grim in 1771, when reports submitted to parliament calculated that, of the 14,311 children admitted between 1756 and 1771, at least 10,000 had died in care.

By the start of the nineteenth century it was recognised that the management of the Foundling Hospital and Workhouse needed to be overhauled. The number of annual admissions was reduced in an attempt to improve conditions within the hospital. Incentives such as tax relief were introduced to encourage respectable Protestant families to take older educated children as apprentices. But the fate of destitute children did not improve significantly. Indeed, limiting the rate of admissions may have resulted in an increase in infanticide generally, while within the hospital children died in alarming numbers. Of the 52,000 infants received into the hospital between 1796 and 1826, 32,000 died, and some 9,600 who could not be accounted for were presumed dead.[5]

The education of girls at the Dublin Foundling Hospital was limited. Its function was to equip them with the means to support themselves, and to instruct them thoroughly in the Protestant religion. The practice of sending foundlings out 'to nurse' caused complications, however, as children who were sent to Catholic nurses were usually instructed in the Catholic religion, and some were informally adopted into Catholic families. Regulations from the start of the nineteenth century stipulated that all children who had been sent out 'to nurse' should be brought back to the hospital at seven years of age, at which time they would undergo three years of basic education and religious instruction. Girls under the new system were trained in laundry work and spinning, and followed a strict daily routine that included a strong emphasis on their religious education. From April to September they rose at 5 a.m. School began at 6 a.m., after prayers. Breakfast was not given out until after an 8 o'clock service, and after breakfast they read the Collect for the following Sunday. Spelling lessons followed, and then there was a lesson from Mrs Trimmer's *Abridgement of the New Testament*. Much of the day was then spent in manual instruction, and this was punctuated with prayers and brief spelling lessons.[6] The enquiry conducted by the Commissioners of Irish Education in 1824 and 1825 highlighted the grim conditions of the hospital. By 1830 it was recognised that the institution should be closed, and from April 1831 no further admissions were made. The remaining children were sent out to nurse, boarded out in the country, or apprenticed out, and some were moved to a building in Cork Street. In 1839 the buildings were converted into a workhouse for the South Dublin Union, marking the end of the Dublin Foundling Hospital and the start of a new system of poor relief established by the Irish Poor Relief Act of 1838.

Under the Irish Poor Relief Act of 1838, the country was divided into 130 unions, each with a workhouse for the confinement of paupers. Administered by a board of guardians, workhouses were penal in character and offered the most basic relief in order not to encourage abuse of a system that relied for support on a local rate. No special provision for children was made at the workhouses, despite the huge dependency of children on the workhouses, especially following the ravages of the famine years. While the law required that each workhouse should keep a school, the Poor Law Commissioners did not examine the proficiency of the teachers, nor did they ensure that adequate furniture and equipment were available at workhouse schools. They did not inspect the schools, nor did they supervise the moral and literary instruction provided.

As a consequence of the failure of the Poor Law Commissioners to oversee education at workhouse schools, the conditions and educational standards at these schools were very poor, and records of school attendance were rarely kept.

Females within the workhouses were classified into three categories: children (those under two years), girls between two years and fifteen years of age, and females above fifteen years. The majority were orphaned, although in some instances parents illegally placed their children in the care of workhouses in order to seek work, or even emigrate. In addition to orphaned and deserted children, workhouses also gave shelter to two other categories of child: illegitimate children (and their mothers) and foundlings. Within these categories were to be found numbers of children classed in official reports as 'blind, deaf and dumb, idiots &c'. Children with epilepsy were categorised with 'idiotic' children. The findings of the Powis Commission (1870) indicated that the numbers of girls at workhouses within these categories were: blind (68), deaf and dumb (78), 'idiotic, epileptic or otherwise afflicted' (68). The diet of workhouse children consisted largely of bread, potatoes, oatmeal and milk, although some workhouses economised by substituting molasses for milk, thereby depriving inmates of essential nutrition. Their diet was again compromised during the years of the Great Famine, when potato blight wiped out the crop on which the majority of the population were dependent in 1845, 1846 and 1848. During these years, workhouses experienced an overwhelming increase in the number of inmates, and by September 1849 there were 255,021 workhouse children (under fifteen years of age).[7] Conditions in the workhouses, especially during the Famine years, were grim. Many of the workhouses went bankrupt and were forced to turn starving children away from their doors. Within the workhouses, hundreds of children died every month. Overcrowding was an acute problem, as existing workhouse accommodation proved inadequate for the increased destitution: 'the pupils were overcrowded . . . the furniture was insufficient and unsuitable, and as the Teachers were in most cases also charged with the general Master or Matronship of the establishment, the school business was neglected, and deemed altogether a secondary duty'.[8] Outside the workhouses, schooling for the female poor was *ad hoc* in the eighteenth and early nineteenth centuries. As shall be seen, even where female education was provided by charitable societies, the emphasis was placed on 'education in female labour' – sewing, spinning, lacemaking, and domestic work.

THE CHARTER SCHOOLS

Against this backdrop of illegal education, and in a climate of Protestant distrust of Catholic influences, it is perhaps not surprising that an 'official' Protestant system of education was proposed. Church pamphlets and letters of the period indicate the increasing concern with the influence of the hedge schools and with the ubiquity of the Catholic Church. In 1723 Edward Synge, Archbishop of Tuam, published a pamphlet titled 'An account of the laws now in force in the Kingdom of Ireland, for encouraging the residence of the parochial clergy, and erecting English schools', in which he recommended that Protestants should 'show . . . love, tenderness, and compassion . . . towards the person even of those whose principles we cannot but detest and abhor'.[9] Further, he advised that his Church should 'endeavour by Christian ways and means to reclaim the papists of this Kingdom from that gross ignorance and error wherein they are all involved and bring them over both to understand and embrace the true religion in its purity'.[10] In 1729, a letter from Bishop Maule stressed the difficulties to be overcome if the number of papists was not to increase.[11] Bishop Tennison of Ossory, reporting on visits around the country in 1731 and 1732, commented with regret on the 'high incidence of mass houses, and a patchy system of English schools'.[12] The situation prompted Hugh Boulter, Archbishop of Armagh and Primate of all Ireland, to propose a system of schools that would counter the effects of Catholic education at the hedge schools, and on 6 February 1733 the Incorporated Society for Promoting English Protestant Schools in Ireland was established. Its schools were known as Charter Schools, and the Society's charter clearly indicated that it aimed to instruct 'children of Roman Catholics and other poor natives of Ireland, in English, writing, and arithmetic, in husbandry and housewifery, or in trades [and] manufactures'. The Society claimed that a Charter School would be 'a fit nursery for servants and other persons proper to fill the offices of low life'.[13] Indeed, some founding members of the Society, which included influential writers such as George Berkeley, Jonathan Swift and Arthur Dobbs, wrote about the usefulness of these schools in preparing boys and girls for service.[14] In addition to providing 'useful Seminaries of Labour and Industry',[15] the Society aimed to 'teach the principles of the Protestant established religion'. Charter Schools were to achieve this by the conversion of the Catholic pupils to 'the pure Protestant faith'. The Society used a system whereby Catholic children were 'transplanted' to schools at great distances from their homes, thereby removing any possible 'contamination' from Popish influences.[16]

The first Charter School was set up in Castledermot in County Kildare, due to the fact that the 'Earl of Kildare had donated £500, given one acre in perpetuity and twenty others at an easy rent. The school opened in May 1734, with an enrolment of ten boys and ten girls'.[17] Minola Charter School (Mayo), Shannon Grove Charter School (Limerick) and Ballynahinch Charter School (Down) were all founded during the first year of the Society's existence, thereby achieving its first general rule of establishing a school in each of the four provinces. By 1744, there were twenty schools in operation and four under construction; only two more had been proposed.[18] The Society was, to a large extent, dependent on English support in its early years. There were annual subscriptions from the Corresponding Society, and in 1739 the King gave £1,000 as a royal bounty and a further £1,000 annually.[19] Official parliamentary support for the schools began in 1747, 'when the Licensing duty on hawkers and peddlers was assigned to the society'.[20] In the early years the schools were mixed, although boys and girls followed different daily routines. Girls worked at spinning and sewing, while boys laboured at the small farms and factories that were attached to the schools. The rules stated that 'girls shall spin linen and woollen yarn for their clothing, and shall make them up; and shall do the same for the boys'. At Castledermot Charter School they were employed in spinning linen yarn, while at Minola the girls worked at spinning both linen and wool. Records noted that they produced eighty-three yards of woollen cloth for boys' suits and sixty yards of linen for shifts and shirts.[21] Girls at the Charter Schools also did the mending for themselves and for the boys, and were responsible for knitting the stockings worn by all the pupils. In addition to providing for themselves, the children at Charter Schools earned income for the school through their labour, and this supplemented the salary of the schoolmaster. Ballycastle Charter School, in Antrim, housed sixty girls who worked at spinning, knitting and washing. Those who laboured at spinning earned one shilling and sixpence per day, while those who knitted stockings earned sixpence a week. Not surprisingly, their schoolwork was compromised by the emphasis on paid labour: the Commissioners of the Board of Education in Ireland (1809) reported that the girls at Ballycastle Charter School were 'deficient' at arithmetic and that their writing was 'indifferent'.[22]

The daily routine of the girls at Charter Schools is documented in the substantial archive of the Incorporated Society, and in the *Third Report of the Commissioners of the Board of Education in Ireland*, 1809.[23] In addition, Charter School pupils gave evidence to the Commissioners of the Irish Education Inquiry, which was published in the *First Report of the Commissioners of Irish Education Inquiry*, H.C. 1825.[24] The girls were provided with two uniforms: a brown frieze dress for weekdays, and a blue dress with a straw bonnet for Sundays. Their diet typically consisted of potatoes, stirabout and broth, and the daily food allowance for each child was 3½d. The meagre diet was considered acceptable, as it was believed that 'as the Charter Schools are designed for the religious education and support of the children of the <u>poor natives</u> [underlined in the original] of Ireland, it is not deemed expedient to nourish such children in a way which, when they fall back again on society, may make them discontented with their lot'.[25] As a consequence of hard labour and poor diet, the girls were reported to have a 'very mean and pauper-like appearance'.[26] They were also susceptible to infectious diseases, such as ophthalmia (inflammation of the eye), which spread through unsanitary institutions at this time, and many died from measles and tuberculosis. Others suffered at the mercy of harsh teachers, and were beaten severely for even minor misdemeanours. At Kevin Street Charter School, girls were beaten on the hands with a cane, another was beaten with a horsewhip, and records note that one girl was stripped to take a beating.

The rules for the governance of the Charter Schools laid down the daily timetable to be followed at the schools (see Figure 1). While the timetable indicated that time was to be given over to 'instruction in learning', the standard of literacy and numeracy at the schools was

6.00–7.00	Children rise and dress; acts of devotion; settling and cleaning house &c.
7.00–8.30	Instruction in learning
8.30–9.30	Breakfast and play
9.30–12.00	Labour
12.00–1.00	Instruction in learning
1.30–2.30	Dinner and play
2.30–5.00	Labour
5.00–7.00	Instruction in learning
7.00–9.00	Supper, acts of devotion, washing, combing &c., bed

Source: Adapted from Appendix to *Third Report of the Commissioners of the Board of Education in Ireland*, 1809 (142) VII. 461, p. 43.

Figure 1 Charter school timetable for summer months, 1 March–1 October 1809.

low. The labour of the children brought financial reward, and often took precedence over literary instruction. In 1788, an official report into Charter Schools noted that 'some children in them [for] six years cannot read. Their reading is neglected, for the purpose of making the children work for the master.'[27] Girls in the Charter Schools were considered to have no use for literary instruction, as popular belief held it that girls who were training to go into service did not need to be able to read, write or cipher. Girls were placed in apprenticeships or in service once they had reached adolescence, and they quickly forgot the small amount of reading and writing that they had learned at school. In giving evidence to the Commissioners, female pupils indicated that they had spent most of their schooldays at labour. Frances Coyle, aged eighteen, testified that she had been in the Charter School system almost all her life, having attended the schools at both Kevin Street and Ballycastle. She had learned to write a little, but could not read, and she had spent most of her time at 'slavish work'. She had eventually been apprenticed out to a Methodist button-maker.[28] Judith Casey, aged sixteen, had attended Baggot Street Charter School and learned a little writing, before serving as an apprentice bonnet-maker. Catherine Carthy attended the Charlemont Street Charter School and Ballycastle Charter School, but had only learned to write her name. She left Ballycastle School to go into a factory, along with fifteen other girls from the school. Some girls were less fortunate, in that they were neither literate nor had they been taught needlework. The Commissioners reported that many girls were 'so ill taught and so ill qualified, that not even the offer of a bounty would tempt the commonest farmer to receive them'.[29] So difficult was it to place some girls that the Society was forced to open a house at Charlemont Place for the 'temporary reception' of girls until they could be prepared for a position. At one point it took in a group of some fifty Charter School girls who had finished an apprenticeship at a flax-hackling factory in Buncrana, when it was found the girls had spent so much time at labour that they had no household skills at all. Household skills were particularly important, as the majority of Charter School girls went into service. In the period 1803–14 alone, 192 Charter School girls were apprenticed to trades, while 742 were apprenticed as servants.[30] With the emphasis on education in 'female labour', it is not surprising that Charter School girls had little or no 'literary instruction'. By contrast, girls who attended the illegal 'hedge schools' during the same period were more likely to follow a similar course of instruction to boys, and were thus more likely to learn rudimentary reading, writing and arithmetic.

THE HEDGE SCHOOLS AND PAY SCHOOLS

Prior to the repeal of relevant penal laws in the late eighteenth century, it was illegal for Irish Catholics to set up a school or to teach Catholic children.[31] Catholics subverted the law by developing a haphazard system of pay schools or hedge schools. In 1824, an official commission calculated that there were about 11,000 schools in Ireland, of which 9,000 were hedge schools. Four out of every five children participated in this unofficial system. Despite their popularity, hedge schools have left a patchy history from which a picture of female participation may be constructed. The unofficial status of these schools and the peripatetic life of many hedge school-teachers have contributed to the paucity of records available. Dowling's study, *The Hedge Schools of Ireland* (1935), constructed the most familiar image of the eighteenth-century hedge school and its master:

> Because the law forbade the schoolmaster to teach, he was com-
> pelled to give instruction secretly; because the householder was
> penalised for harbouring the schoolmaster, he had perforce to
> teach . . . out of doors. He, therefore, settled in some remote
> spot, the sunny side of a hedge or bank, which effectively hid him
> and hid pupils from the eye of the chance passer-by . . . while his
> scholars lay stretched upon the green sward about him.[32]

As laws against education were relaxed, schooling was held indoors, in barns, cabins and huts. The number of hedge schools increased rapidly in the second half of the eighteenth century. The hedge schoolmaster William Carleton, in *Traits and Stories of the Irish Peasantry*, has given some indication of girls' experience of the hedge schools. His record of peasant life illustrates that female education was seen as an agent in securing a good marriage rather than a means to financial independence. Carleton observed that female pupils were, 'for the most part, the daughters of wealthy farmers, who considered it necessary to their respectability, that they should not be altogether illiterate'. Female illiteracy was 'a considerable drawback in the opinion of an admirer, from the character of a young woman to whom he was about to propose'.[33] Girls who attended hedge schools benefited from a curriculum that usually included reading, writing and arithmetic, with the addition of history, geography, Latin and Greek in some schools. In Irish-speaking districts, instruction was given through the vernacular, although English was replacing Irish as the medium of instruction by the beginning of the nineteenth century.

Records of early nineteenth-century pay-schools give some indication of the participation of girls and the work of schoolmistresses. The Parochial School Returns of the Dioceses of Kildare and Leighlin (1824) provide thumbnail sketches of female teachers:

KILDARE TOWN

Mrs. Ravenhill. Holding school in different houses in this parish since 1813, Sundays and Holydays excepted. Roman Catholic. Aged 60 years. Good moral character. Teaches only to Spell and Read. Educated in Fethard, County Tipperary. Income from the payments of the children at 2 pence and 3 pence per week, and this paid irregularily [*sic*] and defectively. House about 12 feet square; mud walls; thatched; £6 would build such a one. Pays rent for it. Very middling accommodation. Not connected with any association. No fixed Inspector. Average attendance:

(a) Summer 1824 – Males 25, Females 15; Roman Catholics 40.
(b) Last winter, 50.
(c) Summer 1823, 56.

Twelve in twenty can read. Can teach to read in six to twelve months. Books – Spelling Books, Primers, Catechism by four Archbishops, taught every day. No Bibles. [34]

The Parochial Returns for Kildare and Leighlin indicate that within that diocese alone there were several schools run by 'husband and wife' teams, in which girls were taught by the mistress and the master taught the boys. It is reasonable to infer that this practice was probably commonplace in Ireland. The Parochial Returns examined over 177 schools. Of these, 138 schools were managed by a master, thirty-one by a mistress, six by a 'husband and wife' team, and a brother and sister ran two schools. [35] With very few exceptions, the schools had both male and female pupils, indicating that parents were committed to giving their daughters elementary education in reading, writing and arithmetic. However, there were fewer girls than boys attending all schools: some 4,199 boys were enrolled in the schools, compared to a total of 2,207 girls. [36]

The reading in hedge schools reflected the interests and ability of the hedge schoolteachers, and also suggests that there was a genuine love of learning to be found at the schools. The parish priest of Powerscourt reported that 'there is throughout this parish a great want of convenient schools. The cabins for school purposes are very wretched. The desire of Education is common to all the people, a trifling assistance well applied would enable the people to indulge their very great desire of educating their children . . . the books found in all the schools are nearly alike: in each of the hedge schools there are spelling books and reading books . . .'[37] The most reliable source of evidence on the reading material is the Appendix to the Report of the Education Commissioners of 1825.[38] Among the texts listed in the report are Sarah Trimmer's *Scripture Lessons*, Mrs Sherwood's *Stories on the Church Catechism*, Fanny Burney's *Cecilia* and Eliza Haywood's *Female Spectator*. As McManus (2002) notes, 'the list was an eclectic mix of both the major and minor literary genres which formed part of the popular reading taste of the time'.[39] Hannah More's (1745–1833) tales also formed an important part of the reading material for girls in the hedge schools.[40] More's moral tracts possibly appealed to the Irish, in spite of their moralising influence and didactic tone, because of the accessible, idiomatic language, and the sometimes entertaining content.[41] While we have some idea of what female pupils may have read in the hedge schools and 'pay' schools, it is not possible to make conclusive comments about their academic progress. The *ad hoc* nature of these schools was such that few records remain, and there are no systematic accounts of pupil participation and performance. It is probable that the schools at the very least provided basic instruction in reading and writing for female pupils, as this kind of instruction was available to girls in the schools of the Kildare Place Society (KPS) from 1811, and indeed the KPS used similar reading books, including the work of Hannah More and Sarah Trimmer. However, as shall be seen, the KPS practice of keeping records allows researchers to get a clearer picture of the nature of female education in schools supported by the Kildare Place Society.

THE KILDARE PLACE SOCIETY SCHOOLS

The Protestant educational society which did most to promote female literacy and to include in its books the prominent women writers of the eighteenth century was the Kildare Place Society, or KPS. It was established in 1811, and it founded and supported schools for boys and girls, and trained both men and women teachers. It also established the Cheap Book Society, a branch of the KPS that developed in recognition of the popularity of Hannah More's *Cheap Repository Tracts* (1795). The Cheap Book Society bought rights to the books of the SPCK and the Religious Tract Society in England and produced them in large quantities, for distribution by Irish booksellers. The books were used in schools and libraries, and were sold by peddlers who travelled the country. For female readers, there was *The Friendly Gift for Servants* (1817), a manual of good conduct extracted from Mrs Taylor's *Present of a Mistress to a Young Servant*.[42] The society also published work by Priscilla Wakefield, Sarah Trimmer and Hannah More.

In addition to popular books, the KPS published its own texts to be used in the schools. They contained versions of well-known tales by prominent English women, which had been adapted and incorporated into primers. The KPS quickly adopted the work of Hannah Letitia Barbauld, whose *Lessons for children from two to three years old* had been published to instant acclaim in 1778. The Dublin edition appeared in 1814. Sarah Trimmer described Barbauld's *Lessons* as having been 'written in the language of the nursery' – with sentence structures that were close to those of the child. Many of the textbook compilers who worked for the KPS adopted Barbauld's techniques. The Society also adopted for its use a very popular book by Lady Eleanor Fenn: *Cobwebs to Catch Flies, or dialogues in short sentences* (1783), and the Dublin edition of her *Infant's Friend: a spelling book* appeared in 1800.

Barbauld's work had inspired one of the most prolific English writers for children – Sarah Trimmer. Her work was appropriate to the use of schools for the poor in Ireland, as she provided a systematically graded reading course, ranging from alphabet and syllabrium, through moral tales to lessons on religious material. Trimmer's work was therefore considered suited to Protestant voluntary education societies, combining as it did both literary and moral instruction. The Dublin edition of her book *The Teacher's Assistant . . . a Plan of Appropriate Instruction for the Children of the Poor*, was adopted for use by the KPS in its early years, and her *History of the robins, designed for the instruction of children . . .* was printed in Dublin in 1819 and again in 1821, for the Irish market.

Irish schoolgirls were also introduced to stories adapted from Barbauld, Hannah More and Maria Edgeworth, which appeared in *The Dublin Spelling Book* (1819) and *The Dublin Reading Book* (1822). Their format and content were derived from Lindley Murray's *English Spelling Book* of 1804 and other schoolbooks by Murray. Evidence clearly indicates that *The Dublin Spelling Book* and *The Dublin Reading Book* 'represent the first Irish attempt to make an organised reading scheme available for the children of the poor'.[43] The stories contained adult admonitions against wasting food, cruelty to animals and general disobedience. Many lessons contained a moral tale, concentrating on the attributes of kindness and charity in young girls. The *Dublin Spelling Book* contained a tale about 'The charitable little girl', who gave her only muffin to a poor woman. Lindley Murray claimed that Maria Edgeworth had given this 'pleasing little narrative' to him. The KPS books endeavoured to provide a consistent image of the 'attentive and industrious little girl' – who would do well at school, help her parents, make and repair her own clothes, and never waste anything. She was depicted as 'completely contented' – for, in the sentiments of Trimmer, such a girl knew 'that it is God who makes some to be poor and some rich; [and] the rich have many troubles which we know nothing of, and . . . the poor if they are but good, may be very happy . . .'[44]

While it is possible to infer something about the *aims* of the society in using English women writers in these schools for the Irish poor, it is difficult to comment conclusively on the influence of these works. This is first because a substantial number of KPS children were monoglot Irish speakers, who would have needed assistance to understand even the most rudimentary passages. The KPS operated its schools at a time when fifty per cent of the population spoke Irish, and Irish was the dominant language of the poorer classes. Inspectors examining the children in the KPS schools in 1826 noted that the children were 'unable to proceed through a sentence in the reading book without hesitation and mistake and displayed the most lamentable ignorance of the subject'.[45] The second obstacle to the success of the books was that many of the lessons directed at the Irish female poor had been lifted from English textbooks (Murray's), and would have had an inappropriate – even alien – content. Few girls at the KPS schools would have experienced the middle-class context and the prosperous meal described in this extract, for example:

> . . . it is time to go in and dine.
> Is the cloth laid? Where are the knives and forks, and plates?
> Call Ann. Are your hands clean? . . . Will you have some lamb,
> some pease? Do not smack your lips, or make a noise, when
> you eat. Take some bread . . . Jane must shake the cloth out of
> doors. The birds will pick up the crumbs.[46]

In addition to such reading lessons, *The Dublin Reading Book* contained some fifteen pages reminding the reader of behaviour expected of her, emphasising the importance of truth, honesty, cleanliness and obedience, and encouraging the reading of the Bible.

While the Quaker utilitarianism of many founding members of the KPS no doubt influenced the secular content of the books, the texts also reflected the committed evangelical Protestantism of some committee members. Religious material and biblical extracts were inserted into reading books – this despite the fact that the KPS had been granted state support on the understanding that it was not a proselytising agency. Catholic hostility to the KPS grew in the late 1820s, as it was contrary to Catholic dogma that the Bible should be read without note or comment. By 1831, the treasury withdrew its support from the KPS and set about establishing a non-denominational state-funded system of elementary schooling: the National system. There was, by this time, a growth in provision of residential care and education via orphanages under Catholic management. Eventually, Catholic teaching orders were to become involved in systematic provision of residential care via reformatories and industrial schools.

ORPHANAGES FOR GIRLS

Orphanages and houses of refuge were sometimes well positioned to provide girls with basic education and domestic training. They were founded specifically for the care of children, and were often influenced by the missionary zeal of their founders. Many of the Protestant orphanages were proselytising agencies, and Catholic women such as Margaret Aylward were anxious to establish orphanages for Catholic girls to prevent their need to enter Protestant institutions. Other religious denominations had their own orphan societies, although these were founded later in the nineteenth century. The Presbyterian Orphan Society was founded in 1866, while the Methodist Orphan Society was founded in 1870. But Protestant orphanages provided shelter for girls as early as 1790, when the Female Orphan House was established on the North Circular Road, Dublin. Incorporated in 1800, it was provided with an annual parliamentary grant of approximately £650, and the labour of the young girls brought additional income of about £400 per year.[47] It was well managed, caring for between 150 and 170 girls, and the Commissioners for National Education in Ireland (CNEI) reported very favourably on this institution in 1827. In 1842, another parliamentary commission reported on the success of the Female Orphan House, recommending it as an example to be followed by other orphan institutions.[48] The education provided included reading, writing, basic arithmetic, spinning, knitting, sewing and domestic work. When the girls reached the age of sixteen, they were placed in service.

Many other Protestant orphan societies were founded in the early decades of the nineteenth century. Most of these were supported by wealthy Protestants in the community, and persons of wealth and rank attended at annual meetings of these societies.[49] But orphan girls, generally, would appear to have been harder to support than boys, and their prospects less certain. The Hibernian Military School, founded originally to educate the orphans of soldiers, decided to restrict the school to boys. The boys, all of whom were raised as Protestants, could be apprenticed to a trade or could join the army or navy; girls, on the other hand, were more difficult to place in employment. During the years of the Great Famine, rural areas witnessed the spread of Protestant schools and 'colonies' that provided shelter and education for Catholics who converted to Protestantism in order to avail of this. Bible societies, such as the Church Mission Society, also cared for orphans. These proselytising Bible societies came under attack from leading Catholic churchmen and laity in the early 1850s. By the 1860s, the activities of such societies had lessened considerably. Catholic orphanages were increasing and the workhouses had been established.

Catholic orphanages were run by laypersons and religious orders. Some changed hands from time to time. St Joseph's Female Orphanage, for example, which had been established in Dublin as early as 1770, was given over to the Irish Sisters of Charity in 1870. A large number of Catholic orphan societies were established at centres such as Cork, Dublin and Waterford. Some were begun with the specific aim of keeping Catholic children out of Protestant orphanages. When Margaret Aylward began fundraising for St Brigid's Orphanage, she urged her supporters to 'save poor orphans whose faith is in danger'. The organisers of St Brigid's openly stated their aim to 'rescue the children of the Catholic church from the enemies of the Catholic church'.[50] The Ladies' Association of Charity of St Vincent de Paul assisted Aylward. The group regularly visited Protestant orphanages to note the attendance of Catholics, and they sent regular reports to Archbishop Paul Cullen. Aylward sent Cullen the testimony of one child, Lizzy Lucas, who had spent two years in the Bird's Nest, Kingstown. The young girl calculated that, of the 127 Catholic orphans there, some 37 had lapsed in their faith. The Bird's Nest orphanages, organised by Mrs Ellen Smyly, were overt in their proselytising aims, and Aylward was determined in her efforts to thwart them. In some instances, the Ladies of Charity physically removed Catholic children from Protestant orphanages. In other cases, Aylward provided destitute Catholics with support, so that they would not turn to Protestant orphanages.

With the exception of religious instruction, the education offered at Catholic and Protestant orphanages was similar. They taught basic reading and writing, and gave the girls domestic skills. It was recognised that poverty contributed to the moral ruin of girls. Homeless girls often turned to prostitution and criminality in order to survive. Young girls therefore needed to be equipped with the necessary skills to support themselves. Those who found themselves temporarily out of work could turn to refuges such as those founded by the Mercy congregation. Girls who entered these refuges had to show evidence of 'modesty, honesty and sobriety', and were put to work in the refuge laundries until a suitable position could be found.[51] It is not surprising to find that, when legislation was passed to provide for the residential care of orphaned and destitute children, the Sisters of Mercy were to play a significant role in coordinating and managing the reformatories and industrial schools for girls in the last decades of the nineteenth century.

REFORMATORIES

In addition to the workhouse schools and orphanages, residential care was also provided to girls in the reformatories and industrial schools that became a feature of the landscape of nineteenth-century education. The reformatories and industrial schools provided instruction and occupational training for thousands of destitute and vagrant girls. Dublin in the mid-nineteenth century was 'infested' with swarms of vagrant children, who survived by hawking, stealing and begging.[52] The majority of these street-urchins or 'city arabs' were without parents or homes, and many became involved in petty crime. Records for 1849–53 indicate a progressive increase in juvenile committals to gaol. In 1852, over one-twelfth of the annual committals were juveniles under the age of 16.[53] That year, in the annual report of the inspectors-general of Irish prisons, the disproportionate number of orphans and deserted children in Ireland was directly linked to juvenile delinquency (see Table 1). Committing vagrant children to prison was considered to increase the incidence of juvenile delinquency, as young vagrants became further educated in crime while imprisoned. Punishments for petty crime were often excessive: one young girl in Cork was sentenced to a month's hard labour for stealing a turnip from a field.[54] Such punishments did little to train or educate children, and indeed the re-committal of juvenile offenders further indicated that, far from reforming young characters, prison was contributing to the problem of juvenile crime.

As vagrancy and criminality became a pressing problem in the mid-nineteenth century, the European practice of establishing

Table 1 Parental information on imprisoned juveniles, 1851

Nos. of imprisoned juveniles	Parental information
830	Without a father
422	Without a mother
1,082	Without parents
105	Illegitimate
205	Deserted by parents
409	Absconded from parents

Source: Thirty-first Annual Report of the Inspectors General of Irish Prisons, 1852.

reformatories suggested a solution.[55] Many state-aided reformatory schools, under voluntary management, had been established on the continent. There it had been found that it was essential to separate hardened criminals from destitute children who were merely exposed to the temptations of crime. Reformatories run on these principles were viable in Ireland, where voluntary agencies had a tradition of involvement in the provision of pauper education, and where the Churches were anxious to 'reform' juvenile offenders and prevent innocents from falling into evil ways. The way forward was paved by legislative provision in England and Scotland in 1854. The passing of the Reformatory Schools Act in Britain was, unsurprisingly, followed by demands for similar legislation in Ireland.

The Reformatory Schools Act for Ireland was passed in 1858, following which institutions were established to 'reform' juvenile offenders and keep them out of the prisons. The Catholic Church responded immediately, and Cardinal Paul Cullen established the Dublin Catholic Reformatory Committee to develop Catholic reformatories. By 1859, five reformatories for girls and one for boys had been established under Catholic management. Records of Catholic reformatories suggest that their managers viewed their mission as being the prevention of 'moral disease' and the 'restoring [of] . . . little outcasts to their place in the human family, as Christians'. In 1858, the Protestant community founded the Dublin Parochial Association, to establish and manage Protestant reformatory schools in Dublin.

Between 1859 and 1909, 1,703 girls were admitted to reformatories.[56] They were invariably committed as a result of a conviction of larceny. While 119 of these were transferred to industrial schools, the majority were detained for between one and five years. If their parents were still living, they were expected to pay five shillings a week towards their daughters' upkeep. Most of the reformatories for girls were managed by Roman Catholic religious orders, and the majority of inmates were Catholic. Less than fifteen per cent of reformatory school inmates were Protestant. Girls, irrespective of their religion, followed a daily routine of prayer, labour and a little secular instruction. Girls at Cork Street Reformatory for Protestant Girls were trained in the use of the sewing machine, and learned laundry work and cooking. In addition, they were taught reading, writing, arithmetic, geography and the Holy Scriptures. The experience of the girls at St Joseph's Reformatory for Roman Catholic Girls, Limerick, was similar: they also learned to read and write, and were instructed in geography, grammar and singing. Dressmaking, the use of the sewing machine, knitting and lacework occupied the girls for several hours each day, and there were daily prayers.[57] The

6.00–6.30	Arise; make beds; morning prayer
6.30–7.30	Cleaning dormitories
7.30–8.30	Mass
8.30–9.00	Breakfast
9.00–10.30	Manual work
10.30–11.30	Some at sewing. Some at laundry work
11.30–1.30	Study and secular instruction
1.30–2.30	Some at needlework, others at garden work
2.30–3.15	Dinner and recreation
3.15–4.00	Catechism and religious instruction
4.00–5.00	Outdoor exercise and recreation
5.00–6.00	Study
6.00–7.00	Needlework and knitting
7.00–8.00	Supper. Recreation. Singing
8.00–8.30	Night prayers. Bed

Source: Royal Commission of Inquiry into Primary Education (Ireland) Vol. VIII, p. 197.

Figure 2 Daily timetable, St Joseph's Reformatory School, Ballinasloe, 1878.

daily schedule for St Joseph's Reformatory School, Ballinasloe, gives an indication of the typical routine for reformatory inmates (see Figure 2).

Few of the reformatories succeeded in providing girls with a basic literary education, and the majority of the inmates were recorded as being able to 'neither read nor write'.[58] Upon discharge, the girls were usually placed in service. Over three thousand girls discharged between 1859 and 1909 went into employment or service. A further 3,656 girls went to friends and 1,118 girls emigrated.[59] A small number were transferred to industrial schools, suggesting that they had been incorrectly committed to reformatories.

INDUSTRIAL SCHOOLS

The idea of providing children with an industrial education was popularised by the utilitarian philosophy that held that literary instruction was neither sufficient nor appropriate for the children of the poor. Industrial schools grew in number following the passing of a Bill to extend the provision of Industrial Schools to Ireland.[60] It provided for the inspection and certification of existing industrial schools, and the founding of new schools. While reformatories were developed to cure juvenile criminals of their ways, industrial schools aimed to erase the potential for crime from young persons. Between 1869 and 1909, 28,391 girls were admitted to Irish industrial schools.[61] Many industrial school inmates were the children of criminals and prostitutes, and were considered to be particularly vulnerable. The largest group involved in establishing these schools were the Catholic religious orders of sisters. By 1873, the Sisters of Mercy had established twenty-five of the thirty-four new industrial schools for girls. However, the Sisters had been active in promoting industrial education since the 1830s, and many female 'houses of industry' supported girls through the grim years of the Great Famine.

Some industrial schools were residential, while others provided instruction and meals on a daily basis. Pupils were usually between six and fourteen years of age, although some industrial schools provided work for young women into their early twenties. Girls at residential industrial schools were usually orphaned, or their parents had either emigrated or been imprisoned.[62] Although many of these schools received some support from the National Board, they were less successful at imparting literary instruction. Instead, the schools aimed to provide girls with practical training and remunerative employment. Typically, girls were trained in needlework, and then began working at piece-work, which was commissioned from the schools. Non-residential pupils could earn money that might make a significant contribution to the family income, while residential pupils earned their 'keep'. Industrial schools afforded their pupils very little formal schooling or 'literary instruction', and few industrial schoolgirls learned to read or write properly.

There were nineteen female industrial schools by 1852.[63] Some of these schools were affiliated to the National Board of Education, which had been established in 1831 in order to support the development of day schools for 'the poorer classes' throughout the country. The CNEI provided monies towards teachers' salaries. One such school was Carrickmacross Female Industrial School, which had been established in 1849 with the support of Lord Bath. The CNEI provided £50 towards the annual salary of the teacher. The school aimed to provide employment for destitute girls from 'the town and neighbourhood of Carrickmacross'.[64] While this school had 144 girls on the school roll, only one-third of this number actually attended the school on a regular basis. The majority of girls were allowed to 'work' at home, doing plain work and lacework in order to earn money. There was little attempt to promote literary education, and, when the CNEI reported on this school, they focused mainly on the value of the sewing completed by the girls. Two years after the school had been established, it was making a good profit from the girls' labour. The CNEI reported that the 'gross value of work executed by the pupils of Carrickmacross Industrial School [was] £213.11s.8d'.[65] However, they also noted that, 'as the great portion of the day is devoted to needlework, the time available for literary instruction does not much exceed a few hours each week'.[66]

Many industrial schools established in the mid-nineteenth century were managed by religious orders, and were usually built in close proximity to a convent. The Sisters of Mercy ran many of the industrial schools for girls. One such school, St Mary's Industrial National School in Limerick, was founded in 1838 to qualify girls 'to act as servants, sempstresses, shop-women [and] elementary teachers; and to provide situations for them'.[67] In its first twelve years, it admitted 1,364 girls, and was successful at finding employment for many of them. The CNEI reported that, between 1850 and 1851, the school had placed 170 girls in domestic positions, while one girl had emigrated to America and two had become National School teachers. Much of the expense of running this school was borne by the convent, as only a small amount of paid work was undertaken in the school. Of the £340 required to board and clothe the girls, £272 was provided by the Mercy order, while the National Board gave a grant of £17.10s. The Sisters provided the girls with a simple diet of bread, soup, rice and milk, and gave some instruction in reading and writing.

Thurles Industrial School was 'founded in the year 1847, by the religious ladies of the Presentation Convent of Thurles . . . with the object of providing food and employment for young females dismissed from service during the famine of that year'.[68] Although the school was attached to Thurles National School, the pupils devoted their time to the manufacture of hemp and flax into sacks, and the manufacture of wool into flannel, stockings and gloves. Another small department did 'fancy-work in wool, cotton and thread'.[69] The girls were paid an average weekly wage of 1s.6d., for ten hours' work per day. The daily schedule included an additional half-hour for secular instruction, and a half-hour for religious instruction. The 'literary instruction' comprised lessons in reading, and no other lessons were provided.

Millstreet Industrial National School was also attached to a Presentation Convent. Here girls were trained and supervised at lacework and embroidery. The institution was regarded as a factory, not a school, since the girls spent much of their time sewing. The *Twenty-first Report of the Commissioners of National Instruction* noted that there were 153 girls working at sewing. The 'materials for the sewing [were] chiefly supplied by the inhabitants of the town', while 'the muslin to be sewn [was supplied by] Messrs MacDonnell and Co., Belfast and Glasgow'.[70] While Millstreet Industrial School did not keep accounts, the District Inspector who visited the school in 1854 calculated that the amount received for the muslin-work and glove-making was £30 and ten shillings.

Kinsale Female Industrial School, attended by 120 females, did not make literary instruction compulsory at all, and pupils, when examined, gave answers which were 'far from satisfactory, and showed how little they understood the subject matter of the lesson'.[71] The school, which had been established by the Sisters of Mercy in 1847, employed the girls at crochet, point-lace and plain work. Girls were paid about four shillings per week, and the women who trained them and supervised their work were paid an annual salary of £9. Religious instruction formed part of the daily routine, and it would seem that industrial schools run by religious orders were emphatic that the moral development of female pupils was more important that literary instruction. The CNEI commended the moral instruction given to girls, suggesting that it had contributed to the girls' 'quiet, contented look, and to their clean, neat persons and dress'. It was suggested that such girls had been 'purified by the

---

TIME TABLE
Lancasterian Industrial National School (for Females) Belfast

---

8.30 a.m.–10.00 a.m.	Religious Instruction
	Breakfast
	Recreation
10.00 a.m.–11.00 a.m.	Literary Instruction
11.00 a.m.–2.00 p.m.	Industrial Training
2.00 p.m.–3.00 p.m.	Dinner

Recreation

3.00p.m.–6.00 p.m. (In summer)	Junior Classes: Literary Instruction
3.00 p.m.–4.30 p.m. (In winter)	Senior Classes: Literary Instruction & Industrial Training

On Saturdays, the period for Industrial Training is taken up in teaching all the younger children to 'mend and darn' their clothes.

Source: Commissioners for National Education in Ireland, *Eighteenth Report*, 1852, p. 750.

Figure 3 Daily timetable, Lancasterian Industrial National School for Females, Belfast, 1852.

principles of religion' and were less likely to become 'idle slatternly females'. The Commissioners concluded that 'the rapid spread of habits of thrift and industry among our Irish female poor . . . cannot be too highly appreciated by all interested in the permanent welfare of this country'.[72]

Most of the industrial schools emphasised industrial training and labour at the expense of formal schooling. As a consequence of this, the majority of industrial schoolgirls were reported to be unable to read or write, while a small proportion could 'read and write imperfectly'.[73] However, some schools managed to devote part of each day to literary instruction (see Figure 3). In Belfast, the Lancasterian Industrial National School for Females was better appointed that many other schools, and some of its teachers had trained at the Marlborough Street teacher-training school established by the National Board. The Lancasterian Industrial National School for Females was 'spacious and comfortable, being sixty feet in length, thirty-two in breadth, and twelve in height; well lighted and ventilated; and having a sufficiency of suitable furniture'.[74] It had three principal teachers and one assistant teacher, and salaries were provided, in part, by the National Board. Lacemaking was a special industry taught to ten girls, while seventy-two learned knitting and sewing, nine learned shirt-making, four learned fancy knotting, and four learned netting.[75] Miss Orr, who had trained at Marlborough Street, gave literary instruction and the graded reading books of the National Board were used. While most of the girls were on the First Book, twenty-two girls had reached the Fourth Book, and arithmetic was taught to forty-one girls.[76] Despite this commitment to academic work, the girls invariably followed the route taken by girls at other industrial schools: the majority became servants or workers in the manufactories. The preparation for domestic and manufacturing labour which girls received in the industrial schools enabled them to join the largest outlets for female labour. By the second half of the nineteenth century, forty-eight per cent of employed women worked as domestic servants. Industrial schools discharged some four hundred girls into service annually. One inspector of reformatories and industrial schools commented favourably on the preparation for work which was given to industrial school girls when he wrote that 'farmers, even with large farms, complain that industrial school children receive a training and instruction in trades which their sons and daughters cannot hope to obtain'.[77] However, there remained some girls who gained neither literary nor industrial training. Girls from St Joseph's Industrial Institute were reported to be 'so totally devoid of knowledge of the common things of life, that they make the effect at first of being completely deprived of ordinary intelligence. Most of them have never seen the interior of a dwelling house, have never handled a breakable article, or used a knife and fork.'[78]

Table 2 Expansion of the industrial schools' system, 1880–1900

Year	Number of schools	Children in the schools	Treasury contributions	Payments from rates	Other
1880	56	5,699	£68,088	£23,253	£15,817
1885	64	6,655	£80,766	£30,100	£18,331
1890	70	7,767	£95,842	£37,262	£20,029
1895	69	7,487	£97,188	£38,944	£16,910
1900	70	7,591	£97,853	£41,944	£19,321

Source: Annual Reports IRIS 1880–1900, cited in Barnes, *Irish Industrial Schools*, p. 75.

It was only in the closing decades of the nineteenth century that industrial schools for girls began to offer somewhat improved conditions. There were a number of reasons for this change. First, the Powis Commission, set up in 1868 to carry out a thorough investigation into primary education in Ireland, commented upon the Industrial Schools Act, which had been passed a decade earlier.[79] This inclusion of the system, together with the certification of approved schools and systematic reporting in the annual *Reports of the Inspector appointed to visit Reformatory and Industrial Schools in Ireland* (1868–1909), brought attention and greater accountability to industrial school managers. Second, the management structures of industrial schools changed after the passing of the Act. The involvement of religious orders was particularly advantageous, as they had the personnel, resources, time and commitment to run these institutions.[80] Third, between 1880 and 1890, there was a period of sustained growth in the industrial schools system. The Industrial Schools Act had empowered local authorities to contribute towards the establishment or alteration of industrial schools, and there were increased treasury contributions (see Table 2).

Barnes (1989) described this period as presenting 'a picture of a flourishing sector in child welfare',[81] the benefits of which were eventually to accrue to female pupils.

NOTES

1 For relevant extracts from primary source material see Aine Hyland and Kenneth Milne (eds), *Irish Educational Documents*, Vol. I (Dublin: CICE, 1987). For secondary sources see for example Desmond Bowen, *The Protestant Crusade in Ireland, 1800–1870* (Dublin: 1988); P.J. Dowling, *The Hedge Schools of Ireland* (Cork: Mercier Press, 1968); Kingsmill H. Moore, *An Unwritten Chapter on the history of education being the history of the society for the education of the poor of Ireland generally known as the Kildare Place Society* (London: Macmillan, 1904); Joseph Robins, *The Lost Children: A study of Charity Children in Ireland, 1700–1900* (Dublin: Institute of Public Administration, 1980).

2 *First Report of the Commissioners of Irish Education Inquiry*, 1825 (400) xii.1. *Second Report of the Commission of Inquiry (Abstract of Returns in 1824, from the Protestant and Roman Catholic Clergy in Ireland, of the State of Education in their respective Parishes)*; 1826–27 (12) xii.1.

3 Robins, *The Lost Children*, p. 8.

4 Ibid., p. 16. Robins notes that in 1737 the bodies of thirteen branded children were found in a sandpit.

5 Ibid., pp. 51, 52.

6 See *Rules for conducting the education of the female children in the Foundling Hospital 1800*, quoted in Robins, *The Lost Children*, pp. 39, 40.

7 *Twentieth Report of the Commissioners of National Education in Ireland*, 1853, Appendix L, p. 632.

8 Ibid., p. 627.

9   Edward Synge, Archibishop of Tuam, *Brief account of the laws now in force in the kingdom of Ireland, for encouraging the residence of the parochial clergy, and erecting of English schools* (Dublin, 1723) in Kenneth Milne: *The Irish Charter Schools, 1730–1830* (Dublin: Four Courts Press, 1997), p. 13.

10   Ibid., p. 14.

11   SPCK, London, ALB, Vol. 15, Lord Bishop of Cloyne, 13 January 1729, cited in Milne, *The Irish Charter Schools*, p. 14.

12   Typescript notes by Tennison, M2462 Representative Church Body Library, cited in Milne, *The Irish Charter Schools*, p. 14.

13   Milne, *The Irish Charter Schools*, p. 26.

14   Ibid.

15   See Timothy Corcoran, *Selected Texts on Education Systems in Ireland from the Close of the Middle Ages* (Dublin: Education Department, University College Dublin, 1928), pp. 44–6.

16   *First Report of the Commissioners of Irish Education Inquiry*, 1825, (400) xii.1, p. 13.

17   Ibid., p. 24.

18   Ibid., pp 347–8.

19   Robins, *The Lost Children*, p. 70.

20   Ibid., p. 32.

21   M.G. Jones, *The Charity School Movement* (Cambridge: CUP, 1938), p. 241.

22   Appendix to the *Third Report of the Commissioners of the Board of Education in Ireland*, 1809, (142) vii. 461, p. 61.

23   *Third Report of the Commissioners of the Board of Education in Ireland*, 1809, (142) vii. 461.

24   *First Report of the Commissioners of Irish Education Inquiry*, 1825, (400).

25   TCD 5264, 7 March 1838. Cited in Kenneth Milne, *The Irish Charter Schools*, p. 79.

26   *First Report of the Commissioners of Irish Education Inquiry*, 1825, (400), xxi, p. 72.

27   *Official Report on the Charter School* (1788), in Corcoran, *Selected Texts on Education Systems in Ireland*, p. 59.

28   *First Report of the Commissioners of Irish Education Inquiry*, 1825, (400), xii, p. 25.

29   Ibid., p. 27.

30   *First Report of the Commissioners of Irish Education Inquiry*, 1825, (400), xii, Appendix 171.

31   See for example *An Act to restrain foreign education* (7 Will. C. 4 (1695)); *An Act to prevent the further growth of popery* (2 Anne c.6 (1703)).

32   P.J. Dowling, *The Hedge Schools of Ireland*, p. 35.

33   William Carleton, *Traits and Stories of the Irish Peasantry* (London: n.p.,1843), p. 302.

34   Martin Brenan, *The Schools of Kildare and Leighlin, 1775–1835* (Dublin: M.H.Gill & Son, 1935), p. 179.

35   See Brenan, *The Schools of Kildare and Leighlin*.

36   Ibid.

37   See Brenan, *The Schools of Kildare and Leighlin*, pp. 477–8.

38   *First Report of the Commissioners of Irish Education Inquiry* 1825 (400) xii.1.

39   Antonia McManus, *The Irish Hedge School and its Books, 1695–1831* (Dublin: Four Courts Press, 2002) p. 182.

40   Ibid., p. 161.

41   Ibid., p. 164.

42   See Harold Hislop, 'The Kildare Place Society: An Irish Experiment in Popular Education' (unpublished PhD thesis, University of Dublin, Trinity College, 1990), p. 202. Evidence based on the presence of Mrs Taylor's *Present . . .* in the list of KPS books dated 1826 (KPS II/24/3).

43   Hislop, 'Kildare Place', p. 164.

44   *The Dublin Spelling Book*, pp. 197–201, quoted in Hislop, p. 148.

45 General report of tour (No. 2) for the year 1826, by W.V. Griffith, 6 February 1827, KPS I/Ms 398, pp. 9–13. Quoted in Hislop, 'Kildare Place', p. 167.

46 A Reading Book (Tablet XIII) [or *The Dublin Spelling Book*, p. 381], in Hislop, 'Kildare Place', pp. 145–6.

47 See Anon., *A Brief Record of the Female Orphan House* (Dublin: 1893), p. 3, and Maria Luddy, *Women and Philanthropy in Nineteenth-Century Ireland* (Cambridge, Cambridge University Press, 1995), pp. 76–7.

48 *Reports of the Inspector of Charitable Institutions*, Dublin 1842, p. 32.

49 See Robins, *The Lost Children*, p. 123.

50 Rev. Mathew Russell, 'St. Brigid's orphans', *The Irish Monthly*, 4, 1876, p. 5. Quoted in Luddy, *Women and Philanthropy*, p. 77.

51 Annual report of the House of Refuge, Baggot Street, 1803. See Luddy, *Women and Philanthropy*, p. 84.

52 Jane Barnes, *Irish Industrial Schools* (Dublin: Irish Academic Press, 1989), p. 13.

53 Barnes, *Irish Industrial Schools*, p. 14.

54 Ibid., p. 16.

55 For a discussion of such developments see Barnes, *Irish Industrial Schools*, pp. 21–6.

56 *Forty-Eighth Report of the Inspector of Reformatory and Industrial Schools of Ireland*, 1910, p. 33.

57 See *Royal Commission of Inquiry into Primary Education (Ireland)* Vol. VII, p. 197.

58 *Nineteenth Report of the Inspector of Reformatory and Industrial Schools of Ireland*, 1881, p. 119.

59 *Forty-Eighth Report of the Inspector of Reformatory and Industrial Schools of Ireland*, 1910, p. 33.

60 *Bill to extend the Industrial Schools Act to Ireland*, 1867 (17) Ill. 215; (102) II; 229; 1867–168 (6) II. 523.

61 *Forty-Eighth Report of the Inspector of Reformatory and Industrial Schools of Ireland*, 1910, p. 43.

62 See *Nineteenth Report of the Inspector of Reformatory and Industrial Schools of Ireland*, 1881, p. 15.

63 *Eighteenth Report of the Commissioners of National Education in Ireland*, Vol. I, 1851, p. xiv.

64 Appendix to the *Eighteenth Report of the Commissioners of National Education in Ireland*, Vol. I, 1851, p. 752.

65 Ibid., p. 754.

66 Ibid., p. 757.

67 Ibid., p. 762.

68 Ibid., p. 760.

69 Ibid.

70 Appendix to the *Twenty-first Report of the Commissioners of National Education in Ireland*, 1854, Vol. II, p. 7.

71 Ibid., p. 9.

72 Ibid., p. 11.

73 *Nineteenth Report of the Inspector of Reformatory and Industrial Schools of Ireland*, 1881, p. 19.

74 *Eighteenth Report of the Commissioners of National Education in Ireland*, 1851, p. 749.

75 Ibid., p. 751.

76 From its inception in 1831, the CNEI had insisted on the use of five graded reading books, which they had published for use in all schools attached to the National Board. Additional reading books, including books for female pupils, were later provided.

77 *Eighteenth Report of the Inspector appointed to visit Reformatory and Industrial Schools of Ireland*, p. 26 [C 2692], 1880, xxxvii, 397.

78 Anon., 'St Joseph's Industrial Institute and the Workhouse Orphans', *Irish Quarterly Review*, 9 January 1859, cited in Maria Luddy, *Women in Ireland, 1800–1918: A Documentary History* (Cork: Cork University Press, 1995), p. 123.

79 *Royal Commission of Inquiry into Primary Education* (Ireland) 1870, (Powis), Vol. I, Part I, p. 480.

80 Barnes, *Irish Industrial Schools*, p. 57.

81 Ibid., p. 75.

Chapter 2
The Education of Girls Within the National System

JUDITH HARFORD AND DEIRDRE RAFTERY

BACKGROUND

> There seems to be no problem of statesmanship which at the
> same time *looks* easier and *is* harder to solve than that of
> establishing a really effective system of national education.[1]

By the early nineteenth century, the British government had recognised that supporting the delivery of education in Ireland via
'voluntary' societies was not proving effective. As noted in Chapter 1,
in 1811 the Kildare Place Society (KPS) had introduced teacher
training and the principles of good school 'management', and had
also provided reading books for use in schools. However, the
Catholic Church became increasingly hostile to the KPS, because
KPS schools incorporated the use of the Bible 'without note or
comment' into daily teaching and reading lessons – a practice which
was contrary to Catholic dogma. Political activists such as Daniel
O'Connell, who supported Catholic emancipation, were quick to
criticise the KPS as being anti-Catholic. John Leslie Foster, in a letter
to the Secretary of the Board of Education in 1811, warned that the
Irish people were taking education into their own hands and that
state intervention was long overdue.[2] Education was increasingly
viewed as a means of monitoring and controlling the increasingly
'vocal' Catholic population. In addition, the provision of a system of
non-denominational national education would, it was believed,
improve Anglo-Irish relations. In 1812, the Commissioners of the
Board of Education recommended the establishment of a Board 'to
superintend a system of education, from which should be banished
even the suspicion of proselytism'.[3] A Committee of the House of

Commons in 1828 made similar recommendations.[4] The Catholic Church continued to put pressure on the government to establish a system of education which would be acceptable to the Catholic people, and to withdraw funding from Protestant voluntary agencies.

In the autumn of 1831, the government of Earl Grey set out to initiate a new scheme of primary education for the benefit of the poor in Ireland. The system was to be known as the National System, although for many this was merely a label, and the system failed to take into account the needs of an evolving nation.[5] The Chief Secretary of Ireland, E.G. Stanley, wrote a letter to the Duke of Leinster setting out the principles of the new scheme. The document, which became known as the Stanley Letter, was essentially the blueprint for the National System of education. The letter noted the failure of former systems of schooling, notably the Kildare Place Society, to accommodate the needs of the entire population and the importance of a system of education which would meet the requirements of the Roman Catholic Church. The new system hoped to provide, 'if possible, a combined literary and a separate religious education . . . a system of National Education for the poorer classes of the community'.[6] It was to be administered by a Board of Commissioners, representative of the major Churches, so as to eliminate any semblance of proselytism which had plagued previous bodies.

The intention of the architects of the new system was to bring all children together for literary instruction, while also providing separate religious instruction for the various denominations. The display of religious and political emblems was prohibited under the rules of the system. The Catholic clergy, who formed the great majority of school managers, were not satisfied with the 'non-denominational' character of the National System. In their view, 'the rule restricting all religious instruction to one period of the day, and forbidding any allusion to the subject at other times, except the commencement or the close of the day [was] very prejudicial to the religious training of the school children'.[7]

In many National Schools, the rule regarding the presence of religious symbols in the class was interpreted rather loosely. On a visit to Blackrock Convent Female National School, Cork, one inspector noted:

> At one end of the room [was] a painting representing Nanno Nagle, the foundress of the Presentation order, teaching young children; at another end [was] a painting of our Saviour on the cross and the Blessed Virgin and Mary Magdalene each side,

and a wooden cross underneath this [was] covered with a curtain during <u>school business</u> (underlined in original).[8]

The inspector eventually requested that the cross be removed because it was contrary to the rule that 'any emblem which might be considered of a denominational character should not appear in the school-room during time for united education'.[9] Several convent schools were 'struck off' the register of national schools because of non-observance of the Board's rules regarding religious instruction.

DENOMINATIONAL DIFFICULTIES

The Catholic hierarchy initially welcomed the new scheme as a compromise measure, and the majority of prelates and clergy were supportive of it in the early 1830s. The hierarchy was conscious of the fact that it could not afford to boycott the scheme since it was not in a position to adequately finance its own system of primary education.[10] Furthermore, the system made explicit provision for denominational religious instruction, with the state bearing most of the expense.[11] Three prelates in particular were behind the new plan: William Crolly, Bishop of Down and Connor and later Archbishop of Armagh, Daniel Murray, Archbishop of Dublin, and James Doyle, Bishop of Kildare and Leighlin.[12] Support was far from widespread, however, and the decision of the Christian Brothers to withdraw their schools fuelled doubts over the system's integrity. Some clergy viewed the scheme as 'secular . . . anti-Catholic . . . Protestant . . . [coming from] a source of Protestantism in England . . . whose primary objective was to proselytize the country and lead the people away from Catholicism'.[13]

Although the National Board had set out to provide a non-denominational system and to foster cooperation between denominations, specifically through the promotion of joint denominational applications, this policy rarely worked. As Daly notes, despite the legal obligation to have mixed denominational representation, few applications included the signatures of both Catholic and Protestant clergy.[14] The Commissioners of National Education (hereafter CNEI) noted that schools were widely conducted along denominational lines.[15] However, the Commissioners themselves helped to sustain the denominational divide by not actively promoting mixed applications.[16] Because of the majority position of Catholics, the system became decidedly Catholic in its structure and ethos. By 1868, just over three-quarters of all children found in National Schools were

Catholic. At that time, a little over one-eighth belonged to the established Church; one-tenth were Presbyterian, and less than one-hundredth belonged to 'other denominations'.[17]

The largely Catholic structure and ethos of the National System had implications for the way in which the curriculum was shaped. A particular feature of the system, as it evolved, was that it included 'female' subjects which were taught with the support of specially produced 'female' reading books. These subjects prepared girls for marriage and motherhood, or for work as a domestic servant.

THE DEVELOPMENT OF THE NATIONAL SYSTEM

Despite the many difficulties which the new system faced, National Schools (schools affiliated to the National Board) flourished. Their number rose from 789 in 1832 to 6,520 in 1867.[18] However, despite the growth in schools and numbers on school rolls, there were high levels of pupil absenteeism. Approximately 75 per cent of Irish children absented themselves from school, compared with almost 56 per cent in England and Wales and about 63 per cent in Scotland.[19] Variations in levels of participation can also be explained in terms of the extent to which children continued to participate in the labour market.[20] High rates of absenteeism were related to the attitudes of parents towards schooling and to the impoverished circumstances in which the majority of pupils lived. Girls were often removed from school to help in the home, to work in factories or to help out on the farm.

High levels of absenteeism meant that standards of education were low. Pupils often remained away from school as long as four or five months at a time, and had forgotten most of what they had learned upon their return.[21] In 1860, out of the 804,000 children on school rolls, just over 38 per cent were on Book I, and just over 6 per cent were on Books IV and higher.[22] The education received by those in the lower classes was very basic, including learning to read and write words of one and two syllables. Such lessons were only beneficial in so far as they prepared pupils for instruction in the higher classes. However, fewer than one-fifth of pupils attending National Schools reached the higher classes.

THE POWIS COMMISSION, 1870

Low standards of attainment and high levels of absenteeism were some of the issues which made an investigation into the operation of the national system inevitable. The ongoing dissatisfaction of the Catholic Church with existing provision for Catholics and the need for the English Treasury to demonstrate accountability and efficiency led to the establishment of a Royal Commission of Inquiry into Primary Education in 1868. Under the chairmanship of Lord Powis, the brief of the commission was to investigate and make recommendations on the operation of the system of primary education in Ireland. The Commission, which sat for two years, gathered evidence from a wide range of witnesses involved in education, including many from educational bodies not associated with the existing system, such as the Christian Brothers. The final detailed report provides an exhaustive analysis of the national system from its inception in 1831 until 1870.[23]

The Commission was critical in its appraisal of the system, noting that, in general, the progress of children in national schools was 'very much less than it ought to [have been]'.[24] In particular, it highlighted the low levels of pupil attainment and attendance, the sub-standard state of many school buildings, and the lack of proficiency of the teaching body (of which 43 per cent was female). It issued a total of 129 recommendations as a means of reforming the system, including the introduction of a system of 'payment-by-results'; a contract of employment for all teachers; management committees for all state-aided schools; formal training for all teachers; the extension of state aid to training institutions under the auspices of religious societies; and the suspension of the National Board's brief to publish textbooks (although the right of the Board to sanction books was retained). Significantly, for the Catholic teaching orders, the Commission recommended that all teachers, religious and lay, would be obliged to provide proof of their competence to teach before being entitled to a class salary and that teachers in convent schools would be examined and classed like other teachers.[25]

The most significant change to follow from the Powis Report was the adoption of a system of payment-by-results, which was put into operation nationally by 1872. This policy was not unexpected, as the Newcastle Commission in England (1858) and the Argyll Commission in Scotland (1864) had both recommended the introduction of payment-by-results in elementary schools. Teachers were paid a basic annual salary, which was then supplemented by additional payments depending on the performance of their pupils in annual examinations. Informed by utilitarian and functionalist principles, the system introduced a mechanical approach to teaching and learning. It was a vehicle for securing 'a better return for the outlay and labour of the National system'.[26] The schedule of payments indicated that greater 'value' was attached to the study of agriculture by boys than to the study of needlework by girls. Female teachers were paid a lower basic salary than were male teachers. Because many female teachers taught female pupils, they did not have the same opportunity as their male counterparts to increase their salary by a significant sum.

THE PARTICIPATION OF GIRLS IN NATIONAL EDUCATION

According to Margaret Byers (1832–1912), founder of Victoria College, Belfast, the state recognised the principle that 'girls should in no sense be left behind their brothers in obtaining the early facilities to prepare them for the duties of life' when it established a national system of schooling in 1831.[27] As the new system progressed, increasing numbers of girls availed of primary instruction. Daly (1979) suggests that this was because parents who had not previously been in a position to pay for their daughters' education could now send them to school.[28] The increase was also influenced by the demise of gainful work in the home. It was noted in the Powis Report that the absence of staple industries in many towns and the general scarcity of occupations for women explained the significant level of female participation in education. In towns (such as Celbridge and Drogheda) where female attendance was lower, this was due to the demand for female labour in factories. Girls were also needed to manage the home while parents worked in factories.[29] In rural areas, the attendance rates of girls corresponded with the farming calendar. Attendance at the Convent of Mercy, Killarney, fluctuated according to the agricultural operations of the season, being lowest at tillage and harvest times, and highest in the summer quarter. Attendance rates for older girls fluctuated according to the season for sowing potatoes, while younger girls were often removed from school in order to spin wool.[30]

By the late 1860s, the overall number of girls attending National Schools had almost reached the same level as boys (see Table 3). However, while the overall number of girls attending National Schools almost equalled that of boys, there were differences within age groups. Younger girls (between the ages of five and seven) attended school to the same degree and often in greater numbers than boys, but attendance figures for older girls were significantly lower. By the age of fifteen and above, there was a significant gap in the numbers of boys and girls on school rolls.[31] Education was not

Table 3 Number of males and females attending National Schools in 1868

	Males	Females	Infants	Total
Ulster	66,414	55,264	16,045	137,723
Leinster	47,373	44,212	18,842	110,427
Connaught	28,844	25,578	4,958	59,380
Munster	67,116	60,548	18,421	146,085
Grand Total	209,747	185,602	58,266	453,615

Source: Powis, Vol. VI, Educational Census: Return showing number of children actually present in each primary school 25th June 1868; with introductory observations and analytical index.

considered as important a priority for girls, and many older girls were removed from school in order to work in the home or to earn a wage to help in the upbringing of younger siblings. Early with-drawal from school had significant implications for the ability of girls to eventually take up the challenge of the Intermediate and Royal University Acts (1878, 1879). It was not until after the intro-duction of the Irish Education Act of 1892 that attendance rates of boys and girls became comparable. The Act introduced the principle of compulsory schooling for all children living in urban areas between the ages of six and fourteen for at least seventy-five days each year. It also prohibited employment for children under eleven, except during particular periods of the year. The Act did not apply to children in rural areas.[32]

LITERACY AND EDUCATION

The increased numbers of children participating in formal schooling resulted in an inevitable increase in levels of literacy. An increase in overall levels of literacy meant an increase in the acquisition of English and a corresponding decline in the use of Irish.[33] The Great Famine was also indirectly responsible for the increase in literacy levels and the proliferation and assimilation of the English language. According to Daly (1986), 'the famine has, at one stage or other, been held responsible for almost every subsequent occurrence in Irish history from the decline of the Irish language and an upsurge in religious devotion to sweeping changes in Irish agriculture and the engendering of a strong hostility to England which inevitably led to the movement for national independence'.[34] As Fitzpatrick (1990)

notes, 'the census returns of literacy show that virtually every young
Irish adult could write (or claimed to be able to write) by 1911,
whereas before the Famine most Irishmen were illiterate. This
improvement was far more dramatic for women, since they were
initially disadvantaged. Men born in the late eighteenth century
were three times as likely to be literate as women.'[35] Over three
million women emigrated from Ireland during the nineteenth
century. More than half of the female generation which reached
adolescence by the time of the Famine subsequently emigrated.[36]
Most emigrated to America and Australia. Knowledge of English
was necessary for those who wished to emigrate or rise in society. As
Fitzpatrick observes, 'the school system was said to foster emigration through the curriculum, the extra-curricular activities of
teachers and the decoration of class rooms'.[37] Girls in particular
utilised their access to elementary education in order to prepare for
a life in America and Britain.[38]

Fitzpatrick further notes that

> adolescent girls showed a growing disposition to go to school,
> overtaking the boys in about 1880. Girls tended to play truant
> less often than boys, to stay at school longer and therefore to
> reach higher standards . . . The superior performance of girls
> reflected not only their possibly stronger desire to better
> themselves, but also their declining importance in the labour
> market . . . Those [girls] who stayed at National School usually
> hoped to become monitors and eventually National teachers, a
> profession dominated by women.[39]

THE NATIONAL SCHOOL CURRICULUM FOR GIRLS

The formal curriculum was the most powerful way in which the
system of education was shaped along gendered lines. The principal
subjects of secular instruction for boys and girls in national schools
were reading, writing, arithmetic, grammar, dictation and geography.
The course of instruction in these subjects was less demanding for
girls, particularly those in classes 4 and 5.[40] Girls of all ages were
taught needlework and those attending convent schools were also
instructed in singing. Girls generally performed as well as boys in
the areas of reading, writing and dictation, displaying less competence in geography and in arithmetic.[41] The requirements of the
National Board in arithmetic were lower in female schools than in

male schools, and girls generally attained a lower standard.[42] Girls attending convent National Schools were singled out as being particularly poor at arithmetic. This was generally judged to be owing to the attitude of the nuns themselves towards the importance of arithmetic for girls.[43] Arithmetic was generally more effectively taught in boys' schools, while in mixed schools the boys excelled.[44]

Needlework formed a central part of the curriculum of girls in national schools from the system's inception. It was considered 'of very great importance' for girls, ranking next to reading and writing.[45] Older girls often remained on in National Schools for the sole purpose of receiving instruction in needlework.[46] The same emphasis on needlework and domestic subjects was evident in the elementary school curriculum for girls in Britain.[47] The ordinary course of needlework extended from the second to the sixth classes. In the lower classes, it comprised instruction in hemming, knitting, plain patching, darning, making pinafores and cutting patterns. In the sixth class, it also included instruction in the different branches of plain sewing and knitting.[48] Although it was noted that instruction for girls in needlework should be accompanied by instruction in reading, writing and arithmetic, timetables in girls' schools reflected the central role of needlework in the curriculum.[49]

Competency in needlework was also regarded as important for female National School teachers. Women were specifically employed for the purposes of teaching 'sewing, knitting, platting [sic] straw and other female work'.[50] Needlework was a compulsory subject for all female teachers seeking classification as well as promotion.[51] The first directress of needlework was appointed by the CNEI in 1888. Part of the brief of the Inspectorate was to ensure that girls were being adequately instructed in sewing or knitting. Inspectors were admonished that any neglect in providing detailed reports on the instruction of needlework in girls' schools would be brought to the serious attention of the Commissioners.[52] Schools for embroidery, crochet, knitting, netting and tatting were established for girls who wished to focus on these skills alone. The Census of 1851 returned 902 pupils in such schools.[53]

It is clear that the National School system institutionalised the dominant ideology regarding the role and function of women in society. Its emphasis on domestic subjects meant that the home was promoted as woman's natural habitat and girls were provided with the necessary skills to enable them to carry out their duties in the home. It also reinforced and legitimated the private/public dichotomy, particularly for middle-class girls, who were not expected to require skills other than that of home-maker. Even working-class girls, many of whom would have had to seek gainful employment to help support their families, would have been equipped with skills appropriate to a working life within the confines of the domestic sphere. The curriculum thus indirectly supported prevailing arguments concerning woman's intellectual capacity for a scholarly education and the suitability of such an education to her future role. This approach to female education was supported by the Catholic Church, an institution which articulated the superiority of men and the subordination of women. The relegation of women to the domestic sphere also facilitated one of the Church's basic ideologies, the reproductive and nurturing function of women.

NATIONAL SCHOOL TEXTBOOKS FOR GIRLS

Textbooks were employed as a powerful vehicle for reinforcing and legitimating existing stereotypes regarding appropriate education for girls. The National School textbooks published by the CNEI, provide compelling evidence regarding what constituted a woman's appropriate place and role in society.[54] The earliest text produced for the exclusive use of girls, *The Reading Book for Use of Female Schools* (1854), illustrates the kind of values and ideas being transmitted to Irish girls via print culture.[55] The text, revised three times, was essentially an anthology of prose and poetical pieces which comprised extracts deemed particularly appropriate for girls. Lessons covered in the text included those relating to looking after children; tending the sick; temper and disposition; duties of a housemaid; duties of a cook and of a housekeeper; good management; domestic arts; and female education. The importance of honesty, benevolence, gentleness, sincerity, cleanliness, politeness, patience and obedience were all highlighted. So-called 'female foibles' such as laziness and vanity were criticised, and knowledge was promoted as being necessary and worthwhile in so far as it promoted industry and diligence, but not as a vehicle for challenging existing norms and mores.[56]

A substantial part of the *Reading Book* was given over to tending to the needs of others. Taking care of other people, whether the sick or children, was represented as a very important female duty. Because of her 'nature' and disposition, woman was depicted as being uniquely suited to 'caring' activities, and the textbook advised that these activities should be carried out selflessly and silently:

In reading to yourself, in a sick room, turn over the leaves gently; even the noise of paper is often very disturbing to invalids ... Wear no creaking shoes, nor rustling garments, nor have any loose pins or needles about you.[57]

The importance of passivity and self-effacement was at all times emphasised:

There is no hand like a woman's hand, no heart like a woman's heart ... The woman feels no weariness, and owns no recollection of self. In silence and in the depth of night, she dwells, not only passively, but so far as the qualified term may express our meaning, joyously ... Her step, as in obedience to an impulse or a signal, would not waken a mouse ...[58]

Cleanliness received a great deal of attention throughout the course of the text. Housemaids were instructed to be active, clean and neat, carrying out their duties in an unobtrusive and almost invisible manner.[59] Cooks were encouraged to be healthy, strong and clean. Female 'cleanliness' was linked to the notion of morality, and convent schools in particular stressed its importance. As one lesson in the girls' *Reading Book* states, 'cleanliness may be recommended under the three following heads: as it is a mark of politeness; as it produces affection; and as it bears analogy to purity of mind'.[60] While the *Reading Book* argued that women felt 'no weariness' and were excellent nurses, women were also portrayed as being inept, ineffectual and unable to cope with minor domestic mishaps. In one lesson, a woman who discovers her dress is on fire becomes alarmed, and finding no one to help her runs about screaming, causing the fire to escalate.[61] An extract on the 'Importance of Exercise to Females' cautioned that 'bodily and mental indolence, to which females are prone, both from nature and education, ought to be vigorously contended against'. However, it reinforced the image of women's physical weakness and inferiority by noting that women shy away from exercise such as walking because 'from physical causes' they find it painful.[62] The virtues of industry and economy were among the few values promoted for both sexes.[63]

The difference between men and women was overtly embraced and celebrated throughout this anthology. Women were portrayed as passive, obedient, helpful and compliant, while men were seen as active and powerful. The question of the inequality of the sexes was accorded some space in the text, but only to reaffirm that inequality is natural and necessary. It noted that, 'as to equality, if by it is meant an equality of property or condition, there is no such thing, nor was there ever such a thing in any country since the world began'.[64] What the text testified to, above all else, is that education for men and women should be different. The kind of education appropriate for women should prepare them for life in the domestic sphere, as carers, helpers, mothers and wives. Education should reinforce and legitimate existing sexual divisions and in no way challenge them. The role of the passive, biddable, content and silent woman is celebrated and girls are taught to adopt and fulfil this role. The lesson entitled 'On Female Acquirements' summarises the role of female education thus:

> Knowledge is not to elevate her above her station, or to excuse her from the discharge of its most trifling duties. It is to correct vanity, and repress pretension. It is to teach her to know her place and her functions . . . to render her more useful, more humble, and more happy . . . she will be happy in her own home, and by her own hearth, in the fulfilment of religious and domestic duty, and in the profitable employment of her time.[65]

In addition to the *Reading Book for the Use of Female Schools* (1854), girls were taught from the *Girls Reading Book for the Use of Schools* (1864); *Manual for Needlework* (1869), and *Short Lessons in Domestic Science* (1885). These books not only idealised the role of the young woman as 'homemaker', but defined such a role as one of service to the husband as 'breadwinner'. In a lesson titled 'Tact and Taste', girls were taught:

> Beautify your homes: make them the resting places of the bread winners: brighten them so that the clouds of the outside world may vanish under their influence . . . go through the house, room after room, to see in what manner it can best be fitted up as the resting place of the bread winners.[66]

Somewhat more practical was the instruction to be found in the *Girls Reading Book for the Use of Schools* (1864). It contained considerably more information on cooking and domestic economy than the *Reading Book for the Use of Female Schools*. While some ten per cent of the latter textbook was devoted to cookery, almost half of the former book contained lessons on cooking and food preparation. It offered 'hints . . . and practical directions for the preparation of homely fare', with specific lessons on breakfast cookery, roasting and baking, soups, boiling, stewing, pies and puddings, and various recipes. It also linked the utility of such lessons with the eventual role of the young reader, as a homemaker and wife, reminding her that 'the housewife must, as soon as breakfast is over, be active and have everything in readiness' for the preparation of dinner.[67]

The *Manual for Needlework for Use in National Schools* (1869), published by the CNEI, gave 'a practical knowledge of plain needle-work', stating clearly that this was 'probably the most important acquirement for females, especially those attending the National Schools of Ireland'.[68] The *Manual for Needlework* comprised a total of thirty-nine lessons ordered under three categories: 'needlework', 'dressmaking' and 'underclothing'. In an endeavour to ensure that 'every girl of ordinary ability . . . will be able to cut out and make up, neatly and tastefully, a plain dress', the *Manual for Needlework* included diagrams and illustrations. Indeed, the illustrative material compared very favourably with that found in the five 'graded readers' published by the CNEI for general use in schools. While the graded readers were packed with text, and contained very few line-drawings or illustrative material, the *Manual for Needlework* provided both visual stimulation and practical instruction by including pictures, sewing patterns and diagrams.

In a detailed study of the textbooks produced exclusively for girls by the CNEI, Mac Suibhne (1996) has indicated that almost sixty per cent of the content was devoted to domestic/family themes, and to the development of 'female character qualities'.[69] Textbooks were thus an extremely powerful mechanism for developing and sustaining authoritative images of what constituted a suitable education for girls. This phenomenon was not unique to Irish education, but was representative of dominant thinking regarding appropriate education for girls.[70] The education system, and textbooks as powerful vehicles for delivering the ideology of that system, was the most effective site for legitimating and perpetuating this sex-role stereotype.

GIRLS AT WORKHOUSE SCHOOLS WITHIN THE NATIONAL SYSTEM

The majority of workhouse schools connected themselves to the national system of education.[71] From 1840, the National Board offered support to the workhouse schools in the form of books and supplies, but they had little control over the running of the schools and the appointment of teachers. The schools remained under the control of the Poor Law Commissioners, and girls had a different experience of school than National School girls. By the mid-nineteenth century, there were 139 workhouse schools for girls attached to the National Board.[72] A small number of gratuities were made to them, in the form of allowances for teachers, and the reports of the inspectors who visited workhouse schools attested to the fact that 'the number of children in attendance at the Workhouse Schools is so large, that unless Assistant Teachers or Paid Monitors be appointed, it will be impossible for the pupils to make satisfactory progress in their education'.[73] The dependency of children on workhouse schools became clear when, in 1852, a parliamentary commission was set up to inquire into the treatment of juvenile criminals and destitute children.[74] The inquiry, which encompassed Ireland, took evidence from Irish witnesses, together with reports and articles, and provided a compelling picture of the fate of workhouse children. In all, there were 76,724 children under the age of fifteen in Irish workhouses. Several thousand of these children had been deserted by parents fleeing the country on famine ships, and many were later reclaimed and sent to America with aid from the Poor Law Guardians.[75] But, for those who remained, industrial, agricultural and domestic training was necessary, in order that they could earn their keep. In theory, this was to be supplied at the workhouse schools. The workhouse schools associated with the National Board were reported upon in the annual reports of the CNEI, and the *Twentieth Report* (1853) is particularly rich in evidence, appearing immediately after the publication of the inquiry of 1852.

Workhouse girls were supplied with a frock, petticoat and cap, although many went ragged and dirty. Diseases spread quickly in the cramped conditions of the schools. In 1853, official reports noted that, at Nenagh Union Girls' School, 70 out of 325 girls had skin diseases. Reports of skin diseases were commonplace, as were reports of infectious eye diseases. At the Tipperary Union Girls' School, 700 girls had ophthalmia, and as a consequence of eye disease some twenty girls had lost both eyes and fifty-nine had lost one eye.[76] The education provided to girls in workhouse schools reflected the expectations of the Poor Law guardians for these girls. Occupational training was considered more useful than academic education. Unlike National School regulations, which stipulated that pupils should receive a daily minimum of six hours tuition, a minimum of three hours of reading, writing and arithmetic was considered sufficient for pupils at workhouse schools. However, even this meagre amount of literary instruction was often sacrificed to labour. Despite the spread of eye disease at Tipperary Union Girls' School in the 1850s, girls were taught basket-weaving, but offered no schooling at all. In addition to occupational training, workhouse girls also provided labour for workhouse industry, such as the grinding of corn for milling. A device known as the capston mill, which required one hundred and fifty girls to push the arms of a rotating horizontal millwheel, was employed at the workhouses at Cork, Midleton, Killarney, Athlone and Dublin South. Some contemporary reports of the use of treadwheels and capstan wheels were scathing:

> The capstan-mill . . . tends to directly increase the stupor of the already dull children, and is attended with considerable danger, as when children fall . . . they are walked over by numbers before the machine can be stopped . . . In Athlone Union the capstan-mill [is] worked by little girls . . .[77]

Less arduous though equally industrious labour included knitting, and weaving straw bonnets. In some instances, this labour continued right through the school lessons. One CNEI inspector who visited workhouse schools attached to the National Board commented on the common practice of 'bringing into the Girls' school spinning wheels, reels, adult girls to practise sprigging, &c, and carrying on these branches of industry while the children are supposed to be engaged at their ordinary lessons'.[78] Perhaps as a consequence of the excessive amount of time spent on labour, offical reports make few comments on actual lesson content, but document the girls' labour in some detail. Inspectors also sometimes commented on the pathetic countenances of workhouse girls. Visiting the Midleton workhouse school in 1868, Mr Coward reported:

> Many of the girls . . . bore the marks of early ill-usage; and their disfigured and careworn countenance and (sometimes) deformed bodies made it painful to see them.[79]

By the middle of the century, it was estimated that there were 15,049 girls attending workhouse National Schools. In some areas, girls were hired out as farm labourers, for seasonal work, and others found work as farm servants, but the majority were engaged in sewing and knitting, while over three thousand girls did domestic work within the workhouse.

Girls at workhouse schools were not only trained in various types of needlework and domestic work, but they also made clothing for workhouse inmates, and for sale by the workhouse guardians. James Kavanagh, an inspector for the National Board, observed that 'the general practice is, that the school-girls make and mend the men's shirts, and all of the clothing both of the women and girls, and make and repair much of the bed clothing of the house . . . [and] wash down their own dormitories and their school-rooms'.[80] He added that a common practice was to 'take in orders from commercial houses and execute the orders so obtained', which led to the abuse of the children as cheap labour by which to raise funds to pay the teachers.[81] The CNEI condemned workhouse schools that engaged the girls in fancy needlework, since such schools had failed to provide adequate preparation for domestic service, which was 'the destiny of most of these girls':

> . . . rough household work should occupy the first rank in the industrial training of the pauper girls . . . a girl might work a collar exquisitely, or embroider a coronet for a duchess, and be unable to patch her own dress neatly or darn her stockings; and she might do all these to perfection, and be unable to wash and make up a shirt, dress a baby, cook a beefsteak, or lay a tradesman's dinner table.[82]

The daily practice of manual labour in place of literary instruction was in part a consequence of the fact that schoolmistresses appointed to workhouse schools were usually untrained, and some were paupers. Poor Law Commissioners were frequently obliged to dismiss schoolmistresses for offences such as drunkenness, petty crime, violence and incompetence.

The incompetence of schoolmistresses was not always without cause: most workhouse schoolmistresses had very large classes in their charge. At Kilrush Union Girls' School in 1852, one young woman teacher had responsibility for 512 pupils.[83] Not surprisingly, none of the girls had any proficiency in writing and arithmetic, while only fifteen of the girls could read at the level of the Second Graded Reader (National School). At Cork Union school, the mistress had responsibility for 234 pupils, despite being 'very deficient in skill both in teaching and in examining'.[84] In the middle of the nineteenth century, the National Board Inspector James Kavanagh described the duties undertaken by the mistress of a workhouse school:

> The teacher . . . is no longer a mere schoolmistress; she undertakes the chief control and immediate direction of an average family of about 200 girls, from 3 or 4 to 15 years of age . . . she super- intends their dormitories, and sees them rise, wash, and dress;

she conducts the morning and night prayers of those of her own communion; she invokes a blessing on the meals, all of which are taken in her presence; she provides for their entire clothing, most of which is made and all repaired under her direction; she has entire charge of them in school . . . she daily inspects all as to health and personal cleanliness . . . she is present at their recreation . . . she directs all their industrial employment . . .[85]

Although some workhouses employed 'an old pauper woman' to sleep in the girls' dormitories at night, the burden of managing a workhouse school was invariably placed on young shoulders.[86] At least 25 per cent of the workhouse schoolmistresses were twenty years of age or younger, and the average age of mistresses was twenty-three. Most worked for a period of about three years. The salaries afforded to workhouse schoolmistresses ranged from ten to twenty-five pounds per annum, depending on how they were 'classed'. Fewer than one-third of workhouse teachers had any training, and some were almost illiterate. The mistress of Dromore Union was described thus by the CNEI: 'Spells and writes badly, knows little arithmetic, and no geography whatever.' The mistress at Donegal Union did not 'know even the rudest outlines of the Map of the World'. In receipt of an annual salary of £10, she defended her lack of mathematical knowledge to the CNEI saying that she 'took a girl to reduction, but indeed it's little figuring she ever done'.[87]

The number of pupils in the mistresses' charge did not influence the size of their salary. At Tralee Union in the mid-nineteenth century, there were 629 girls in the charge of two mistresses. Neither woman was 'classed' or trained; one earned ten pounds and the other fifteen pounds per annum, and both had rooms and rations worth thirteen pounds per annum.[88] At Limerick Union, three teachers managed a workhouse school for 730 girls. One of the women was paid twenty-five pounds per annum, as she was trained. The other two mistresses earned ten pounds per annum each, with apartments and rations. The incentive to the three mistresses to accrue income from the girls' labour was criticised by the CNEI, who commented that 'the proficiency of the pupils in the literary branches appears to have been rather checked by the introduction of industrial branches, such as muslin-embroidery, shirt-making &c'.[89]

By the last decades of the century, the number of children attending workhouse schools declined, and many workhouse girls had been placed in employment. Often girls were placed in positions in houses in the vicinity of the workhouse, and were sometimes selected by visitors to the workhouse schools. Visiting the workhouse school at Parsonstown, Mr Harvey reported to the Powis Commission:

> On the day of my visit, one of the older girls was leaving the workhouse, having been chosen as a servant by a person in the neighbourhood; and I was glad to find that the school was visited regularly by a number of ladies in and about Parsonstown.[90]

By 1868, it was calculated that there were 7,589 girls under the age of fifteen attending workhouse schools.[91] In 1872, the Local Government Board for Ireland replaced the Poor Law Commission. The Local Government Board favoured the practice of boarding out the workhouse children with families. This practice had been adopted by some thirty-five Protestant orphan societies, and had proved successful in providing foster homes and apprenticeships for orphaned children. As Luddy (1995) noted, boarding out was seen as particularly important for girls. It was 'in the homes of respectable cottagers that poor girls could acquire . . . skills in domesticity'.[92] This, in turn, prepared them for marriage and motherhood. By the end of the nineteenth century, boarding out had been widely adopted within the workhouse system, and this, together with the introduction of industrial schools and the work of the Protestant Orphan Society and the Catholic religious orders, helped the workhouses to rid themselves almost completely of children. In 1898, the Pauper Children Act provided for the education of remaining workhouse children in National Schools, and this further reduced the need to provide workhouse schooling.

CONVENT SCHOOLS AND THE NATIONAL SYSTEM OF EDUCATION

The proliferation of convents in the early years of the nineteenth century facilitated the development of a network of convent schools, many of which joined the National System. Convent schools emphasised the importance of morality, obedience and piety, as well as subjects traditionally prescribed for girls. Because of the type of curricula provided and the close relationship between convent schools and the community, convent schools managed to attract great numbers of children for whom formal education would not, heretofore, have been considered a priority. The education provided spanned the literary, industrious and religious and attracted children from very young ages, some of whom remained on until their late teens.[93] Parents favoured a convent education for their children because nuns were often instrumental in providing pupils with situations, and because the moral training provided was deemed superior. Parents were also more comfortable entrusting the education of their daughters to nuns, whom they valued as models of piety, purity and morality.[94] Finally, convents enjoyed higher social status than ordinary national schools, because the majority were fee-paying and because they focused on the acquisition of accomplishments, such as dancing, drawing and French conversation.[95]

By the time of the 1868 educational census, 133 schools of the 229 convent schools listed in the returns were affiliated to the National Board. Almost 10 per cent of all children in school at this time were in convent schools, and just under one-fifth of all girls.[96] Convents also enjoyed higher attendance rates. The average daily attendance rate at National Schools in 1860 was about 32 per cent, compared with 38 per cent at convent schools.[97] Convent schools were valued because of the religious, social and economic benefits they brought the country. They were supported by the hierarchy because it was believed they would increase devotional piety.[98] The nuns who taught at the convent schools were powerful symbols of the ideal woman: chaste, pure and devout. Convent schools were highly effective sites for attracting future postulants and for moulding future generations of Irish women in the values and doctrine of the Catholic Church. These nuns were valued as agents of social control and moral regeneration. Schools were effective platforms for inculcating into young girls the importance of obedience, piety and morality. Nuns, as educators, had increased powers to go out into the community and carry their message to a wider audience. Even those who were cloistered were typically given special dispensation from the local bishop to go out into the community as educators and nurses.[99] Finally, nuns were considered a valuable economic resource. The cost of employing nuns was one-third of the cost of employing lay teachers, since nuns did not sit state examinations required for classification as salaried teachers and were hence paid on a capitation basis per pupil.[100] In 1874, the average salary paid by the National Board to lay teachers was about £37, while nuns earned about £13.[101] It was noted in the Powis Report that it would be financially beneficial to have more nuns and Christian Brothers working within the national system.[102] The issue of subjecting nuns to state examinations remained contentious throughout this period.

It was generally accepted that 'the people of Ireland would rise in rebellion against [the] National System if they saw their nuns dragged from their cloisters, gathered to some common hall and submitted there to Government inspection'.[103] However, as the century progressed, increasing pressure for accountability led to calls for nuns to have formal qualifications.

EDUCATIONAL PROVISION FOR GIRLS AT CONVENT NATIONAL SCHOOLS

Convent schools followed similar curricula to ordinary National Schools, but placed even greater emphasis on the importance of morality, deportment and accomplishments. The policy of the Catholic Church at the time was to educate girls to be 'holy women and accomplished ladies'.[104] A strong emphasis was placed on fostering in girls the values of order, neatness and obedience. The instruction provided in convent schools in the areas of cleanliness, singing, needlework and reading (in the higher classes) was deemed superior to that provided in ordinary National Schools. Convents were, however, considered less effective in the areas of arithmetic, grammar and geography.[105] Arithmetic was singled out as particularly deficient, especially among senior classes.[106] Overall, the Powis Commission found the progress of children in non-national convent schools, as in National Schools, below an acceptable standard.

A fundamental belief central to the curricula in convent schools was instruction in manners, deportment, order and politeness, features of the French convent tradition.[107] The education of girls at this time was influenced by the French educationalist Fénelon, who held that women's moral and intellectual training were closely linked.[108] Among the areas in which pupils in convent schools were periodically examined and graded were conduct, order and punctuality, politeness, deportment, and application.[109] Convent schools also promoted the importance of deference and compliance. Children were taught to know their 'respective stations in life' and were warned about the ills of being 'restless and unhappy in their proper spheres'.[110] Visitors to convent schools found girls 'marked by an unusual subduedness of look and manner, not downcast, but deferential'.[111] Across the majority of convent schools, girls were found to be submissive, neat, orderly, obedient, clean, truthful and modest. It was noted in the Powis Report that 'the neat dresses, the clean faces, and well-combed hair of the girls, and their pleasant, modest ways [compensated] in great measure for their other defects'.[112] It was further observed that 'this part of the convent schools' training [did] much for the coming generation, by civilizing through these means its mothers'.[113] Hence, religious orders viewed their role as including the preparation of girls to be the mothers of future generations.

Class distinction was a dominant feature of convent life and convent schooling. Nuns themselves were ranked according to their social class, and this demarcation was repeated at the level of the school. Nuns were ranked as lay sisters or choir sisters.[114] Lay sisters usually came from less privileged backgrounds and were responsible for the domestic chores in the convent. Choir sisters were generally from wealthier families and were involved in activities such as nursing, teaching and the governance of the convent. One of the prevailing arguments made to justify this distinction was that lay sisters were not proficient in Latin and could not recite office in choir. As Clear (1987) notes, assigning inferior status to women who cooked and cleaned allowed convents to preserve class bias and divisions of labour.[115]

Nuns maintained and perpetuated existing class distinctions in their schools. Schooling was always separate for different social classes, even among those orders devoted largely to the instruction of the poor. Girls of different social classes were at all times prevented from mixing with each other, since 'richer parents would not send their children if there was any danger of them associating with the poor children'.[116] In Ardee Convent National School, Louth, the Sisters of Mercy operated a separate school for daughters of shopkeepers and farmers. These girls were taught French, vocal and instrumental music, and the 'usual English course'. On Sundays, secular and religious instruction was provided to servants and girls who worked in the fields.[117] Dundalk Convent National School, Louth, also a Sisters of Mercy school, provided a separate department for the children of the middle classes, in which they were taught music, French and the English course. They also operated a school on Sundays for servants and labouring classes, in which instruction was provided in reading, writing, the making up of shop bills, and letter writing for those wishing to emigrate.[118] Lurgan Convent National School had three distinct departments, all under the National Board: an infants' school for poor children, a school called St Mary's for poor girls, and a school called St Joseph's for girls of a 'higher social class'. The girls in St Joseph's were mainly daughters of tradespeople living in Lurgan. Each paid 2s. 6d. or 5s. a quarter. The room in which they were taught was separate and approached by a different route.

The role of the religious teaching orders in providing education to the poorer classes was viewed as even more significant than their role in providing education to the middle classes, as education was viewed as one of the most powerful ways of civilising the poor. Orders such as the Sisters of Mercy, the Sisters of Charity and the Presentation nuns were actively engaged in providing instruction to the poor. They were motivated not only out of a desire to educate, but out of a perceived need to exercise a moral and religious influence over a vulnerable section of society. They were valued not for their pedagogical expertise, but for their 'humble and solid piety, and particular talent in instructing the ignorant'.[119] Nuns regularly used visits to the sick or destitute to impress on parents the benefits and value of education.[120] They also promised food and clothing as an incentive to poorer families to send their children to school. They were frequently obliged to vary the times and dates of the allocation of food or clothing, since parents often sent their children to school for a number of days prior to distribution, only to keep them at home thereafter.[121] Breakfast was provided to girls attending Bagnalstown Convent National School, Carlow, a Presentation school.[122] Clothing was supplied to pupils from Clonakilty Convent National School, managed by the Sisters of Mercy.[123] The more destitute girls from Fir House Convent National School, managed by the Carmelite order, received bibs and frocks, and occasionally lunch.[124] Poorer pupils from Newtown Smyth and Rahoon Convent National Schools, Galway, received food and clothes.[125] Children from Enniscorthy Convent National School, managed by the Presentation order, were encouraged to bring bread and lunch for their poorer and destitute classmates.[126] Occasional strategies used by convent schools for attracting pupils were frowned on by other National School teachers. A teacher from Armagh Female National School complained that nuns teaching in the nearby convent, a Sacred Heart school, had induced girls to attend the convent by sending them presents.[127]

Girls from poorer classes were instructed largely in the acquisition of domestic arts, such as needlework, or in basic domestic chores, which prepared them either for their role as a wife and mother, or for taking up a position as a domestic servant. Many schools operated a separate department for this purpose.[128] The greatest emphasis was placed on the acquisition of skills in plain and fancy needlework, which was considered 'a most essential branch of female instruction'. Even infants in convent schools learned how to sew.[129] Girls regularly left ordinary National Schools for convents because these offered instruction in needlework, and prizes were awarded in needlework to encourage attendance. Parents often removed their daughters from ordinary National Schools in favour of convent schools because 'fancy work' received greater attention. Many older girls attended convent schools specifically for the purpose of learning plain needlework.[130]

Additional crafts and skills which would enable girls to earn a livelihood were also taught, and products were often sold and the profits handed over to the pupils.[131] Embroidery was taught at Bagnalstown Convent National School,[132] crochet-work at Blackrock Convent National School,[133] lace-work and feather-flower work at Youghal Convent National School[134] and dress- and shirt-making at Newtown Smyth Convent National School.[135] Older girls and their mothers attended classes in lacemaking and Irish crochet at Scoil Ursula National School during the 1830s. The work produced was sold to the USA and other countries.[136]

EMPLOYMENT PROSPECTS FOR GIRLS FROM CONVENT NATIONAL SCHOOLS

The type of career open to girls leaving convent schools reflected the emphasis placed by convents on particular subjects deemed appropriate for women. Typically, girls left convent schools to become teachers or nursery governesses, enter a trade, work in a mill or go into service.[137] Teaching or governessing were deemed respectable occupations for middle-class girls as they were associated with the private sphere and with a nurturing role. Going into service was deemed particularly appropriate for girls from poorer families as, again, it was confined to the domestic sphere, the natural habitat for women. Nuns were instrumental in sourcing employment for girls, in an endeavour to keep 'girls of industry and talent' longer at school.[138] Three girls from Bagnalstown Convent National School, Carlow, procured employment as governesses in France, one in Germany, four in America, five in Australia and others in Ireland. Fifty-seven found employment in industrial work, the remainder in 'respectable service'.[139] Seven girls from Youghal Convent National School, Cork, trained as national teachers, while three became private teachers and two monitors.[140] Of the eighteen girls who left the fifth class of Baggot Street Convent National School, Dublin, managed by the Sisters of Mercy, twelve went into business, five found work as governesses and one became a national school-teacher. Of the twenty-six who left from the fourth class, three became dressmakers, the majority remaining at home.[141] Girls from

Newtown Smyth Convent National School, Galway, went on to become headmistresses in model schools, teachers, governesses to private families, milliners, shopkeepers' assistants and ladies' maids. More than seventy girls were trained in the industrial department to support themselves.[142] Fifty-three girls from Rahoon Female Convent National School, Galway, found employment with the National Board as teachers, while seven found employment as teachers in private families. More than a hundred girls were trained as milliners, shop assistants and dressmakers.[143] Some girls became nuns.[144] The majority of girls from poorer backgrounds had few options but to take up work as domestic servants.[145]

Towards the end of the nineteenth century, there were calls for the primary curriculum to be modified to meet the needs of a changing society. A growing number of individuals concerned about the narrow focus of the curriculum, particularly its over-emphasis on literacy and numeracy, advocated a more pragmatic and func-tionalist approach towards elementary education. Influenced by curricular developments in England and Scotland, many lobbied for the introduction of manual and practical instruction into the primary school curriculum. Ideologically, this was justified because it would aid in the development of moral qualities such as accuracy, industry and perseverance; have a beneficial effect on the general health of pupils by increasing their interest in other school subjects; foster a sense of individuality in the pupil; inspire respect for bodily labour; prepare students for the higher education given in technical schools; and develop expertise in subjects such as agriculture.[146]

For girls, it was widely felt that the existing provision, despite its considerable émphasis on domestic arts, was too literary and quite removed from the day-to-day experiences of life in the private or domestic arenas. This was particularly the view of some members of the Catholic Church, who found the existing curriculum too academic and lacking in practical application. Writing in 1884, one clergyman noted:

> An average Irish girl who has just completed her course of education at a National school, and is nearly full-grown, cannot 'cut out' or 'make-up' even her own clothing. She cannot knit or sew or spin. She cannot milk cows or make butter. She is totally unskilled and inexperienced in the art of cookery. In fact, through her utter ignorance of the useful industries, she can render no service which any one wants or care for: she can produce no commodity for which there is any demand. Until she has been trained and practically instructed in some useful

industry, she is literally not worth the cost of her maintenance
. . . the system is too theoretical and speculative, and not sufficiently practical and utilitarian.[147]

The Royal Commission on Manual and Practical Instruction in
Primary Schools under the Board of National Education in Ireland,
or the Belmore Commission, as it was commonly known, was
established in 1898 to examine the extent to which manual and
practical instruction should be included in the primary school
curriculum.[148] The Commissioners heard evidence from a range of
bodies and individuals involved in primary education, among them
the Commissioners of National Education, who noted that there
existed a 'general feeling' that the current system of primary
education placed too great an emphasis on literary instruction, and
not enough emphasis on 'manual instruction and the cultivation of
habits of observation'.[149] The Commission heard evidence that
existing provision for girls was too literary and not of any practical
import. Provision, it was suggested, should be shaped to reflect the
future role and needs of girls. Girls living in towns needed to be
trained to work as shopassistants and telegraph clerks, while those
in rural areas needed to acquire the necessary skills to equip them to
work in the areas of domestic service and the home.[150]

One of the principal recommendations of the Commission was
that cookery, laundry work and domestic science should be taught
in all girls' schools where practicable. These additional subjects were
to complement the existing provision of instruction in sewing and
knitting. In order to encourage schools to make provision for the
teaching of such subjects, financial assistance was made available to
girls' schools to provide them with the necessary buildings and
equipment, and a liberal system of grants was promised to managers and teachers who cooperated. Needlework, it was advised,
should continue to form a central part of the curriculum for girls. It
should begin in kindergarten and continue up, as part of hand and
eye training, into the higher classes. Advanced needlework should
occupy the time given over to woodwork in schools for boys.[151]

The Commission's recommendations formed the basis of the
Revised Programme of Instruction which was introduced in 1900.[152]
The Revised Programme, which brought to an end the 'payment by
results' era, promoted a more child-centred approach to education,
while at the same time placing greater emphasis on manual and
practical subjects. Under the terms of the new programme, English
and arithmetic were made compulsory, and, in schools with Irish-
speaking pupils, teachers were instructed to employ the vernacular

Literary Programme

Reading (which should include text books on suitable industrial subjects, and on Domestic Economy, with knowledge of the subject matter).

English Composition, including Letter-Writing on various subjects, which should embrace Geography, Grammar, &c., skill in Penmanship to be taken into account.

Industrial Programme

Plain Needlework (in its various developments, including Shirtmaking). This must be one of the three industrial subjects to be taken up daily in each of the two years of a Sixth Class Course. Subjects in Classes A and B (as below), any two of which may be adopted at the choice of the Manager, and within the capacity of the Teacher.

Class A

1. Dressmaking (plain); Underskirt-making. 2. Fine Underclothing; Baby Clothes. 3. Knitting and Crocheting of Jerseys, Caps, Wraps, Vests, Petticoats, Socks, Stockings, Gloves, Slippers, and similar articles. 4. Good repairing of garments, hose, house and table linen, &c., such as darning (damask and invisible), fine drawing, re-lining, re-binding, re-fitting, re-buttonholing, turning; also plain ingrain marking. 5. Clothwork, viz.:– Girls' Jackets, Children's Cloaks and Newmarkets, Little Boys' Suits, Braiding, Tailor-buttonholing. 6. The washing, carding, spinning, and weaving of wool. 7. Treatment of flax and weaving of linen.

Class B

1. Lace-making – Youghal, Limerick, Carrickmacross, Inishmacsaint, or other recognised kind. 2. Mountmellick Work – Sprigging (on Handkerchiefs, &c.), ornamental marking of Linen. 3. Art Needlework, including Embroidery from Celtic patterns. 4. Gold and Silver Lace Work – Ecclesiastical Embroidery. 5. Hangings – Furniture Embroidery. 6. Glove-making. 7. Artificial Flowermaking. 8. Basket-making – Indian Matting – Straw Matting; Straw Chairs, Straw plaiting, &c.: other articles produced from Straw, or Wicker. 9. Other kinds of Cottage Industries, such as Wood Carving, Net Mending, where local or suitable.

Source: Royal Commission on Manual and Practical Instruction in Primary Schools under the Board of National Education in Ireland; Final Report of the Commissioners, 1898, p. 46.

Figure 4 Alternative scheme for girls of sixth class, 1889.

to assist in the teaching of English. Kindergarten methods, manual instruction, drawing, object lessons, elementary science, singing, school discipline and physical drill were also obligatory in schools where there were teachers holding certificates of competency in these areas. Cookery and laundry were made compulsory in all girls' schools where there were competent teachers and suitable appliances and needlework was made obligatory for girls in schools with female teachers or workmistresses.[153]

THE 'ALTERNATIVE' SCHEME FOR GIRLS (1889)

As the national system was modified to reflect the needs of a changing society, the inherent gendering of the curriculum became more marked. Needlework became an even more central part of the curriculum for girls, and technological advances allowed for the introduction of new subjects such as cookery, laundry work, domestic science and hygiene, also deemed essential for girls. As part of an ongoing policy of developing the curriculum along gendered lines, the CNEI introduced an 'alternative scheme' in 1889 for sixth-class girls attending National Schools in which a female teacher was employed (see Figure 4). Under the new programme, the industrial course of instruction was more highly developed and the literary course was condensed.[154] Anticipating opposition to the new course, the CNEI decided to allow school managers to apply for special exemption where necessary. By 1896, it was found that about one-third of schools had adopted the new course. The Commissioners issued an explanatory memorandum with the new programme, in which they recommended that girls who had passed the two stages of fifth class should devote the remainder of their time to industrial education in order to get prepared for 'the practical duties of their homes, or for employment in profitable industries'.[155] In order to facilitate this, it was recommended that sixth-class girls should devote about two hours each day (out of the ordinary school timetable) to plain needlework and special industrial instruction.

The Belmore Commission pronounced that the two hours devoted to industrial instruction under the 'alternative scheme' were unwarranted, believing many of the subjects the scheme embraced to be unsuitable for primary school pupils. The Commissioners recommended the termination of the scheme, suggesting instead that the first four subjects (dressmaking; fine underclothing; knitting and crocheting; repairing of garments) should be provided as additional subjects to be taken either inside or outside of school hours. The Commissioners also observed that, if school managers desired that special provision be made for industrial instruction of girls, they should utilise the Special Industrial Departments, which were recognised in connection with certain National Schools. These Departments totalled sixty-one on 31 December 1896. It was recommended that the only industrial subjects appropriate for girls in National Schools were dressmaking, cookery and related subjects, which formed 'an essential part of a girl's education, having regard to the efficient discharge of her household duties'.[156] However, it was also noted that other industrial subjects were taught in some of these departments, including book-binding, net-mending, weaving, dairy management, poultry-keeping and bee-keeping, under the title of 'cottage industries'.

COOKERY INSTRUCTION FOR GIRLS

At the beginning of the 1890s, the provision of cookery classes was random and confined largely to convent national schools and to the practising schools of the training colleges for females. This was for the most part owing to the financial difficulties associated with adequately resourcing the subject. Only eighty-three national schools were listed as providing instruction in cookery in 1896. With the increased emphasis on domestic subjects for girls, a practical knowledge of cookery assumed a central role in the primary school curriculum. The Belmore Commission promoted cookery as 'a most important branch of practical instruction' for girls, a subject 'of special importance in Ireland where the labouring and artizan classes [were] sadly ignorant of the art of cookery, their food in consequence being seldom prepared in as economical or nutritious a manner as it might be'.[157]

In 1896, the Commissioners secured permission to engage some special 'itinerant' teachers of cookery and laundry work. The teachers recruited, four in total, were trained under the Royal Irish Association for Promoting the Training and Employment of Women, and had obtained diplomas from the National Union for the Technical Education of Women. They travelled throughout the country providing instruction at the various National Schools. The exemplar course embraced twenty demonstration and practice lessons in household cookery suitable for pupils of classes 4, 5, and 6.[158] Instruction in cookery was instrumental in promoting the popularity of the education provided by National Schools and impacted positively on the attendance rates of girls.[159] Cookery became a central part of the curriculum for Irish girls, with some believing that, 'if Irish cookery were better, Irish husbands would be more sober'.[160]

LAUNDRY WORK AND DOMESTIC SCIENCE FOR GIRLS

In the closing years of the nineteenth century, laundry work was considered as a school subject by the National Board. The Board examined existing provision in England as a means of informing practice in Ireland. Under the London School Board, laundry work was an obligatory subject for girls in the higher standards. A lesson was usually of two hours' duration, one hour being devoted to a demonstration and one hour to practical work. The Belmore Commission recommended 'the encouragement and extension of instruction in laundry work' to Irish National Schools.[161] With developments in science and technology, domestic economy and hygiene assumed more prominent roles in the primary school curriculum for girls. Instruction for boys in agriculture was considered by the Commissioners to complement instruction for girls in domestic economy.[162] Domestic economy included instruction in food, clothing, cleanliness, the dwelling and simple ailments. Hygiene consisted of knowledge of air, breathing, ventilation, water, alcoholic liquors and food. The practice up until the late 1890s was to acquire the requisite information solely from textbooks. One of the recommendations of the Belmore Commission was that the theoretical aspect of these lessons be illustrated and supplemented by experiments performed, where possible, by the pupils themselves.

The religious orders placed a considerable emphasis on the acquisition of skills in domestic economy. Housewifery, the 'practical application of domestic economy', had been introduced at the Loreto Convent National School, Bray, in the late 1880s. It was exclusively at the expense of the Loreto community, as the subject had not yet been approved by the Commissioners of National Education. It had proved 'both useful and attractive' to the senior girls in the school.[163] In 1896, domestic economy was taken up by 151 schools: 1,570 students were examined, of whom 1,030 secured passes. Hygiene was pursued in twenty-five schools: 535 pupils were examined and 379 passed.[164] Hence, despite technological advances and the changing nature of Irish society, the role of women was still viewed as firmly fixed in the private or domestic sphere and the system of education was shaped to reflect and reinforce this role demarcation. Woman's role within an emerging modern Ireland was viewed as largely unchanged, and nowhere was this more obvious than in the values and ideologies promoted by the education system.

NOTES

1   T. W. Rolleston, 'National Ideals of Education,' *New Ireland Review*, Vol. xvii, 1902, p. 17.
2   J.L. Foster to Secretary of Board of Education, 22 April 1811, cited in *Fourteenth Report of the Commissioners of the Board of Education in Ireland*, 1812.
3   Letter of the Right Hon. E.G. Stanley, Chief Secretary to His Excellency the Lord Lieutenant, addressed to His Grace the Duke of Leinster, October 1831, cited in *First Report of the Commissioners of National Education in Ireland*, 1834, p. 1. Hereafter The Stanley Letter.
4   Ibid.
5   *Freeman's Journal*, 1 July 1889.
6   The Stanley Letter, pp. 2–3.
7   *Royal Commission of Inquiry into Primary Education (Ireland), Vol. II: Reports of Assistant Commissioners*, 1870, p. 1.
8   MS Blackrock Convent Female National School, form no. 197, roll no. 5940, Ursuline Convent Archives, Blackrock, Cork.
9   Ibid.
10 Emmet Larkin, *The Making of the Roman Catholic Church in Ireland, 1850–1860* (Chapel Hill: University of North Carolina Press, 1980), p. xx.
11 Patrick Corish, 'The Catholic Community in the Nineteenth Century', *Archivium Hibernicum*, xxxviii, 1983, pp. 26–33.
12 Donald Akenson, *The Irish Education Experiment* (London: Routledge & Kegan Paul, 1970), p. 202.
13 *The Nation*, 19 December 1898.
14 Mary Daly, 'The Development of the National School System, 1831–40', in Art Cosgrove and Donal McCartney (eds), *Studies in Irish History* (Dublin: University College Dublin 1979), p. 155.
15 *Third Report of the Commissioners of National Education in Ireland*, 1836, p. 66.
16 John Coolahan, *Irish Education: History and Structure* (Dublin: Institute of Public Administration, 1981), p. 15; Akenson, *The Irish Education Experiment*, p. 215.
17 *Royal Commission of Inquiry into Primary Education (Ireland), Vol. I, Part I. Report of the Commissioners; with an appendix*, 1870, p. 259.
18 *Royal Commission of Inquiry into Primary Education (Ireland); Vol. VII: Returns from National Board*, 1870, p. 362.
19 Norman Atkinson, *Irish Education: A History of Educational Institutions* (Dublin: Allen Figgis, 1969), p. 101.
20 See David Fitzpatrick, ' "A Share of the Honeycomb": Education, Emigration and Irishwomen', in Mary Daly and David Dickson (eds), *The Origins of Popular Literacy in Ireland: Language, Change and Educational Development 1700–1920* (Dublin: Department of Modern History, Trinity College Dublin, 1990), pp. 167–87; John Logan, 'The Dimensions of Gender in Nineteenth Century Schooling', in Margaret Kelleher and James Murphy (eds), *Gender Perspectives in Nineteenth-Century Ireland* (Dublin: Irish Academic Press, 1997), pp. 36–49.
21 *Royal Commission of Inquiry into Primary Education (Ireland), Vol. III: Minutes of Evidence taken before the Commissioners, from 12 March to 30 October 1868*, 1870, p. 185.

22   There were five graded readers published by the Commissioners of National Education. In theory, a child progressed from one book to the next when a particular standard of education had been reached.

23   *Royal Commission on Nature and Extent of Instruction by Institutions in Ireland for Elementary or Primary Education, and Working of System of National Education* (Powis); Vol. i., pt. i. Rep., App. 1870 [C.6] xxxviii pt. i. 1; Vol. i. pt. ii. App., Special Reps. on Model Schools, Central Training Institution and Agricultural Schools 1870 [C. 6a] xxviii pt. ii. 1; Vol. ii. Reps. of Assistant Coms. 1870 [C. 6–i] xxviii pt. ii. 381; Vol iii. Mins. of Ev. 1870 [C.6–II] xxviii pt. iii. 1; Vol. iv. Mins. of Ev. 1870 [C. 6–iii] xxviii pt. iv. 1; Vol. v. Analysis of Ev., Index 1870 [C.6–iv] xxviii pt. iv. 547; Vol. vi. Educational Census 1870 [C. 6–v] xxviii pt. v.1; Vol. vii. Returns from National Bd. of Education 1870 [C. 6–vi] xxviii pt. v. 361; Vol. viii Miscellaneous Papers 1870 [C.6–vii] xxviii pt. v. 917.

24   *Royal Commission of Inquiry into Primary Education (Ireland), Vol. I, Part I: Report of the Commissioners; with an appendix*, 1870, p. 522.

25   Ibid., pp. 522–34.

26   Ibid., p. 522.

27   Margaret Byers, 'Girls' Education in Ireland: Its Progress, Hopes and Fears', paper read at the Annual Meeting of the Schoolmasters' Association, Dublin, 28 December 1888, p. 1, Victoria College Archives, Belfast.

28   Daly, 'The Development of the National School System, 1831–40', p. 161.

29   *Royal Commission of Inquiry into Primary Education (Ireland), Vol. II: Reports of Assistant Commissioners*, 1870, pp 18, 30.

30   Ibid., pp. 454–5.

31   *Royal Commission of Inquiry into Primary Education (Ireland), Vol. VII: Returns from National Board*, 1870, pp. 368–9.

32   See *Bill to Improve National Education in Ireland* 1892 (420), iv 645.

33   Mary Daly, 'Literacy and Language Change in the Late Nineteenth and Early Twentieth Centuries', in Daly and Dickson eds, *The Origins of Popular Literacy in Ireland*, p. 154.

34   Mary Daly, *The Famine in Ireland* (Dublin: Historical Association, 1986), p. 117.

35   Fitzpatrick, '"A Share of the Honeycomb": Education, Emigration and Irishwomen', p. 168.

36   Ibid., p. 173.

37   Ibid., p. 176.

38   David Fitzpatrick, 'The Modernisation of the Irish Female', in Patrick O'Flanagan, Paul Ferguson and Kevin Whelan (eds), *Rural Ireland, 1600–1900: Modernisation and Change* (Cork: Cork University Press, 1987), p. 176.

39   Fitzpatrick, '"A Share of the Honeycomb": Education, Emigration and Irishwomen', p. 172.

40   See *Twenty-Seventh Report of the Commissioners of National Education in Ireland*; 1860, Appendix D, Programme of Instruction for Pupils in the National Schools, or the Minimum amount of proficiency required for each Class, pp. 1–4.

41   *Thirty-Seventh Report of the Commissioners of National Education in Ireland*; 1870, Appendices, Table 6, Exhibiting the Proficiency of the Pupils examined by the Inspectors during the year 1870, under each head, pp. 371–4.

42   *Royal Commission of Inquiry into Primary Education (Ireland), Vol. II: Reports of Assistant Commissioners*, 1870, p. 465.

43   Ibid., p. 17, p. 465.

44   *Royal Commission of Inquiry into Primary Education (Ireland), Vol. I, Part I: Report of the Commissioners; with an appendix*, 1870, p. 290.

45   *Royal Commission of Inquiry into Primary Education (Ireland), Vol. III: Minutes of Evidence taken before the Commissioners, from 12 March to 30 October 1868*, 1870, p. 185.

46   *Eighteenth Report of the Commissioners of National Education in Ireland*, 1851, p. 210.

64 Female Education in Ireland

47 See C.S. Bremner, *Education of Girls and Women in Great Britain* (London: Swan Sonnenschein and Co., 1897).

48 *Royal Commission on Manual and Practical Instruction in Primary Schools under the Board of National Education in Ireland*; First Report, Minutes of Evidence 1897 [C. 8383] [C. 8384] xliii.1 . . . Final Report., Minutes of Evidence., Apps. 1898 [C. 8923] [C. 8924] [C. 8925] xliv.1, 77, 531 (Belmore Commission). Final Report of the Commissioners, 1898, p. 45.

49 *Royal Commission of Inquiry into Primary Education (Ireland), Vol. III: Minutes of Evidence taken before the Commissioners, from 12 March to 30 October 1868*, 1870, p. 79.

50 *Royal Commission of Inquiry into Primary Education (Ireland); Vol. I, Part I: Report of the Commissioners; with an appendix*, 1870, p. 45.

51 *Royal Commission on Manual and Practical Instruction in Primary Schools under the Board of National Education in Ireland; First Report of the Commissioners and Minutes of Evidence*, 1897, p. 5; see also *Royal Commission of Inquiry into Primary Education (Ireland), Vol. III: Minutes of Evidence taken before the Commissioners, from 12 March to 30 October 1868*, 1870, p. 184.

52 *Royal Commission of Inquiry into Primary Education (Ireland), Vol. VII: Returns from National Board*, 1870, pp. 190–1.

53 See 'The Cultivation of Female Industry in Ireland', *Englishwoman's Journal*, Vol. ix, August 1862.

54 See Lorcan Walsh, 'Images of Women in Nineteenth-Century Textbooks', *Irish Educational Studies*, Vol. 4, No. 1, 1984, pp. 73–87.

55 Deirdre Raftery and Judith Harford, 'Reading for Maidens and Maids: The Use of Eighteenth-Century Englishwomen's Writing in the Education of Irish Girls' (forthcoming), University of Southampton Conference, 'Women's Writing in Britain, 1660–1830', July 2003.

56 Mrs. Sandford, 'On Female Acquirements', *Reading Book for the Use of Female Schools* (Dublin: Commissioners of National Education, 1850), pp. 329–30.

57 Anon., 'On Attending the Sick,' *Reading Book for the Use of Female Schools*, pp. 28–9.

58 Literary Gems, 'The Sick Chamber', *Reading Book for the Use of Female Schools*, pp. 180–1.

59 Mrs. Parke's Domestic Duties, 'Duties of a Housemaid', *Reading Book for the Use of Female Schools*, pp. 58–61.

60 Addison, 'On Cleanliness', *Reading Book for the Use of Female Schools*, pp. 128–9.

61 Anon, 'Advice in Case of Fire,' *Reading Book for the Use of Female Schools*, p. 51.

62 *Quarterly Journal of Education*, 'Importance of Exercise to Females', *Reading Book for the Use of Female Schools*, pp. 265–6.

63 Goldsmith, 'On Generosity and Justice', *Fifth Reading Book for the Use of Schools* (Dublin: Commissioners of National Education, 1869), p. 23.

64 Watson, 'On Equality', *Reading Book for the Use of Female Schools*, pp. 194–5.

65 Mrs. Sandford, 'On Female Acquirements', *Reading Book for the Use of Female Schools*, pp. 329–30.

66 F.M. Gallagher, 'Tact and Taste', *Short Lessons in Domestic Science* (Dublin: Commissioners of National Education, 1885), p. 219.

67 *Girls' Reading Book for the Use of Schools* (Dublin: Commissioners of National Education, 1864), p. 133.

68 *Manual for Needlework for Use in National Schools* (Dublin: Commissioners of National Education, 1869), Preface.

69 Seosamh MacSuibhne, *Oblivious to the Dawn: Gender Themes in 19th Century National School Reading Books in Ireland, 1831–1900* (Sligo: FDR, 1996), pp. 112–15.

70 See, for example, Carol Dyhouse, 'Good Wives and Little Mothers: Social Anxieties and the Schoolgirl's Curriculum, 1890–1920', *Oxford Review of Education*, Vol. 3, No. 3, 1977, pp. 21–35; Anna Davin, *Growing Up Poor: Home, School and Street in London, 1870–1914* (London: Rivers Oram, 1997).

71 Of the 163 Poor Law Unions established by 1853, 141 had connected their schools to the National Board. See *Twentieth Report of the Commissioners of National Education in Ireland*, 1853, Appendix L, p. 631.

72 The number of girls' Workhouse National Schools in each province were: Ulster (28), Munster (49), Leinster (34), and Connaught (28). Source: Commissioners of National Education in Ireland, *Twentieth Report*, 1853, Appendix L, p. 635.

73 *Eighteenth Report of the Commissioners of National Education in Ireland*, Vol. I, 1852, p. xxvii.

74 *Report from the Select Committee on Criminal and Destitute Juveniles*, 1852 (515), vii.

75 Barnes, *Irish Industrial Schools*, p. 12.

76 *Twentieth Report of the Commissioners of National Education in Ireland*, 1853, Appendix L, p. 660.

77 Ibid., p. 676.

78 Ibid., p. 636.

79 *Royal Commission of Inquiry into Primary Education (Ireland)* (Powis), Vol. I, Part I, p. 475.

80 *Twentieth Report of the Commissioners of National Education in Ireland*, 1853, Appendix L, pp. 678–9.

81 Ibid., p. 678.

82 Ibid.

83 Ibid., p. 647.

84 Ibid.

85 Ibid., p. 652.

86 See *Royal Commission of Inquiry into Primary Education (Ireland)* (Powis), 1870, Vol. I, Part I, p. 476, and *Twentieth Report of the Commissioners of National Education in Ireland*, 1853, Appendix L, p. 652.

87 *Twentieth Report of the Commissioners of National Education in Ireland*, 1853, Appendix L, p. 650.

88 Ibid.

89 Ibid., p. 648.

90 *Royal Commission of Inquiry into Primary Education (Ireland)* (Powis), 1870, Vol. I, Part I, p. 477.

91 Ibid., p. 278.

92 Luddy, *Women and Philanthropy*, pp. 90–1.

93 *Royal Commission of Inquiry into Primary Education (Ireland), Vol. III: Minutes of Evidence taken before the Commissioners, from 12 March to 30 October 1868*, 1870, p. 79.

94 ALS, Sr. M. Perpetual Succour to Mother Patrick, 25 July 1911, Dominican Generalate Archives, Dublin.

95 See, for example, An Old Convent Girl, 'A Word for the Convent Boarding Schools', *Fraser's Magazine*, Vol. x, 1874, pp. 473–83.

96 *Royal Commission of Inquiry into Primary Education (Ireland); Vol. I, Part I. Report of the Commissioners; with an appendix*, 1870, p. 260.

97 Mary Peckham Magray, *The Transforming Power of the Nuns: Women, Religion and Cultural Change in Ireland, 1750–1900* (New York: Oxford University Press, 1998), p. 81; see also Tony Fahey, 'Female Asceticism in the Catholic Church: A Case Study of Nuns in Ireland in the Nineteenth Century', unpublished PhD Thesis, University of Illinois, 1981, pp. 97–8.

98 Larkin, *The Making of the Roman Catholic Church in Ireland*, p. 23.

99 MS Important Contracts, 1771, Ursuline Convent Archives, Blackrock, Cork.

100 Tony Fahey, 'Nuns in the Catholic Church in Ireland in the Nineteenth Century', in Cullen (ed.), *Girls Don't Do Honours*, p. 20.

101 Return of grants made by the Irish National Education Board to convent and monastic schools for 1863, 1864, and 1874 . . . 1875 (451) lxi, p. 341, cited in Fahey, 'Nuns in the Catholic Church', in Cullen (ed.), *Girls Don't Do Honours*, p. 20.

102 *Royal Commission of Inquiry into Primary Education (Ireland), Vol. IV: Minutes of Evidence taken before the Commissioners, from 24 November 1868 to 29 May 1869*, 1870, p. 1242.

103 Rev. T. Quin, 'Convent Schools, Correspondence' (Belfast: 'Morning News' Office, 1883), p. 8.

104 *Irish Times*, 8 October 1883.

105 See *Special Reports to Commissioners of National Education in Ireland on Convent Schools 1864* [405] xlvi. 63, p. 7; p. 56; p. 86; p. 93. See also *Royal Commission of Inquiry into Primary Education (Ireland), Vol. I, Part I: Report of the Commissioners; with an appendix*, 1870, pp. 283–4.

106 *Special Reports to Commissioners of National Education in Ireland on Convent Schools 1864*, p. 30; p. 86; p. 93. See also *Royal Commission of Inquiry into Primary Education (Ireland), Vol. I, Part I: Report of the Commissioners; with an appendix*, 1870, p. 284; *Royal Commission of Inquiry into Primary Education (Ireland), Vol. II: Reports of Assistant Commissioners*, 1870, p. 234.

107 Anne V. O'Connor, 'The Revolution in Girls' Secondary Education in Ireland 1860–1910', in Cullen (ed.), *Girls Don't Do Honours*, p. 39; See also 'Convent Boarding Schools for Young Ladies', *Fraser's Magazine*, Vol. ix, 1874, pp. 778–86.

108 See Jules Renault, *Les idées pédagogiques de Fénelon* (Paris: P. Lethielleux, 1879).

109 MS Immaculata Boarding School, Roll Book, 1889–92, Dominican Convent Archives, Cabra.

110 *Prospectus of the Immaculata Boarding School*, 1835, cited in *Annals of the Dominican Convent, St. Mary's Cabra, 1647–1912*, p. 102, Dominican Archives Cabra.

111 Rev. W. Fraser, 'The State of our Educational Enterprises: A Report of an Examination of the Working, Results, and Tendencies of the Chief Public Educational Experiments in Great Britain and Ireland' (Glasgow: Blackie and Son, 1858).

112 *Royal Commission of Inquiry into Primary Education (Ireland), Vol. II: Reports of Assistant Commissioners*, 1870 [C. 6I.] p. 138.

113 Ibid.

114 For a comprehensive examination of the social background of recruits to the religious life in the second half of the nineteenth century in Ireland, see Caitriona Clear, 'Walls within Walls: Nuns in Nineteenth-Century Ireland', in Chris Curtin, Pauline Jackson and Barbara O'Connor (eds), *Gender in Irish Society* (Galway: Galway University Press, 1987), pp. 134–51. For an examination of the role of the lay sister, see Luddy, 'Lay Sisters', in *Women in Ireland, 1800–1918*, pp. 80–2 and Christine Trimingham Jack, 'The Lay Sister in Educational History and Memory', *History of Education*, 2000, Vol. 29, no. 3, pp. 181–94.

115 Catriona Clear, *Nuns in Nineteenth Century Ireland* (Dublin: Gill & Macmillan, 1987), p. 99.

116 *Royal Commission of Inquiry into Primary Education (Ireland), Vol. II: Reports of Assistant Commissioners*, 1870, p. 3.

117 *Special Reports to Commissioners of National Education in Ireland on Convent Schools, 1864*, p. 163.

118 Ibid., p. 167.

119 ALS, Sister M. Charles Molony to Mother M. Joseph McLoughlin, 18 August 1836, Ursuline Convent Archives, Blackrock, Cork.

120 *Special Reports to Commissioners of National Education in Ireland on Convent Schools 1864*, p. 8; p. 38; p. 87; p. 163.

121 *Royal Commission of Inquiry into Primary Education (Ireland), Vol. II: Reports of Assistant Commissioners*, 1870, p. 451.

122 *Special Reports to Commissioners of National Education in Ireland on Convent Schools, 1864*, p. 12.

123 Ibid., p. 32.
124 Ibid., p. 71.
125 Ibid., p. 95; p. 100.
126 Ibid., p. 213.
127 Ibid., p. 11. See also p. 95.
128 Ibid., p. 13.
129 Ibid., p. 72.
130 *Royal Commission of Inquiry into Primary Education (Ireland), Vol. II: Reports of Assistant Commissioners*, 1870, p. 467.
131 *Special Reports to Commissioners of National Education in Ireland on Convent Schools, 1864*, p. 7.
132 Ibid., p. 12.
133 Ibid., p. 29.
134 Ibid., p. 56.
135 Ibid., p. 95.
136 *Ursuline Convent, Souvenir Book*, 1952, p. 25, St Angela's College Archives, Cork.
137 *Special Reports to Commissioners of National Education in Ireland on Convent Schools 1864*, p. 5.
138 Ibid., p. 13.
139 Ibid.
140 Ibid., p. 57.
141 Ibid., p. 64.
142 Ibid., p. 96.
143 Ibid., p. 101.
144 Ibid., p. 133.
145 *Royal Commission of Inquiry into Primary Education (Ireland), Vol. III: Minutes of Evidence taken before the Commissioners, from 12 March to 30 October 1868*, 1870, p. 79.
146 *Royal Commission on Manual and Practical Instruction in Primary Schools under the Board of National Education in Ireland; Appendices to the Reports of the Commissioners, 1898*, Appendix A, Document I, pp. 5–6.
147 Thomas Nulty, *The Relations Existing between Convent Schools and the Systems of Intermediate and Primary National Education* (Dublin: Browne and Nolan, 1884), pp. 35–6.
148 *Royal Commission on Manual and Practical Instruction in Primary Schools under the Board of National Education in Ireland* (Belmore Commission).
149 *Royal Commission on Manual and Practical Instruction in Primary Schools under the Board of National Education in Ireland; Appendices to the Reports of the Commissioners, 1898*, Appendix A, Document I, p. 5.
150 *Royal Commission on Manual and Practical Instruction in Primary Schools under the Board of National Education in Ireland; Third Report of the Commissioners, 1897*, pp. 24–6.
151 *Royal Commission on Manual and Practical Instruction in Primary Schools under the Board of National Education in Ireland; Final Report, 1898*, pp. 42–7.
152 See Michael Tierney, 'The Revised Programme in National Schools', *New Ireland Review*, Vol. xv, 1901, pp. 77–84.
153 See *Revised Programme of Instruction in National Schools*, in *Appendix to the Annual Report of the Commissioners of National Education*, 1902.
154 *Royal Commission on Manual and Practical Instruction in Primary Schools under the Board of National Education in Ireland; Final Report of the Commissioners*, 1898, p. 46.
155 Ibid.
156 Ibid., p. 47.
157 Ibid., p. 42.
158 Ibid., pp. 42–3.

159 *Report of Mr. F.H. Dale, His Majesty's inspector of schools, Board of Education, on Primary Education in Ireland;* 1904 [Cd. 1981.] xx. 947.
160 'Letters from Ireland, VI', *New Ireland Review*, December 1901, p. 206.
161 *Royal Commission on Manual and Practical Instruction in Primary Schools under the Board of National Education in Ireland; Final Report of the Commissioners*, 1898, p. 44.
162 J.M. Goldstrom, *The Social Content of Education 1808–1870: A Study of the Working Class School Reader in England and Ireland* (Shannon: Irish University Press, 1972), pp. 76–8.
163 *Royal Commission on Manual and Practical Instruction in Primary Schools under the Board of National Education in Ireland; Final Report of the Commissioners*, 1898, p. 45.
164 Ibid., pp. 42–5.

Chapter 3
Intermediate Education for Girls

SUSAN M. PARKES

BACKGROUND

The demand for state support for secondary education (known as 'Intermediate education' in Ireland) had been growing since the middle of the nineteenth century. Following the introduction of the state supported National School system of primary education in 1831, the 1835 Wyse Report of a Select Committee on Foundation Schools had recommended the setting up of a system of state second-level schools on a county basis. Twenty years later the Endowed Schools' Commission of 1857–58 recommended the establishment of a state education board to provide grants to secondary schools.[1] However, the long controversy in the nineteenth century between the Church and state over denominational rights in education in Ireland prevented the establishment of a state system of second-level schooling. The protracted struggle between the Catholic Church and the state regarding the secular Queen's Colleges in Belfast, Cork and Galway had made the government reluctant to intervene at secondary level.[2]

The provision of secondary education was, in the first half of the nineteenth century, undertaken by Protestant voluntary and endowed schools such as the Royal Schools in Ulster, the Grammar Schools of Erasmus Smith, Royal Belfast Academical Institution and Catholic religious orders such as the Jesuits, the Carmelites, the Vincentians and a network of diocesan colleges.[3] From the 1850s, Protestant high schools for girls emerged in response to the growing desire of girls to access second-level education. These included the Ladies' Collegiate Institute, Belfast (1859), Alexandra College, Dublin (1866) and Strand House School, Londonderry (1860). In addition, there were a number of co-educational schools such as

Methodist College, Belfast (1868), Wesley College, Dublin (1845) and the Quaker Newtown School, Waterford (1798). The female Catholic religious orders who provided education for middle-class girls included the Loreto (Institute of the Blessed Virgin Mary), the Dominicans, the Ursulines, the Sisters of St Louis and the Society of the Sacred Heart. The demand for education for middle-class girls had been increasing with the growth of wealthy commercial and manufacturing families in the cities and towns, particularly in Belfast, Dublin and Cork. The need for a middle-class girl to earn a living rather than being financially dependent on her male relatives – father, brother or husband – was apparent. The meagre education in languages, needlework, art and music that was offered to girls to prepare them for society and marriage was seen to be insufficient. One of the only respectable careers open to middle-class women who needed to support themselves was to be a governess in an upper- or middle-class home or to open a small private school in their own house. In either case, women needed to be well educated.

THE LEADERSHIP OF ISABELLA TOD AND MARGARET BYERS IN BELFAST

Among the leading advocates in Ireland for the right of women to an academic education were Isabella Tod (1836–96) of Belfast, who founded the Ladies' Institute, Belfast, (1867), Margaret Byers (1832–1912) of the Ladies' Collegiate School, Belfast (1859) and Anne Jellicoe (1832–80) of Alexandra College, Dublin (1866). These three women, in different ways, worked together for the campaign for girls' education. They were all influenced by the high-school movement in England, which had begun in the 1840s with the opening of Queen's College, London, founded by the Christian socialist, Reverend F.D. Maurice, for the purpose of educating young women, many of whom wished to become governesses. The need to provide formal higher education for English women led to the establishment of Bedford College, London (1849), endowed by Elizabeth Reid as a non-denominational college modelled on London University.

Two of the young women educated at Queen's College (1848) were Frances Buss and Dorothea Beale, who became the key pioneers of the girls' high-school movement. In 1857 Miss Buss founded her own school, North London Collegiate School, and in 1858 Miss Beale became headmistress of Cheltenham Ladies' College, which had been founded five years previously. These two schools became models for girls' high schools and boarding schools. Frances Buss emphasised the need for a rigorous and ordered programme of academic studies similar to that undertaken by boys, including Latin, mathematics and science, while Dorothea Beale sought to develop a high standard of girls' education which, while academic in nature, recognised the distinct needs of girls, whose role in society would differ from that of their male counterparts. This difference of approach was to continue for many years within girls' education, as to whether it should be modelled exactly on boys' education and so prove equality of achievement, or whether the 'separate sphere' of the girls' lives should be accepted and educational provision adapted to suit their specific needs.[4] The ideas that shaped the high-school movement in England were to be given a voice in Ireland through Tod, Byres and Jellicoe, and they played a key role in the development of 'academic' education – particularly for Protestant girls. It will be seen that the agency of certain nuns within religious orders, such as the Dominican, Loreto and Ursuline orders, enabled Catholic girls to attain a similar education.

Isabella Tod was born in Edinburgh in 1836, of a Scottish–Irish family. She returned to live in Belfast, and, although little is known of her private personal life, she became a major public figure in the development of girls' education in Ireland and an advocate of women's rights.[5] Influenced by the high-school movement in England, she was a founding member of the Ladies' Institute in Belfast in 1867 and became its first secretary. The Institute provided lectures for young women and promoted women's educational opportunities. Queen's College, Belfast, was still closed to women, so professors from the College were invited to give lectures at the Institute. Tod enabled her entry into public life in 1867, when she addressed a meeting of the National Society for Promotion of Social Science, which held its annual meeting that year in Belfast. The Society had been set up in 1854 and was an offshoot of the British Association for the Advancement of Science. Membership was open to women and it became an important platform for women social reformers. Tod's paper was titled 'On Advanced Education for Girls in the Upper and Middle Classes', and on that occasion a male friend read it for her. In 1874 she published her ideas in a pamphlet titled 'On the Education of Girls of the Middle Classes', in which she argued strongly against the idea of a 'practical' and vocational education for girls. She advocated that a girl needed a broad general education, not just for marriage but as a full human being who could contribute to public life and gain employment. Many women had to earn their living and it was essential that those destined to become governesses or teachers should have a thorough education. Tod argued in favour of a broader curriculum for girls that would include Latin and Greek, modern languages such as German and French, mathematics and English language and literature. She suggested that a study of science and logic or political economy could be added and that the study of music should be regarded as a subject in its own right and not just as an accomplishment. Tod concluded by discussing the pressing need for women teachers for girls' schools, and argued for the establishment of a system of written and oral examinations, which would set standards and provide recognised qualifications.[6]

Tod was a close friend of Margaret Byers, who founded the Ladies' Collegiate School in Belfast in 1859 to educate middle- and upper-class girls.[7] These were the daughters of the rising wealthy manufacturing and professional families of the city. Born in Co. Down, of a Presbyterian family, Margaret Byers had been educated at a ladies' college in Nottingham. She had married a missionary and travelled, but was widowed quickly. She returned to Belfast and set up her own school, the Ladies' Collegiate School, later to be called Victoria College, Belfast. The school rapidly developed both a secondary and higher education department, and in 1873 moved into purpose-built accommodation in Lower Crescent. The new building was opened by one of the pioneers of women's education in England, Maria Grey, who had founded the Women's Education Union.[8] Byers emphasised the need for young women to undertake serious academic study so as to be able to find a 'respectable job' and earn a living. Byers was to be one of the main advocates for the inclusion of girls in the Intermediate examination system and for the opening of university education to women.

ANNE JELLICOE AND ALEXANDRA COLLEGE DUBLIN, 1866

Alexandra College, Dublin, was founded in 1866 as a college of higher education for girls. Anne Jellicoe, a Quaker and a committed social reformer, had been born in Mountmellick, Co. Laois, and had set up an embroidery and lace school in Clara, Co. Offaly, to provide work for women.[9] She became deeply involved in the debate about the employment of women and in 1861 she addressed the first Dublin meeting of the National Association for the Promotion of Social Science on the topic 'On the Conditions and Prospects of Young Women Employed in the Manufactories of Dublin'. As a result of this interest and work she became a co-founder of the Queen's Institute in Dublin in 1861.[10] This organisation was first known as the Irish Society for Promoting the Training and Employment of Women, and its management committee included both men and women. Anne Jellicoe and Ada B. Corlett were members from the start, whilst Ada Corlett became one of the honorary secretaries. The purpose of the society was to find suitable employment for middle-class women, but this proved difficult as these women had a limited education and could not compete in the labour market. The Queen's Institute was thus the first technical college for women, and it sought to arrange for women's classes in commercial languages and in law-writing. However, Jellicoe also saw a need for a proper academic college, where girls who wished to become governesses could receive a full liberal education. With the help of the recently appointed Church of Ireland Archbishop of Dublin, Dr Richard Chenevix Trench, she founded Alexandra College in 1866.[11] Chenevix Trench had been Professor of Divinity at King's College, London, and was a close friend and colleague of F.D. Maurice, Professor of English Literature and Modern History at King's College, who had been a founder and first Principal of Queen's College, London, in 1848. Modelled on Queen's College, London, the new Alexandra College aspired to offer girls not only a secondary education but also a university-style liberal education, to fit them for careers as teachers. The College was located in Earlsfort Terrace, Dublin, and Jellicoe used the powerful influence of Church of Ireland clergy and professors of Trinity College Dublin to support her venture, which was to be highly successful. Alexandra College became a model for other girls' academic schools in Ireland, and it was to play a major part in obtaining support for the inclusion of girls in the Intermediate Education Act of 1878 and in the opening to women of the new Royal University of Ireland in 1879. In 1873 a 'feeder high school' for the College, known as Alexandra School, was established next door to the College. Its first headmistress, Isabella Mulvany, was to be one of the first women graduates of the Royal University in 1884, and a leader of the campaign for the higher education of women.

EXAMINATIONS FOR WOMEN, 1869

One of the great needs of girls' secondary education in the mid-nineteenth century was to establish a standard of academic achievement that would equal that attained by boys. A system of public examinations open to both boys and girls was one way of showing that girls could reach the same standard and had intellectual ability equal to that of boys. It was hoped that the universities would be able to provide such a service, as had happened in England. In 1858 the Oxford and Cambridge Local Examinations had been instituted for boys' secondary schools and in 1863, following pressure from the leading girls' high schools, the examinations were opened to girls. Furthermore, the Schools' Enquiry Commission in England (1864–68), which investigated the existing endowed and proprietary schools for boys, took evidence from Frances Buss of North London Collegiate School, Dorothea Beale of Cheltenham Ladies' College and Emily Davies, the leading pioneer of women's higher education, who founded Girton College, Cambridge in 1869.[12] The Commission recommended that a system of girls' day schools under public management should be developed to offer an academic curriculum. The Endowed Schools' Act of 1869, which followed the Commission's report, enabled many of the old school endowments to adapt to provide for a new network of girls' grammar schools.[13] In the same year Cambridge University instituted a series of Cambridge Higher Local examinations, for students over eighteen years of age. These examinations were open to women and could be taken by students studying in higher education.[14]

Thus 1869 was a significant year in the development of women's higher education both in England and in Ireland. The three universities of Cambridge, Dublin and the Queen's University of Ireland all introduced external examinations for women. In Belfast, Margaret Byers, anxious to enhance the work of the Ladies' Collegiate School, had petitioned the Oxford and Cambridge Board to allow an examination centre in the city for the Local Examinations, but this had been refused, as it was said that Belfast was too far away. The Ladies' Institute, Belfast, then requested the Queen's University of Ireland to allow women to take university local examinations.[15] In 1860 the Queen's University had introduced a system of external examinations for boys held annually in Dublin and at other local centres. These examinations were offered at two levels – junior for candidates under sixteen and senior for older candidates. In 1869, in response to the request from the Ladies' Institute, Queen's University agreed to open this system of external examinations to girls.[16] The Ladies' Institute, while pleased with this achievement, was concerned when it emerged that the London School of Medicine for Women would not accept a QUI certificate for entry to courses. A successful lobby succeeded in changing this. Although the Queen's University examinations for women did not lead to the award of a degree, they provided the first step in raising the standard of girls' education. As a consequence, the Ladies' Collegiate School entered its pupils for these examinations. By 1874 thirteen candidates from the Ladies' Collegiate School had gained honours certificates from QUI. The results were published in the local press, and this was very encouraging for the schools. The following year the Ladies' Institute petitioned Queen's College Belfast to allow women to attend lectures in the college in order to study for the university certificates, but this privilege was refused.

TRINITY COLLEGE DUBLIN AND EXAMINATIONS FOR WOMEN, 1869

In Ireland a similar opening occurred for women when the University of Dublin, Trinity College, Dublin, introduced Examinations for Women in 1869. The Council of Alexandra College and the Governesses' Association of Ireland sent a memorial to Trinity College, Dublin, requesting the University to provide examinations which women could take as a recognised qualification, and the Board agreed. Anne Jellicoe was anxious to provide external qualifications for students attending Alexandra College and in 1869 she had established the Governesses' Association of Ireland (GAI) to promote the higher education of women as teachers. The GAI was modelled on the Governesses' Benevolent Institution (founded in England in 1841) and, while one of its functions was to provide an employment register, its main purpose was to try to improve educational opportunities for women.[17]

The TCD Examinations for Women were to exist until 1900, by which time their usefulness had been overtaken by the Intermediate system and the Royal University degrees. Though the number entering for the TCD exams was small, they provided an important qualification for women prior to the introduction of the Intermediate system.[18] The TCD examinations were held once a year and were offered in three grades: Junior (below eighteen years), Intermediate and Senior. The obligatory subjects in the Junior Grade were English grammar and composition, elementary arithmetic, history of England and geography of Europe. Optional subjects, of which the candidate had to offer one in Junior Grade, were French, Italian, Spanish, German, Latin, Greek, Mathematics, botany, zoology and the theory of music. In the Intermediate and Senior Grades, the study of the history of Greece and Rome was added to the obligatory subjects. In addition, scientific subjects such as mechanics, astronomy, physics, chemistry, geology and logic were included in the optional list, of which the candidate had to choose two for examination. The GAI provided scholarships for students to attend Alexandra College in order to prepare for the examinations, and these proved valuable for girls in need of financial support.[19]

INTERMEDIATE EDUCATION (IRELAND) BILL, 1878

Throughout the 1870s the demand for state support for secondary education increased, particularly among the Catholic schools, which considered that the Protestant schools had more than a fair share of endowments. The prominent Catholic boys' schools, such as Blackrock College, founded by the Holy Ghost Fathers, and Castleknock College, run by the Vincentians, were seeking a system which would bring state financial support and equality of status with the Protestant schools. The 1871 census had revealed that there were 587 superior schools in Ireland (252 male, 162 female, and 160 mixed) serving 21,225 pupils, of which only 50 per cent were Catholic, whereas Catholics constituted 77 per cent of the total population of 5,412,377.[20] The education of middle-class Catholic girls was largely provided by the religious orders. The religious orders most involved in the provision of schooling to middle-class Catholic girls included the Loreto, Dominican and Ursuline orders. These three orders would later spearhead the campaign for the provision of higher education to Catholic women.[21]

The Conservative government of Disraeli (1874–80) sought a formula for channelling money into secondary schools that would appear to be upholding the principle of non-denominational education but would have the consent of the Catholic Church. The Church of Ireland had been dis-established in 1869 and a million pounds of its assets had been set aside for educational or social use. The Irish Chief Secretary, Sir Michael Hicks-Beach, decided to use this fund to establish a system of public examinations through which the money would be distributed equitably. A system of 'payment by results' had been operating in the primary national school system since 1872, and this seemed a possible mechanism to use for secondary schools. Sir Patrick Keenan, Resident Commissioner of National Education, was an expert in the system and had advised the government on its introduction into schools in Trinidad (1868). A fruitful partnership between Keenan, Hicks-Beach and the Catholic hierarchy developed which brought about the Intermediate Education Act of 1878. In 1876, Keenan had drafted a lengthy memorandum regarding a plan to support second-ary schools. Discussions were held between the Chief Secretary and the Catholic hierarchy and a draft of the Bill was drawn up based on Keenan's scheme. However, the final introduction of the Bill was delayed by various factors, including the 'obstruction' tactics of the Irish parliamentary party in the House of Commons, the promotion of Hicks-Beach to the post of Colonial Secretary and his replacement in Ireland as Chief Secretary by James Lowther.[22]

The introduction of this Intermediate Education Bill was of crucial importance to the women committed to the development of girls' education, but it was not until well into 1877 that it was realised by the women educators that girls' schools were in danger of being excluded.[23] In January 1878, prior to his departure, Hicks-Beach had included in the draft scheme the education of girls. It stated that the word 'student' implied girls as well as boys, but added that, in order to conserve funds, the payment by results for girls should be lower than for boys. However, when this draft of the Bill was sent to Cardinal Cullen, the Catholic Archbishop of Dublin (1850–1878), he objected to the inclusion of girls. In his reply to the Chief Secretary, Cardinal Cullen criticised four main issues in the draft Bill. First, he objected to the fact that Protestant schools would be keeping their previous endowments while Catholic schools would get no extra money other than that earned through payment by results. Second, he took issue with the fact that the Bill did not include payment for teachers' salaries. Third, he raised an objection to the powers of the proposed Intermediate Board, which he felt were not sufficiently defined. His final objection related to the inclusion of girls. He wrote to the Chief Secretary regarding the terms of the Bill that were intended to extend to intermediate schools for both girls and boys:

> This might do very well for infant or primary schools where children of both sexes learn the mere fundamental rudiments of knowledge, but this should not be extended to higher schools in which the training and teaching separate into diverging channels for different sexes. In the Intermediate schools the boys begin to teach themselves for the army or navy, for the bar or the magisterial bench, for the medical or surgical professions or for other occupations to which they alone can aspire: the females go in a different direction and require other sorts of training and teaching; and it seems strange that regulations for the two classes should be united in the one bill . . . .[24]

Further discussion followed between the Catholic hierarchy and the Chief Secretary. Dr Woodlock, Bishop of Ardagh and Clonmacnoise (1879–1940), reported to Cardinal Cullen that he considered that the hierarchy had persuaded the government to omit girls' schools from the Bill. He wrote that, in the discussions, Dr McCabe (Auxiliary Archbishop of Dublin 1877–97) had remarked that 'such examinations might be useful for advanced girls in the national schools', but 'our Convent schools, which have the chief part of the education of our young ladies of the middle classes, are very well conducted . . . And that neither the nuns nor the mothers of the girls of Ireland consent to the pupils presenting themselves at a centre for examinations, or to strangers entering convents as examiners'.[25]

Meanwhile, in Belfast, the women's lobby was alerted to the fact that the Education Bill was now unlikely to include girls' schools. The government decided that in order to try to move the Bill more quickly it should be introduced first into the House of Lords, and this was done on 21 June by the Lord Chancellor, Lord Cairns, in an eloquent speech.[26] However, the inclusion of girls in the Bill had been dropped and the word 'student' was taken to refer to boys only. A deputation from the Belfast Ladies' Institute led by Isabella Tod and Margaret Byers crossed immediately to London to address Lord Cairns on the issue. Mr James Corry, MP for Belfast, who was a supporter of the women's cause, assisted the deputation. On 2 July the Bill went to committee stage and a question was raised by Earl Spencer, a Liberal peer who had served in Gladstone's government, as to whether the prizes and exhibitions would be open to competition by women. Lord Cairns replied that the Bill, as it was framed, did not include women but that it could be extended by parliament at a later stage. However, such a decision would warrant a review of the rules, the subjects, the venue of the examinations and an increase in the funding. On 4 July, Earl Granville, another Liberal peer who had served in Gladstone's government, raised the matter again, saying that he had been advised that, legally, the word 'student' could apply to both sexes. Lord Cairns this time gave an evasive answer, adding: 'I expect that to-morrow my right honourable friend, the Chief Secretary of Ireland, will receive a deputation of ladies and gentlemen on the subject.'[27] The next day Earl Granville presented a petition from the Ladies' General Educational Institute requesting that female students might be permitted to share in the benefits of the Intermediate Education (Ireland) Bill. Ten days later the Bill passed to the House of Commons and at the second reading on 15 July the matter of the exclusion of girls was raised again. Gladstone, leader of the Liberal Party, strongly supported the Bill, stressing that 'there is great anxiety in Ireland that the benefits of this measure should be extended to young women as well as to young men. We have upon the whole, done less justice to women as compared to men.'[28] He also emphasised that, as the scheme had come from a religious endowment, the money should be applied as widely as possible. Mr James Corry, MP for Belfast, who was supporting the women's cause, brought it to the attention of the House that extra funding would be needed to allow the scheme to be extended to girls' education. The MP for Halifax, Mr Stansfield, also spoke strongly in support of extending the Bill to girls, emphasising the need for 'a sound education for girls' and noting the success which Irish girls had had in the university examinations offered by Trinity College, Dublin, and by the Queen's University. He also drew attention to the Endowed Schools' Act of 1869 in England, which had made special provision for girls' education. With pressure mounting for the women's cause, the government was persuaded to add an amendment to the Bill. On 25 July, during the committee stage of the Bill in the House of Commons, the new Irish Chief Secretary, James Lowther, proposed that an additional clause should be added which read: 'For applying, as far as conveniently may be, the benefits of this Act to the education of girls.'[29] The amendment was accepted as worded and the Intermediate Education Bill passed to its final reading on 12 August. Another important amendment was achieved by The O'Conor Don, MP for Roscommon, whereby 'Celtic language and literature' was included as a subject in the schedule for examination, and the history of Ireland was joined with that of Great Britain as a subject for examination.[30] The final Bill had an easy passage – possibly, as McElligott suggests, because, owing to the lateness of the Bill, many of the MPs had already left London for the 'grouse-shooting season'.[31]

WORKING OF THE INTERMEDIATE EDUCATION SYSTEM, 1878–1898

The passing of the Intermediate Education Act was well received in Ireland not just by the women advocates of higher education, but by schools generally. The Act provided a system of funding for both Catholic and Protestant secondary schools without appearing to give grants directly to denominational schooling. It received the support of the Catholic hierarchy and of the Irish parliamentary party, and it was seen as one way of redistributing the wealth of the disestablished Church of Ireland on an equitable basis. Under the terms of the Act the Intermediate Board was empowered to institute a system of public examinations which were to be offered in three grades, Junior, Middle and Senior. Results fees were to be paid in two ways, first to the schools, based on the overall performance of their pupils in the examinations, and, second, to individual pupils in the form of exhibitions and prizes. From the outset the Board decided to award separate exhibitions and prizes to girls and thus avoid competition between the sexes. The Board comprised seven commissioners appointed by the government. They were chosen to represent the main educational and religious groups in the country: Catholic, Church of Ireland (Anglican) and Presbyterian. The first seven commissioners were John Ball, Lord Chancellor of Ireland; Earl Belmore; James Corry, MP for Belfast; The O'Conor Don, MP for Roscommon; Christopher Palles, Chief Baron of the Irish Court of Exchequer; Baron O'Hagan and George Salmon, Professor of Divinity at Trinity College, Dublin. For the women, the appointment of Corry, who had been one of their key advocates, was pleasing. However, though the membership of the Board was raised to twelve in 1900, women were never appointed to the Board in the years of its existence, from 1878 to 1924. The leaders of women's education had therefore to find other ways of influencing the development of secondary education. There were to be few women examiners appointed, even when a pool of women graduates from the Royal University became available. In domestic economy there were always women examiners, including Fannie Gallaher, author of the standard textbook *Lessons in Domestic Science* (1885), and by 1900 the list of examiners included Jane Barlow (English), Mary Hayden, MA (English), Maud Joynt, MA (English), and Mary Story, MA (English).[32] Other examiners included Margaret Dixon, MA (Natural Philosophy), Mary Robertson, MA (Chemistry), Florence Conan (Drawing), Annie Patterson, Mus. D. (Music), and, in Domestic Economy, Mary Daly, Elizabeth Moore, and Mary Todd Bellingham.

The Intermediate examination programmes were to be the same for boys and girls, and this was a fundamental issue in the quest for equality. The only differences were in the grouping of the subjects. The programme consisted of seven divisions:

1. the ancient language, literature and history of Greece;
2. the ancient language, literature and history of Rome;
3. the language, literature and history of Great Britain and Ireland;

4. the language, literature, and history of France, Germany and Italy, or any one of them, either separately or together, with the Celtic language and literature;
5. mathematics, including arithmetic and book-keeping;
6. natural sciences; and
7. such subjects of secular education as the Board may from time to time prescribe.

No examination was offered in religion and the Board was not allowed to make any payment in respect thereof. The managers of the schools therefore retained the right of religious control but the act contained a conscience clause to protect the individual pupil's religious rights. It stated that no payment would be made to a school unless the Board was satisfied that no pupils had been permitted to attend religious instruction that had not been sanctioned by their parents or guardians; and that 'the time for giving such religious instruction is so fixed that no pupil not remaining in attendance is excluded directly or indirectly from the advantages of the secular instruction'.[33] The examination rules that related specifically to girls were, first, that their examinations would be held apart from those of the boys but on the same day; girls could present themselves for examination in two or more divisions but one of these must be the third division (English), fourth division (modern languages), or fifth division (mathematics). For boys, one of the two divisions presented could include Classics – Greek or Latin; and, finally, the girls could pass the mathematical division by taking arithmetic alone, whereas the boys were required to pass in two sections, arithmetic and either Euclid, algebra, book-keeping, trigonometry or mechanics. These exemptions recognised that some of the smaller girls' schools would not be in a position to offer Classics or higher mathematics at a senior level. Two of the subjects which were offered in the seventh division, music and drawing, proved very popular with girls' schools, as did botany in division six.

FIRST YEAR OF INTERMEDIATE EDUCATION EXAMINATIONS, 1879

The first examinations were held in June 1879, and out of a total of 4,268 candidates who 'announced their intention of presenting themselves for examination' 797 were girls.[34] The actual number of girls who sat the exams was 736 out of a total of 3,954 candidates. Of these, only around sixty per cent obtained a pass, that is, 482 girls and 1,845 boys. Separate examination centres for girls were established, in acknowledgement of the fears that particularly the Catholic convent schools had expressed about the 'dangers' of 'mixed' centres. Thirteen girls' centres were organised in Armagh, Belfast (two), Cork, Dublin (three), Dundalk, Galway, Kilkenny, Londonderry, Navan and Oldcastle. The majority of female candidates (521), as was to be expected in the first year, sat for the Junior Grade, while in the Middle and Senior Grades female candidates numbered 156 and 59 respectively. The most popular subjects chosen were English, mathematics and French, music and drawing. The fact that one hundred girls sat Junior Grade algebra indicated that higher mathematics was beginning to be taught in girls' schools, while three candidates attempted Senior Grade trigonometry but none passed. In natural science the numbers were small except for botany and geography, and in Classics only 47 female candidates as opposed to 1,386 male candidates took Junior Grade Latin.[35]

Under the payment-by-results system, schools were paid on a rising scale for each successful candidate who obtained a pass grade. The more passes obtained in each grade, the higher the fee. This system undoubtedly encouraged schools to enter as many pupils as possible for as many subjects as possible, and, throughout the forty years of the Intermediate Board examinations, a pass rate of around 50 per cent to 60 per cent was maintained. The pressure on candidates and school staff was to be severe, and the competition between schools was to prove very strong. Schools published their results and the winners of prizes and exhibitions 'raced' each other to gain the most. For the girls' schools this provided evidence of their academic achievements, and a strong rivalry between the Protestant and Catholic sectors spurred on the competition.[36] Convent schools were initially reluctant to enter their pupils for the public examinations and this was to continue for a number of years. After ten years, only 207 girls from Catholic schools had passed the Intermediate examinations. In an article in the *Irish Ecclesiastical Record* in 1883 the editor wrote:

> Girls have to travel sometimes to distant 'centres' to mingle with strangers; in fact they must rough it for a week or more without adequate protection. Then the physical strain and nervous excitement is oftentimes decidedly and permanently injurious to the more susceptible temperament of females. If high culture can only be secured at the sacrifice of female delicacy, and the rewards of the Intermediate system can only be purchased by permanent injury to health, we think the nuns

are quite right in preferring maidenly modesty and healthy development of their pupils to the honours of the Intermediate Board.[37]

However, this view was not universally held: in 1886, the *Freeman's Journal* noted:

> There is scarcely a Catholic school left in Ireland capable of educating female pupils up to the not very exacting standard prescribed by the Intermediate Commissioners. This is truly a serious state of affairs, and we think that time is not far distant when the ecclesiastical authorities will have to choose between prohibiting the pupils, male or female, of Catholic schools from competing at the Examinations, and prohibiting certain Catholic schools from taking in pupils without having previously made satisfactory arrangement for their education, so that in the race for prizes and honours with Protestant boys and girls they may not be handicapped by the ignorance of their teachers.[38]

Dr William Walsh, who became Archbishop of Dublin in 1885, recognised that, unless the leading Catholic girls' schools began to offer the Intermediate examinations, ambitious Catholic girls would attend a Protestant school such as Alexandra College. Therefore he encouraged and supported the Catholic convent schools to enter their pupils.[39]

One of the key issues of the Intermediate programme was that certain subjects carried more marks than others did. This reflected the relative importance given to them in the curriculum. For instance, whereas Classics, Latin and Greek each carried 1000 marks, as did English, modern languages carried only 700 marks, mathematics 500 each, and sciences 400 each. Music and drawing, which were popular subjects with many girls' schools, carried 500 marks each. As the prizes and exhibitions were awarded on an aggregated total of marks, those entering were encouraged to choose the subjects with higher marks, and this in turn influenced the importance given to those subjects in schools. Exhibitions were awarded on the basis of one for each ten successful candidates who obtained a minimum of passes in three divisions in each grade. The prizes were awarded on a similar basis. In 1879 there were twenty-two exhibitions awarded to girls and 109 to boys. These scholarships were to prove valuable in encouraging pupils to continue their education. A Junior Grade exhibition was £20 for three years, a

Middle Grade £30 for three years and a Senior Grade £50 for three years. The latter award was particularly important to girls, as it enabled a student to attend university and continue her education.

In 1878, the leading girls' schools were determined to show their readiness to enter for the public examinations. In January 1879 Margaret Byers of the Ladies' Collegiate School, Belfast, advertised that her pupils would be entering for the Intermediate Board examinations. Although some of the young women were too old to be eligible to win prizes and exhibitions, they were entered as an example to others and to indicate the high standard of academic ability that could be achieved. In 1880 the Ladies' Collegiate (which became Victoria College in 1880) gained first place in Ireland in the Middle Grade for girls, and by 1888 it had won forty-eight distinctions, as opposed to twenty-three attained by its rival Alexandra College, Dublin, and twenty by the Ladies' Collegiate School, Derry.[40] The Catholic convent schools were less ready to enter for the examinations, but competition with the Protestant schools and encouragement by local Catholic bishops were to spur them on. The Dominicans in Eccles Street, Dublin, began to enter pupils in the 1880s: St Dominic's High School, Belfast, entered in 1894 and the Dominicans in Galway in 1897. The Loreto convent schools in St Stephen's Green and Rathfarnham entered pupils in the 1880s, and in 1896 pupils from Loreto Rathfarnham gained three Senior Grade exhibitions. In Cork, the Ursulines, encouraged by Bishop O' Callaghan, founded St Angela's High School in 1880 and one of the first pupils, Mary Ryan, was to win first place in Ireland, beating her nearest rival from Victoria College, Belfast. She later became one of the first women graduates and the first woman professor in Ireland.[41] The Ursulines in Sligo and in Waterford followed suit and St Louis' Convent, Monaghan, became one of the most successful Catholic schools in the examinations. Pupils from Alexandra School entered for the Junior and Middle Grade examinations with much success. Isabella Mulvany – affectionately known as 'Dr Mull' at Alexandra College – was herself a product of the system, having won Intermediate Board exhibitions, and became one of the first women graduates of the Royal University in 1884.

By 1885, there were eighty-nine girls' schools receiving results fees and this indicated the growing strength of the sector. In Dublin alone there were twelve schools receiving fees, including Alexandra, the Loreto and Dominican convents, Miss Wade's Morehampton House School, Rutland School for Girls and the Masonic Female Orphan School. In Belfast there were eight schools, including Victoria College and Methodist College. In Cork there were five schools in receipt of fees, including the High School for Girls and Rochelle Seminary. The Ulster province had the greatest number of schools, with forty-two institutions listed. In Antrim the schools receiving fees were located in Ballymena, Carrickfergus, Lisburn and Randalstown. In Armagh there were four schools located in the city that were in receipt of fees, two more in Portadown and one in Lurgan. The convent schools in Ulster that were receiving fees were St Louis, Monaghan, and Loreto, Omagh. In Donegal there were two schools and in Down there were eight in receipt of fees, including Banbridge Academy and Sullivan Upper School. In Londonderry there were six schools entering pupils, including the Ladies' Collegiate and Strand House, and in Tyrone the schools in receipt of fees were located in Cookstown, Dungannon and Strabane. Leinster was less well provided for, but there were nine convent schools receiving fees – Loreto Convents in Kilkenny, Navan, Gorey and Wexford; Convents of Mercy in Tullamore, Longford and Arklow; Convent of the Annunciation in Mullingar and one in Kildare. The Quaker Friends' School at Mountmellick also entered pupils. In Munster and Connaught there were eighteen schools benefiting from the examinations, including five in Cork City, the Convent of Mercy at Macroom, the Loreto Convent, Killarney, Leamy School, Limerick and Ranelagh School, Athlone.[42]

PROBLEMS WITH THE INTERMEDIATE EXAMINATION SYSTEM

The main difficulty the girls' schools faced in the early years of the Intermediate system was that, as had been forecast in 1878, there was insufficient money to sustain the payment of results fees and exhibitions. In 1882 there was a crisis when the Intermediate Board considered whether it should curtail its expenditure on girls' schools and set up a separate system of examinations for girls' schools. A petition was submitted by some of the boys' headmasters requesting that more money should be directed to the boys' schools. The women's lobby immediately sprang into action and set up a representative organisation for girls' schools, known as the Association of Irish Schoolmistresses and other Ladies Interested in Education (AISLIE). The opening meeting was held at the invitation of Mrs Jellet, the Provost's wife, in the Provost's House, Trinity College, on 28 January 1882, and around seventy representatives of the Protestant girls' schools attended. The Association grew rapidly and branches were founded in Cork, Derry, Galway and

Sligo. It later became known as the Central Association of Irish Schoolmistresses (CAISM). The driving force behind the association was Alice Oldham (1850–1907), the first secretary. Oldham was on the staff of Alexandra College and was one of the first women graduates of the Royal University in 1884. A formidable opponent and a consummate organiser, she led the campaign for women's rights in both Intermediate and university education from the 1880s until her death in 1907. In her own account of the early history of the CAISM, which she wrote in 1890, she stated:

> The first work undertaken by the association, was the present-ing to Her Majesty's government of a memorial in conjunction with the Schoolmasters' Association, praying for an additional grant to facilitate the working of the Intermediate Act . . . In the same year (1882) action was taken by the association in refer-ence to a point on which we had since to contend repeatedly with the Intermediate Board – the lowering of the standard, and narrowing of the scope of their programmes for girls . . .[43]

In 1882, when the Board excluded mechanics and trigonometry from the girls' programme, a memorial signed by 3,000 persons was sent in protest to the Board. The CAISM worked closely with the Irish Schoolmasters' Association and used their support to retain the separate prizes for girls. In 1889, when a proposal was again before the Board to reduce its financial problems by changing the rules so that girls would have to compete with boys, the two Protestant organisations lobbied against it. The Ulster Schoolmistresses' Association and the CAISM sent a joint memorial, and eventually the proposal was defeated. The Council of Alexandra College added its voice, declaring that they were not prepared 'to grant the alleged inequality of advantages as between girls and boys, and that if some "educational advantages" were given to the girls, this was only fit as the boys had had many educational advantages in former years'.[44]

The total numbers entering for the examinations grew steadily in the 1880s and 1890s and the proportion of girls remained at about one-third. By 1898 the total number presented for the examinations was 9,073, of whom 2,368 were girls. The largest number of entrants was in the Junior Grade (1,189), while in the other grades the numbers were much smaller – Preparatory Grade (744), Middle Grade (312) Senior Grade (123). Both staff and pupils, despite the pressures, enjoyed the challenge and pleasure of undertaking academic work. Mary Colum, the writer, who was a pupil at St Louis Convent, Monaghan, wrote in her autobiography *Life and the*

Dream (1928) that, despite the rigours of convent boarding-school life, she much enjoyed the pleasure of academic study:

> Class hours and study were long and though we studied books and subjects assembled for us by an educational body called the Intermediate Education Board for Ireland, which at the start must have emanated from the head of some English bureaucrat, the whole way we were taught was Continental. In fact my school was French in tradition, having been founded by a French religious order for the education of girls . . . But the language which really fascinated me at school was Latin. I can never forget the rapture with which, by the aid of a dictionary, I first poked a meaning out of the second book of Virgil . . .[45]

Catholic girls began to make use of the education offered. Hanna Sheehy Skeffington, along with her three sisters, the daughters of David Sheehy, MP, attended the Dominican Convent, Eccles Street, which had opened in 1883. The Dominicans had made a strong case to Archbishop Walsh of Dublin stating that, if Catholic girls were not to be tempted to attend a Protestant college, the Catholic schools must offer the Intermediate examinations. Education was expensive for many families and the Sheehy family was no exception. All the Sheehy girls won exhibitions and prizes under the Intermediate Board and gained a thorough academic education. Hanna was a serious student and scholar and was significantly influenced by the strong-minded and well-educated women of the Dominican order who taught her.[46] Hanna Sheehy attended classes at St Mary's Dominican College in Merrion Square, while two of her sisters attended classes at the Loreto Convent in St Stephen's Green.

PALLES COMMISSION ON INTERMEDIATE EDUCATION, 1898

In the first five years the weaknesses of the 1878 Act were apparent to schools of both sexes. The Intermediate Board had no finance to offer for capital building grants (for instance for science laboratories) which could improve teaching facilities. There was no provision for teachers' salaries other than the fees earned through payment by results. The inequality of marks allocated to various subjects militated against the growth of science and modern languages. The examination system led to 'cramming' and put much pressure on staff and pupils, and some parents of girls protested and refused to allow their daughters to enter for the examinations. In fact in most girls' schools, both Catholic and Protestant, only a minority of pupils chose to enter for the public examinations. One possible alternative to the payment-by-results system was to change to a system of state grants, but this would have required the introduction of a state school inspectorate to visit schools in receipt of grants. The voluntary schools, however, and in particular the Catholic schools, were fearful of such supervision, as it could be seen as state interference and a threat to their autonomy.

The criticisms of the Intermediate system led eventually to the setting up in 1898 of the Palles Commission on Intermediate Education.[47] The Commission consisted only of members of the Board itself, and therefore there were no women appointed. The chairman of the Board, Chief Baron Palles, had himself requested the establishment of a commission and the government had agreed, provided the Board undertook to do it itself. Six women witnesses were called to give evidence and many more submitted completed questionnaires. The women used the occasion to support the continuation of the Intermediate system, which, despite its faults, had done so much to raise the standard of girls' education, and had opened up the opportunity of entry to higher education. The six women witnesses called to the Palles Commission were Margaret Byers, head of Victoria College, Belfast; Henrietta White, principal of Alexandra College, Dublin; Margaret McKillip, head of Victoria High School, Derry; Isabella Mulvany, head of Alexandra School; Alice Oldham, hon. secretary of the Central Association of Irish School Mistresses; and Eliza Boyd, assistant mistress at the Royal School, Raphoe.

The calling of these women witnesses indicated the growth in importance of girls' education since 1878, and they were able to make a major contribution to the Commission's report. The overall outcome of the report was to recommend the continuation of the system of payment-by-results with minor modifications and, while the introduction of a Board inspectorate was suggested, it did not materialise until 1909, when a temporary inspectorate was set up. The examination curriculum was reformed and grouped into four courses, in an attempt to make the subjects more equally weighted, and it was hoped that this would ease some of the strain of the examination. The concept of a separate programme for girls was described as 'a retrograde step' and was rejected.[48]

Byers, in her evidence, strongly supported the Intermediate system despite attempts by members of the Commission to draw attention to the stress which girls were reportedly suffering. She noted that 'the good effect of the Intermediate System far preponderates over the evil, and defects of the system are remediable'.[49] She emphasised how poor the education and schooling of girls had been prior to the introduction of this system, and, where there were no facilities, the 'school programme was almost limited to such subjects as could be displayed in the drawing room . . . Solid learning used to strengthen the minds of boys was almost entirely excluded.'[50] She added that 'in 1878, when the Irish Intermediate Bill was passed, it was a great joy to women educationists all over the three kingdoms that for the first time the British Government recognised the claims of women to secondary education'.[51] In her opinion, the benefits of the system had resulted in better-educated middle-class women who were better able to superintend their children's education and domestic affairs. She agreed with 'the opinion of an eminent London physician who declared that he had seen far more victims of inaction and idleness than that of wholesome and interesting work'.[52] Students from Victoria College had performed well in the examinations of the Royal University and had gone to Girton and Newnham Colleges at Cambridge, and to Edinburgh University. Byers submitted to the Commission a copy of a memorial that had been sent to the Intermediate Board in 1890, emphasising the need to retain the separate prizes for girls. It had been signed by both the Ulster Schoolmistresses' Association and the CAISM, as well as by many individual girls' schools throughout Ireland.[53]

Henrietta White, principal of Alexandra College, in her evidence to the Palles Commission, was equally supportive of the retention of the examination system.[54] White had been appointed principal of Alexandra in 1890 and she was an outstanding leader of the struggle for women's rights to higher education.[55] She had been a student at Newnham College, Cambridge, and was determined to develop Alexandra as a college of higher education. She noted that the advantages of the Intermediate system included the stimulation of activity in schools, the endowments provided and a more relevant programme of studies. She fully supported the equality of pro-grammes for boys and girls and was critical of domestic economy being seen as a substitute for natural sciences for girls. However, she drew attention to one of the evils of the results system, namely that of schools competing to get the best pupils in order to earn more results fees. In 1897, members of the CAISM had circulated a memorial to members condemning the practice of offering 'free places' to clever pupils in order to attract them:

> We allude to the practice of heads of schools and colleges offering parents free education or education at very reduced

terms for their children if they have ability to win prizes and high result fees under the Intermediate system, and will enter for the examinations . . . This is injurious to the best interests of education and dishonouring of the teaching profession.[56]

The memorial was signed by a large number of headmistresses and assistant mistresses of Dublin, Belfast and Cork, including Edith Badham of St Margaret's Hall, Dublin; Isabella Mulvany of Alexandra School, Dublin; Margaret Byers of Victoria College, Belfast; Anna Hunter of Princess Gardens School, Belfast; E.C. Shillington of McArthur Hall, Methodist College, Belfast; Jane Marshall of Rochelle School, Cork, and Harriet Martin of Cork High School. To reduce the pressure of examinations, White recommended the abolition of the preparatory grade examination. She also recommended the introduction of pass and honour papers to cater for a wider range of pupils, and the introduction of a system of inspection for schools. She pointed out that more women examiners should be appointed and, despite the critical questioning by members of the Commission, she refused to agree that the Intermediate system had not been beneficial to girls' education.

Isabella Mulvany, head of Alexandra School, was also interviewed.[57] The school entered pupils for three grades: Preparatory, Junior and Middle. Mulvany suggested to the Commission that the Preparatory Grade should be abolished and a system of inspection introduced which would improve standards, buildings and facilities. She noted that, even in a school as large and prestigious as Alexandra, many girls did not enter for the examinations and that, out of a possible total of 187 pupils eligible to sit for the examinations, only fifty-seven last year entered and only twenty-five passed. She considered that the Board should extend its power into other crucial areas such as teacher qualifications and registration, and not just confine itself to organising an examination system.

Another strong supporter of the Intermediate system was Margaret McKillip, head of Victoria High School, Londonderry, who praised the public examinations and the encouragement which they had given to academic success in her school. Girls from Victoria High School had gone on to Girton College, Cambridge, and had taken Royal University degrees. McKillip said that before the introduction of the examinations 'there had been no taste whatever for education on the part of girls or their parents'.[58] In her opinion the Irish Intermediate system had 'created a desire for education' and had produced a 'generation of capable, responsible and industrious women'.[59]

The CAISM had sent in its own submission to the Commission in support of the system and its benefits for the education of girls. It made specific recommendations for improvements, which included the abolition of the Preparatory grade, the grouping of subjects at senior level, practical science examinations, the making of history as a separate subject and, most importantly, the appointment of women examiners and women inspectors.[60] As an experienced teacher for Intermediate examinations, Alice Oldham considered that the number of girls entering for the examinations would be increased not by providing an alternative girls' programme, but rather by ending the competitive nature of the examinations with the stress involved. She noted that the ending of a system of payment-by-results was being considered at primary level and that the Bryce Commission in England in 1895 had recommended inspection as the best method of accountability. She emphasised the need for qualified teachers and registration and, above all, that girls should have the opportunity to study the same programme as boys:

> My anxiety about these subjects is simply and purely this, that my experience is that the girl who does learn these subjects is educated in a totally different way; her mind is opened and is enlarged. For instance, a girl who has learnt Latin knows something of classical life, the past life of Europe, and her whole horizon is much larger.[61]

Another advocate of higher education who made a submission was Mary Hayden, lecturer in St Mary's University College and a Junior Fellow of the Royal University. Hayden drew attention to the stress girls were under and the 'cramming' which girls were obliged to do in preparation for the examinations. She suggested that the Preparatory grade should be abolished, that the number of subjects taken in the examinations should be limited and that a system of inspection should be introduced.[62] The only assistant schoolmistress to be interviewed was Eliza Boyd, a graduate of the Royal University and a housemistress at the Royal School, Raphoe. She spoke out strongly on the needs of the smaller girls' schools in the provinces. The lack of provision for teachers' salaries or buildings was worse for small schools. In the Intermediate system, she stated, the majority of the money was earned by the large schools who needed it least, while nothing was being done to assist rural girls' schools or to make secondary education accessible to poorer areas. She added:

the chief defect of the Intermediate system is, in my opinion, the failure to effect its avowed object, namely, to bring within the reach of the poorer people a cheap and easily accessible means of obtaining a better education than was to be obtained under the National System, one which not only prepares for university education, but qualifies for commercial pursuits.[63]

Many written submissions in support of the Intermediate system were presented by women to the Palles Commission. Query sheets were sent out to all schools that were in receipt of grants and a large number of girls' schools replied. The convent schools in particular used this means to express their views publicly. Among those that sent in answers were the Ursuline High School, Cork, St Louis Convent, Monaghan, the Dominican Convent, Sion Hill, the Dominican Convent, Eccles Street, the Convent of Mercy, Queenstown, Cork, and the Loreto convents in Navan, Mullingar and Rathfarnham. They were less enthusiastic about introducing a system of state inspection and wished to retain the present system of payment-by-results. The Dominican convents stated that 'compared with other educational systems this one appears to be eminently impartial and satisfactory in its results; therefore any proposal to institute inspection . . . could not be approved'.[64] The Catholic girls' schools were not represented in person at the Commission, as their congregations did not allow religious heads to give evidence. However, James Macken, an examiner in English, was asked by the Loreto order to present their views.[65] He spoke on behalf of Loreto Abbey and thirteen other Loreto schools (excluding Navan and Mullingar), which had entered pupils for the examinations. The Loreto submission emphasised the value of examinations extending the girls' curriculum from English, music and a language to include science, mathematics, geography and history. The advantages of the system were its impartiality and definite programmes of work. Nevertheless, the Loreto schools were aware that the freedom of the school was restrained, and that was a danger of 'narrowing the education of the scholar' and neglecting 'general education'. They recommended the introduction of practical examinations in music, orals in modern languages and more marks given to botany so that more girls would be encouraged to take it. It was suggested that large numbers of girls did not enter for the examinations because among Catholic convent girls there was a fear that the work was too exhausting. In addition, there was the prevailing view that, while boys had to prepare for careers, girls did not:

A large number of parents of girls consider that the Intermediate system is not suitable for girls and that if they entered into the competition they would not be trained in the subjects and accomplishments which they regard as more fitted to form part of the education of girls.[66]

RECOMMENDATIONS OF THE PALLES COMMISSION

The outcome of the Palles Report was to be a disappointment for women. Although the report recommended various changes in the system, there was no major shift from a system of payment-for-results to one of inspection and the Preparatory Grade for younger pupils was not abolished until 1913. The report recommended a gradual change towards the payment of a 'normal school grant' based on the triennial average performance of each school in the examinations. The 1900 Intermediate Education (Ireland) Act allowed the Board to change its own rules for the distribution of its income, provided the approval of the Lord Lieutenant and parliament was obtained.[67] The Act also gave the Board the power to hire inspectors, but, while a temporary inspectorate was introduced in 1901, the government was not prepared to finance both an inspectorate and a payment-by-results examination system. Approval for the appointment of a permanent inspectorate was not achieved until 1909 and none of the new appointees was a woman. Although the membership of the Intermediate Board was increased from seven to twelve in 1900 there were still no women commissioners appointed, and this position was to continue for the remaining life of the Board.

Thus the Intermediate system continued for another twenty years. The number of girls entering for the examinations increased steadily. By 1915 the number entering Junior Grade had risen to 2,526, Middle Grade to 1061, and Senior Grade to 501.[68] The new Department of Agriculture and Technical Instruction after 1900 encouraged the teaching of science, and grants were awarded to schools to build laboratories for practical work. The number of girls sitting experiential science slowly increased, and the course in domestic economy and hygiene, which was recognised as a science subject, proved popular with girls' schools. As the number of graduate women teachers increased, the academic standard of the school was raised and schools were fortunate in having a distinguished group of headmistresses, both religious and lay, to lead them. In 1903 an article in the journal *Lady of the House* portrayed headmistresses of ten Protestant girls' schools and praised their achievements. The schools included not only the large ones such as Alexandra College and School, Dublin and Victoria College, Belfast, but also two in Derry – Strand House and Victoria High School, two in Dublin – Rutland School and Morehampton House School, two in Cork – Rochelle School and Cork High School, and in Belfast – McArthur Hall, the girls' residence for Methodist College, Belfast.[69]

DALE AND STEPHENS' REPORT ON INTERMEDIATE EDUCATION, 1905

The government continued to try to reform the Intermediate system, but the strong resistance from the voluntary secondary schools regarding the introduction of a state inspectorate hindered progress. Fear of state intrusion was strong. In 1905 a government report on secondary education by two English inspectors, F.H. Dale and T.A. Stephens, suggested ways of moving away from a system of payment-by-results towards one based on school grants and inspection. They suggested a reduction in the number of examinations from three to two grades, and the establishment of a central state authority to supervise schools. Regarding the education of girls, the report commented on the number of private schools that did not enter for the public examinations, and noted the reluctance of parents and school managers to enter girls 'owing partly to fear of overpressure, and partly to a desire for a different type of education from that based on the syllabuses for the Board'.[70] There had been a decrease in the number of girls entering the previous year and the report blamed the unsuitability of some of the examination courses for girls. It noted that 'many parents will not allow their daughters to enter for the Intermediate examinations, and that many persons hold strongly the view that the programme of work in a girls' school should, for the bulk of the work differ in important particulars, partly as to the subjects, partly as to the incidence of the work, from the programme usually followed in the boys' schools'.[71] The report also noted the lack of provision of secondary education for poorer pupils and pointed out that, as most of the secondary schools were fee-paying, there was little or no opportunity for pupils, either male of female, to proceed from a primary National School.

One key area that affected girls' education was the lack of qualifications and adequate remuneration for staff, both male and female. Among the Catholic schools there was a large number of religious teachers, and in 1903, out of a total of 344 women teachers employed, only eighty-four were laywomen. Women teachers also were less well qualified than male teachers. In 1903, in Catholic girls' schools, the proportion of graduates to non-graduates was eight per cent for women compared to 11.5 per cent for men in boys' schools. Among Protestant women the percentage of graduates was higher, being mostly from the Royal University. The number of women teachers employed in Protestant girls' schools was 435, of whom 30 per cent were graduates, whereas for men teachers in Protestant boys' schools 55.5 per cent were graduates. The Dale and Stephens Report was very critical of the employment of so many unqualified teachers and noted that the poor salaries failed to attract able recruits. The average wage among seventy intermediate schools was estimated at £82 6s 7d for men, but only £48 2s 7d for women. The introduction of formal qualifications for teachers was essential and a system of registration was imperative.[72]

PROFESSIONAL TRAINING FOR SECONDARY SCHOOL TEACHERS

The professional education of secondary teachers was only in its infancy in 1905. In England a movement to establish a register of teachers was under way, but in Ireland little as yet had been achieved. Among Catholic schools the religious congregations provided basic teacher training within their schools, but there was little available to lay teachers. However, education was becoming a recognised academic subject in universities, and in 1898 the Royal University had introduced a Diploma in Education consisting of both theoretical and practical studies. Trinity College, Dublin, also introduced in 1898 a Diploma in Education in the theory, history and practice of education and in 1905 instituted a chair of education. Both university diplomas were open to women and, although the numbers taking the examinations were small, the majority of them were women. Other women in search of professional qualifications had undertaken the Cambridge Syndicate Teachers' Certificate, which was based on a course offered by the pioneer Cambridge Women's Training College, founded by Elizabeth Hughes in 1885.[73] The Ursuline convent in Waterford had arranged for classes for students to study for the Cambridge Teachers' Certificate through a scheme developed by St Augustine's De La Salle Training College, Waterford. When the first Register of Secondary Teachers was published in 1919, most holders of the Cambridge Certificate were women in religious congregations, while laywomen had obtained the Diploma in Education from the Royal University or Trinity College, or, after 1908, from the National University of Ireland.[74] Women were in the forefront of the campaign for minimum qualifications and registration for teachers, as they, more than their male counterparts, needed formal recognition of their professional status.

Though the recommendations of the 1905 Dale and Stephens Report were far-reaching, they were not immediately implemented. They were, however, influential in guiding future education policy. Criticism of the Intermediate examinations continued to grow, one of the most direct being Patrick Pearse's *The Murder Machine* (1908), which described the system as anti-intellectual and anti-Irish, based on rote learning and cramming.[75] D.P. Moran, supporter of the 'Irish-Ireland' movement and editor of the *Leader*, considered that the elite Catholic secondary schools were educating their pupils in an 'English' based curriculum and were ignoring Irish literature and history.[76] As the Gaelic Literary Revival gained momentum, the number of girls entering for the Celtic (Irish) examination increased. In 1900, out of a total entry of 1,997, ninety girls only sat the Celtic examinations, of whom four were in Senior Grade. By 1910, out of a total of 3,933 girls, the number sitting Celtic had risen to 1,688, eighty-one of whom were in Senior Grade.[77]

Women who had benefited by the examinations system were strong in its defence. In 1907 Dr Isabella Mulvany wrote an article in a new journal, *The Irish Educational Review*, in which she defended the Intermediate exams and explained how beneficial they had proved for girls' education (see Appendix 4). At the first examinations in 1879, out of a total entry of 736, the majority of girls had sat only three subjects, English, arithmetic and French. However, by 1905, out of a total entry of 2,659, the subjects taken included history, geography, Latin, geometry and science. The overall effect on girls' schools had been to raise the standard of achievement, make the work more thorough and greatly increase the number of girls receiving an academic education. However, Mulvany regretted that there were still many girls who did not enter for the examinations:

> Is further proof of the potency and success of the Intermediate Education Act in uplifting the educational level for girls necessary? Yet, to judge from the comparative number of boys and girls entering, there must be a much larger number of girls remaining outside the scheme. In 1905, 7018 boys entered and 2659 girls, a disparity which can only take origin in either indifference or prejudice of the parent or guardian. It is difficult to overcome prejudice (impossible if, as in a case known to the writer, the prejudice is against allowing a daughter to share in

a scheme financed by 'a Gladstonian Act of Spoliation'!) but can we not try to remove indifference?[78]

Mulvany concluded that the Intermediate programme now contained all the essential subjects for a 'sound secondary education' and provided a satisfactory substructure for university work which was now opening up for women.

ESTABLISHMENT OF SECONDARY TEACHER REGISTRATION COUNCIL, 1914

Throughout the first twenty years of the twentieth century the pay and conditions of secondary teachers continued to cause concern. However, women teachers benefited from a number of government measures, which aimed at improving the professional status of secondary teachers generally. The first of these in 1914 was the introduction of state registration for teachers laying down minimum professional qualifications, and, in the same year, a state teachers' salaries grant which provided improved salaries for lay teachers, many of whom were women. Another measure which greatly assisted women in their quest for equality was the founding in 1909 of the Association of Secondary Teachers of Ireland (ASTI). It was to argue and lobby the case for improved conditions, in terms of both employment and pay, for both men and women lay teachers. From 1911, a Ladies' Branch was formed and women were accepted as full members of the association, and in the early years they were to be particularly vocal in support of the profession.[79]

The Secondary Teachers' Registration Council and the Teachers' Salaries Grant were both the work of the Irish Chief Secretary, Augustine Birrell, who did much to support education in Ireland. Established in 1914, the Secondary Teachers' Registration Council was to regulate and register qualified secondary teachers and women teachers benefited from the official recognition of their professional status.[80] In order to qualify as a registered teacher, a person had to be a graduate of a recognised university and to hold a professional education diploma. The Registration Council consisted of representatives of the universities, the teaching profession, the Intermediate Board and the Department of Agriculture and Technical Instruction. Two women members were appointed to the first Registration Council: Henrietta White, principal of Alexandra College, Dublin, and Elizabeth Steele, of Victoria College, Belfast. A large number of women teachers were entered in the first register, which was published in 1919 and this now placed them on an equal professional basis with their male colleagues. Graduates of the Royal University of Ireland and of Trinity College, Dublin, were in a position to apply for registration, while those graduates who had already taken a postgraduate diploma in education could register straight away. A period of seven years was allowed for teachers to obtain the necessary qualifications, and women teachers were able to make use of this leeway. The opening of Trinity College to women in 1904 and the founding of the National University of Ireland and of Queen's University, Belfast, in 1908 resulted in a much greater number of women graduates entering the teaching profession. After 1908 the Catholic religious congregations allowed their sisters to attend university lectures at the University Colleges of the National University, and so the Catholic girls' schools were able to have graduate staff and raise the standard of academic teaching.

Similarly, the introduction of the Teachers' Salaries Grant in 1914 gave both male and female lay teachers improved teachers' salaries through a payment by the state directly to schools that employed one lay teacher in a ratio of one to forty religious teachers.[81] Girls' schools, particularly those under Protestant management, employed a greater number of lay staff and so gained much from this new grant, which was the important beginning of direct state support for secondary teachers' salaries. The Catholic girls' schools gained less from the Salaries Grant as there was a supply of nuns as teachers, and this was a saving on the grant. The ASTI also had argued strongly from its inception in 1909 for improved teachers' working conditions and it proved an effective voice for both men and women. The Ladies' Branch of the ASTI continued until 1920 and it played a major role in the organisation in the early years. However, when the Association become a trade union affiliated to the Trade Union Congress in 1919, a number of the women resigned. Faced with the growing political divide between the north and south of Ireland, the Belfast Women's Branch seceded in 1920, along with some members of the Leinster Branch. After 1920 women became ordinary members of the trade union and, as Coolahan has observed, ceased to be as proactive as they had been in the early years.[82]

MOLONY VICE-REGAL COMMITTEE ON CONDITIONS OF SERVICE AND REMUNERATION, 1918

It was indicative of the increased status of women teachers in these decades that, when the Molony Vice-Regal Committee was set up in

1918 to examine the salaries and remuneration of secondary teachers, four women were appointed to the Committee.[83] This was the first time that women had been appointed to sit on a government education committee. The two senior members were Henrietta White and Mary Ryan, Professor of Romance Languages at University College, Cork. The other two women appointed to the Committee were Elizabeth Steele, Victoria College, Belfast, and Annie McHugh, St Brigid's High School, St Stephen's Green, both of whom represented the Association of Secondary Teachers of Ireland. McHugh was a graduate of the National University and had a Cambridge Teachers' Certificate and a Higher Diploma in Education from the National University of Ireland. She was a person of much determination and, in the end, refused on behalf of the union to sign the Molony Report. Along with two other members of the Committee, Professor Robert M. Henry, Professor of Latin, Queen's University, Belfast, and William John Williams, Lecturer in English at the Royal College of Science, Annie McHugh presented a minority report disagreeing with the recommendations, among which were the appeal procedures for teachers. Elizabeth Steele, on the other hand, did sign the final report but presented a reservation clause concerning the appeal procedures for teachers.

The 1918 Vice-Regal Committee was chaired by the Rt Hon. Thomas F. Molony, Lord Chief Justice, and twenty witnesses including two women, Charlotte Rowlette, Hon. Secretary of the CAISM, and Ida Marshal, principal of Carleton House School, Portadown, were interviewed. The report, although its terms of reference were technically confined to salaries and conditions, did, in fact, range over much wider educational issues. It recommended the ending of the system of payment-by-results and the introduction of grants for schools monitored by a system of inspection. Secondary teachers required not only better salaries but also security of tenure and provision of pensions.[84] One of the most radical suggestions of the Committee was that women should receive equal pay to men. Clause 127 stated: 'We do not recommend that there should be any difference in salary between men and women and that a minimum salary should be laid down of not less than £189 per annum and that this salary should rise by a series of annual increments to a maximum of £450 per annum.'[85] However, three members of the Committee did not agree with this recommendation, stating that: 'The payment of lower salaries to women is universal in secondary schools in England, Ireland, and Scotland and is, we think, founded on social and economic reasons.'[86]

The most difficult area of controversy for the Committee was the matter of an independent appeals tribunal to hear teachers' dismissal cases. Secondary teachers still lacked security of tenure and could be dismissed with no redress. The ASTI considered that such a tribunal should be impartial and not under the control of the school management authorities. In the final report the Committee decided that an independent tribunal was not required, although – as already noted – three members, Williams, Henry and McHugh, refused to sign the report on this issue. Coolahan (1984) in his history of the ASTI considered that the union could have compromised on this particular issue, as it did eventually in 1937.[87]

The recommendations of the Molony Committee had little immediate effect on the conditions of women teachers, but it provided a useful platform on which to publicise their views. They had also made a major contribution to the educational debate arising out of the Committee's discussions. The publication of the Molony Report coincided in 1919 with the publication of the Killanin Report on primary teachers' salaries.[88] Both reports recommended the establishment of a central coordinating authority for education which would provide greater financial resources for education in general and in particular for salaries. The Intermediate Board would be abolished along with the National Board for primary education. Influenced by these two reports, the government introduced an Education Bill in 1919 that proposed to establish such an authority, backed up by new local education authorities. However, strong opposition to the Bill from the Catholic Church, which feared a loss of control, and from nationalists, who viewed the new proposed authority as yet another 'English board', defeated the Bill through a lengthy campaign of opposition and it was dropped. There was to be little extra money available for salaries and, in spite of the introduction of the professional registration of teachers from 1919 and of an incremental salary scale based on qualification and service in 1925, women teachers continued to be paid a lower rate.

By 1920, Intermediate education for girls in Ireland was firmly established. From the tentative beginnings of pioneers such as Isabella Tod, Anne Jellicoe and Margaret Byers, girls' schools now offered a rigorous academic education and, as a norm, girls entered for the public examinations. The curriculum of girls' schools had been widened from the 'lady-like accomplishments' of the drawing room to include Classics, modern languages, higher mathematics and science. Despite its shortcomings and faults, the Intermediate examination system had proved a major asset for girls' schools, and its recognised standards and its exhibitions and prizes had provided an important level of achievement. The initial struggle to include girls' schools in the terms of the 1878 Bill had proved most worth-while and the ensuing success of the girls in the examinations indicated the equality of their academic ability. The payment-by-results system, despite the strain imposed on pupils and staff, had assisted the schools to expand their facilities and pay better salaries to their teachers. The CAISM had played a major part in the campaign to improve the status of secondary teachers, and the introduction of a professional register and the provision of a state salary grant owed much to the activities of women teachers. Above all, the Intermediate examination system had laid the foundation of women's higher education and, when full access for women to the universities was granted at the beginning of the twentieth century, there were sufficient numbers of qualified young women to take advantage of the educational opportunities offered. In the forty years from 1878, a 'quiet revolution' had taken place and girls were accepted as equal to boys in the Intermediate education system. It remained for young women in possession of the Intermediate certificates to be allowed access to a university education equal to that available to young men.

NOTES

1   *Select Committee on Foundation Schools and Education in Ireland* (Wyse), 1835 (630) xxiii; *Report of Her Majesty's Commissioners appointed to inquire into the Endowments, Funds and actual condition of Schools endowed for the purpose of Education in Ireland (Kildare)*, 1857–58 (2336 i–iv.) xxii. Parts i–iv.
2   See T.W. Moody and J.C. Beckett, *Queen's, Belfast, 1845–1949* (London: Faber & Faber, 1959); J.A. Murphy, *The College – A History of Queen's College/University College, Cork, 1845–1995* (Cork: Cork University Press, 1995).
3   There were twenty-three diocesan colleges by 1870.
4   See Felicity Hunt (ed.), *Lessons for Life, The Schooling of Girls and Women, 1850–1950* (London: Blackwell, 1987); Josephine Kamm, *Hope Deferred: Girls' Education in English History* (London: Methuen, 1965); Margaret Tuke, *A History of Bedford College for Women, 1849–1937* (Oxford: OUP, 1939); Carol Dyhouse, *Girls Growing up in Late Victorian and Edwardian England* (London: Routledge & Kegan Paul, 1981); Deirdre Raftery, *Women and Learning in English Writing, 1600–1900* (Dublin, Four Courts Press, 1997).
5   Maria Luddy, 'Isabella M.S. Tod', in Mary Cullen and Maria Luddy (eds), *Women, Power and Consciousness in 19th Century Ireland* (Dublin: Attic Press, 1995), pp. 197–230.
6   Isabella M.S. Tod, 'On the Education of Girls of the Middle Classes', in Dale Spender, *The Education Papers: Women's Quest for Equality in Britain, 1850–1912* (London: Routledge & Kegan Paul, 1981), pp. 230–47.
7   Judith Harford, 'The Movement for the Higher Education of Women in Ireland: The Role of Margaret Byers and Victoria College Belfast', *History of Education Researcher*, 75, May 2005, pp. 39–49.
8   The Women's Education Union was founded in 1871, to advance the secondary education of girls. Maria Grey and her sister, Emily Shirreff, were founder members. In 1872 the Union formed the Girls' Public Day School Trust, which founded high

schools in London. By 1890 there were thirty of these GPDST schools, which were closely modelled on the North London Collegiate School.

9   Anne V. O'Connor, 'Anne Jellicoe (1823–1880)', in Cullen and Luddy (eds), *Women, Power and Consciousness*, pp. 125–59.

10 Patricia Phillips, 'The Queen's Institute, Dublin (1861–1881), the First Technical College for Women in the British Isles', in Norman McMillan (ed.), *Prometheus's Fire: A History of Scientific and Technological Education in Ireland* (Carlow: Tyndale Publications, 2000), pp. 446–63.

11 Anne V. O'Connor and Susan M. Parkes (eds), *Gladly Learn and Gladly Teach: A History of Alexandra College and School, 1866 –1966* (Dublin: Blackwater Press, 1984).

12 See Raftery, *Women and Learning in English Writing, 1600–1900*; Ann B. Murphy and Deirdre Raftery (eds), *Emily Davies: Collected Letters, 1861–1878* (Charlottesville and London: University of Virginia Press, 2004).

13 The Endowed Schools' Act reformed educational endowments, thus making it possible to extend them to girls' education. The Act stated that 'in framing schemes under the Act, provision shall be made as far as conveniently maybe, for extending to girls the benefit of endowments'. See Sheila Fletcher, *Feminists and Bureaucrats: A Study in the Development of Girls' Education in the Nineteenth Century* (Cambridge: Cambridge University Press, 1980).

14 Raftery, *Women and Learning in English Writing, 1600–1900*, pp. 174–219.

15 The Queen's University had been founded in 1845 and consisted of three constituent colleges in Belfast, Cork and Galway which, though non-denominational and state-funded, were not yet open to women.

16 Moody and Beckett, *Queen's, Belfast*, Vol. I, pp. 267–8.

17 O'Connor and Parkes, *Gladly Learn and Gladly Teach*, pp. 20–2.

18 Trinity College Dublin, Library, College Muniments, Mun. Women/9.

19 Trinity College awarded two scholarships (one for Junior Grade and one for Senior Grade) on the results of the examinations to women students desiring to continue their studies.

20 *Census of Ireland*, 1871, *General Report*, 1876 (c.1377.) lxxxi.

21 Deirdre Raftery, 'The Higher Education of Women in Ireland, 1860–1904', in Susan M. Parkes (ed.), *A Danger to the Men? A History of Women in Trinity College, Dublin, 1904–2004* (Dublin: Lilliput Press, 2004), pp. 12–13. See also Deirdre Raftery, 'Ideological Differences in the First Formal Progammes of Education for Roman Catholic and Protestant Women in Ireland' (Montreal: *Proceedings of the International Standing Conference of the History of Education*, 1995), p. 1.

22 Emmet Larkin, *The Catholic Church and the Emergence of the Modern Irish Political System, 1874–79* (Dublin: Four Courts Press and Catholic University of America Press, 1996), pp. 257–314.

23 *Bill, intituled, an Act to promote Intermediate Education* 1878 (275) iii 543 and *Bill, intituled, an Act to amend the Intermediate Education (Ireland) Act, 1878*, 1882 (258) ii 523.

24 Quoted in T.J. McElligott, *Secondary Education in Ireland, 1870 – 1921* (Dublin: Irish Academic Press, 1981) p. 28.

25 Quoted in Larkin, *The Catholic Church, 1874–79*, p. 287.

26 Hansard Parliamentary Debates, 3, Vol. ccxli, 8, 21 June 1878

27 Ibid., 742, 4 July 1878.

28 Ibid., 1504–5, 15 July 1878.

29 Ibid., 304, 25 July 1878.

30 The O'Conor Don later served as a member of the Intermediate Education Board.

31 McElligott, *Secondary Education in Ireland*, p. 39.

32 Jane Barlow was a well-known author and graduate of the RUI and Mary Hayden, Maud Joynt and Mary Story were all graduates of the RUI and leading figures in the higher education movement.

33   *Intermediate Education (Ireland) Act*, 1878.
34   *Report of Intermediate Education Board for Ireland for 1879*, 1880 (c.2600) xxiii.
35   Ibid.
36   See Raftery, 'Ideological Differences in the First Formal Progammes of Education for Roman Catholic and Protestant Women in Ireland'.
37   Quoted in McElligott, *Secondary Education in Ireland*, p. 53.
38   *Freeman's Journal*, 2 September 1886.
39   Judith Harford, 'The Movement for the Higher Education of Women in Ireland: Gender Equality or Denominational Rivalry?', *History of Education*, Vol. 34, No. 5, 2005, pp. 497–516.
40   Harford, 'The Movement for the Higher Education of Irish Women: The Role of Margaret Byers and Victoria College, Belfast'.
41   Sister Ursula Clarke, *The Ursulines in Cork, 1771–1996* (Cork: Ursuline Convent, 1996).
42   *Report of the Intermediate Education Board for Ireland for 1885*, 1886 (c.4688.) xxvi.
43   Alice Oldham, 'A Sketch of the Work of the Association of Irish Schoolmistresses and Other Ladies Interested in Education, from its Foundation in 1882 to the Year 1890', *Annual Report of the Association of Irish Schoolmistresses and Other Ladies Interested in Education* (Dublin: 1890).
44   O'Connor, 'The Revolution in Girls' Secondary Education in Ireland, 1860–1910', in Cullen (ed.), *Girls Don't Do Honours*, p. 50.
45   Mary Colum, *Life and the Dream* (London: Macmillan, 1947), pp. 26–7.
46   Margaret Ward, *Hanna Sheehy Skeffington – a Life* (Dublin: Attic Press, 1970), pp. 7–10.
47   *First Report of the Commission on Intermediate Education (Ireland)*, with Appendix (Palles), 1899 (c.9116, c.9117) xxii; *Final Report*, 1899 (c.9511.) xxii. 629; *Minutes of Evidence*, (c.9512) xxiii.i; Part II of *Appendix to the Final Report*, 1899 (c. 9513) xxiv.i.
48   Palles Commission, 1899, *Final Report*, p. 18.
49   Palles Commission, 1899, *Minutes of Evidence*, pp. 295–301.
50   Ibid.
51   Ibid.
52   Ibid.
53   Palles Commission, 1899, *Appendix to the Final Report*, p. 44.
54   Palles Commission, 1899, *Minutes of Evidence*, pp. 178–89.
55   O'Connor & Parkes, *Gladly Learn and Gladly Teach*, pp. 53–86.
56   Palles Commission, 1899, *Minutes of Evidence*, pp. 179–89.
57   Ibid., pp. 529–33.
58   Ibid., pp. 511–18.
59   Ibid.
60   Palles Commission, 1899, *Appendix to Final Report*, pp. 121–5.
61   Palles Commission, 1899, *Minutes of Evidence*, p. 462.
62   Palles Commission, 1899, *Appendix to the Final Report*, p. 222.
63   Palles Commission, 1899, *Minutes of Evidence*, p. 650.
64   Palles Commission, 1899, *Appendix to the Final Report*, p. 121.
65   Palles Commission, 1899, *Minutes of Evidence*, pp. 472–81.
66   Ibid.
67   *Bill to amend Law relating to Intermediate Education in Ireland*, 1900 (c.210.) ii.
68   *Report of the Intermediate Education Board of Ireland for 1915*, 1916 (c.8369.) viii.
69   *Lady of the House* (Christmas, 1903). A note was included in the article, regretting that the religious principals of the Catholic girls' schools were not permitted to be interviewed, and therefore the report was incomplete.
70   *Messrs F.H. Dale and T.A. Stephens, His Majesty's Inspectors of Schools, Board of Education, on Intermediate Education in Ireland*, 1905 (Cmd.2546) xxviii. 709, pp. 26–7.
71   *Dale and Stephens Report*, p. 55.
72   Ibid., p. 42.

73 Pam Hirsch and Mark McBeth, *Teacher Training in Cambridge: The Initiatives of Oscar Browning and Elizabeth Hughes* (London: Woburn Press, 2004).

74 *Register of Intermediate Teachers in Ireland* (Dublin: Alex Thom, 1919).

75 Padraig Pearse, 'The Murder Machine', in P. MacAonghusa and Liam Ó Réagáin (eds), *The Best of Pearse* (Cork: Mercier Press, 1967), pp. 30–52.

76 Senia Paseta, *Before the Revolution: Nationalism, Social Change and Ireland's Catholic Elite* (Cork: Cork University Press, 1999), pp. 28–52. The 'Irish-Ireland' movement of the 1890s sought to 'de-Anglicise Ireland' by encouraging the study of the Irish language, history, culture and sport. One of its leaders was Douglas Hyde, a founder member of the Gaelic League in 1893.

77 *Report of the Intermediate Education Board for Ireland for 1900*, 1901 (c.588.) xxi; *Report of the Intermediate Education Board for Ireland for 1910*, 1911 (c.5768.) xxi.

78 Isabella Mulvany, 'The Intermediate Act and the Education of Girls', *Irish Educational Review*, Vol. 1, No. 1 October 1907, pp. 14–20.

79 John Coolahan, *The ASTI and Post-Primary Education in Ireland, 1909–1984* (Dublin: Cumann na Meánmhúinteoirí, Eire, 1984) pp. 17–18.

80 *Intermediate Education Act (Ireland)*, 1914.

81 *Proposed Scheme for the Application of the Teachers' Salaries Grant*, 1914 (c.7368.) lxiv.

82 Coolahan, *The ASTI*, pp. 55–6.

83 *Report of the Vice-Regal Committee on the condition of Service and Remuneration of Teachers in Intermediate Schools, and on the distribution of grants from public funds for intermediate education in Ireland* (Molony), 1919 (c.66.) xxi.

84 The average salary paid to lay teachers (521 males and 432 females) was £154 per annum for men teachers and £102 per annum for women teachers.

85 *Report of the Vice-Regal Committee on the condition of Service and Remuneration of Teachers in Intermediate Schools* (Molony), pp. 18–19.

86 Ibid., p. 36.

87 Coolahan, *The ASTI*, pp. 44–6.

88 *Vice-Regal Committee of Inquiry into Primary Education (Ireland) 1918* (Killanin); *Final Report of the Committee*, Vol. I: *Report*, 1919 (c.60.) xxi: *Report of the Committee*, Vol. II: *Summaries of Evidence, Memoranda and Returns*, 1919 (c.178.) xxi.

Chapter 4
Women and Higher Education in Ireland

SUSAN M. PARKES AND JUDITH HARFORD

BACKGROUND

The development of higher education for women in Ireland was closely linked with that of Intermediate education. As the number of girls undertaking academic study at second level increased, a demand for entry to university education was created. However, opposition to the higher education of women was even stronger than that encountered by Intermediate education for girls. Fears were expressed about what would happen to women and to society if access to higher education were granted. Educated women, it was argued, would lose their femininity and damage their health through too much study.[1] The term 'blue-stocking' was used throughout the period to mock an intellectual woman. It was also feared that educated women would make less effective wives and mothers, and, since most women were destined to marry and live at home, higher education was considered to be a waste of time and money. It was argued that, since women lived in a 'separate sphere' from men, their education should be separate and distinct.[2] Moreover, the presence of young women in a male college would be a serious distraction and, worse still, a danger to morals. However, despite these obstacles, the women's campaign for admission to higher education intensified throughout the latter half of the nineteenth century.

The movement for the higher education of women in Ireland was, in the initial stages, strongly influenced by the English experience, which was led by a small number of middle-class women. The founding of Girton College, Cambridge, in 1869 by Emily Davies and the subsequent opening of Newnham College, Cambridge, in 1872, provided models for other women to follow. These women's colleges were residential and single sex, and offered rigorous academic study. At Oxford, Somerville College and Lady Margaret Hall, both founded in 1879, followed a similar pattern. However, neither Oxford nor Cambridge was prepared to allow women students to take degrees, although from the 1880s they were allowed to sit for the university examinations.[3] In London, three women's colleges, Bedford College (1849), Westfield College (1882) and Royal Holloway College (1886), became recognised colleges of London University, and the new civic university colleges such as Liverpool, Manchester and Leeds (which comprised the Victoria University from 1880 to 1887) were all open to women. Similarly the four universities in Scotland (Edinburgh, Glasgow, St Andrews and Aberdeen) were by 1892 open to women, and the new University of Wales was founded in 1893. The last university to open its degrees to women was Durham in 1895. In the United States, women's colleges such as Vassar (1865), Wellesley (1875) and Bryn Mawr (1885) offered higher education to women, and at Harvard and Columbia Universities women's colleges were established, namely Radcliffe (1893) and Barnard (1889) respectively.[4] In addition, a number of American universities such as Cornell, Michigan and Boston were co-educational from the outset. All of these developments meant that Irish women were now in a strong position to argue the case for access to university education.

EXISTING UNIVERSITY PROVISION FOR IRISH WOMEN

In 1869 there were three universities in Ireland, none of which was open to women. Trinity College, University of Dublin, had been founded in 1592 as a Protestant Reformation university, though from 1793 it was open to Catholics and Dissenters. The Queen's University of Ireland, which had been founded in 1845, comprised three constituent Queen's Colleges in Belfast, Cork and Galway.[5] These Colleges were secular, non-denominational and state-funded. They were condemned by the Catholic Church as 'godless colleges', and Catholic students were forbidden to attend them. In 1854, as a countermeasure, the Catholic University had been founded with John Henry Newman as the first rector, but this university had been unable to gain a charter or state funding. 'The Irish University Question' continued to be a dominant political issue for the remainder of the nineteenth century.[6]

For women, the first important step forward was the introduction of Examinations for Women in 1869 in both Trinity College, Dublin, and the Queen's University of Ireland. These examinations, though aimed more at secondary-school level, provided the universities with experience of the academic ability of women students and of the standard of knowledge that could be achieved by them. Equally important was the work of pioneering women such as Isabella Tod and Margaret Byers, who had been actively lobbying for higher educational provision for Irish women. With the opening of the Ladies' Collegiate School (1859) and the Belfast Ladies' Institute (1867), and with the introduction of the system of public examinations under the 1878 Intermediate Education (Ireland) Act, the demand for university education had grown.

A significant opportunity to press the women's case came in 1873, when Gladstone, the Liberal Prime Minister, introduced his Irish University Bill.[7] This Bill proposed to establish a single university in Ireland that would include Trinity College, the Queen's Colleges and the Catholic University College. Isabella Tod and the Belfast Ladies' Institute petitioned the House of Commons to allow women's higher education to be included in any public endowment, which would be awarded under the Bill. Tod, in a public speech in Belfast, asked:

> Why should women be left out of account? Whatever the reasons may be, all friends of education, all who care more for the education of the people than for carrying out any particular theory as to the mode, should make a united effort to obtain consideration of the claims of women now, while the whole question is under discussion. If we neglect this opportunity, no other may occur for fifty years to come. The indifferentism will get hardened in new grooves, and we shall soon find ourselves worse off than English women, who are claiming and getting some share of school endowments, if not of college endowments . . . [8]

Tod went on to point out that, while the existing examinations for women now offered by the universities were a very efficient help to women, they only tested teaching but did not provide it. She concluded:

> We must draw the attention of the government and the legislature to the facts of the case, and claim from them that in arranging for the higher education of one half of the nation they shall not shut out the other half from its advantages.[9]

In a follow-up to this request the Belfast Ladies' Institute wrote to the Senate of the Queen's University requesting that women be allowed to take degrees. They stated that 'more might be done by the University for the education of women than the institution of special examinations, valuable as they were, as long as the means of good teaching was so scanty, and so irregularly distributed'.[10] The Institute recommended that women should be allowed to share in the university teaching and stated that 'so far as we have been able to ascertain there is nothing in the constitution of the Queen's University to prevent it from being open to women'.[11]

At the same time, encouraged by the Belfast efforts, the Queen's Institute in Dublin petitioned both Queen's University and Trinity College, Dublin, to admit women to sit for degrees. The Queen's Institute had been founded in 1861 by Anne Jellicoe (who later founded Alexandra College) and A.B. Corlett. It was an offshoot of a similar society in England and aimed at providing middle-class women with a technical education and assisting them to obtain suitable employment.[12] In a letter dated 9 October 1873 addressed to the Provost and Board of Trinity College, A.B. Corlett, secretary of the Queen's Institute, enclosed a draft memorial that was to be sent to both universities. It stated that:

> The higher education of women occupies now a remarkable share of public attention. Good results were predicted from the separate examinations granted to women by universities; but it is now alleged the profession of teaching has not been elevated by them, nor have those who have passed successfully derived any advantage from possessing these certificates.[13]

The lack of public confidence in the separate women's examinations and the failure to create a group of women graduates who could teach in women's colleges were a disappointment, and what was needed was for women to be able to matriculate and obtain degrees at the universities:

> It concerns the honour of Ireland that her universities should inaugurate such enlightened policy by inviting women desirous of obtaining the highest education to study in the schools. Nor should it be overlooked that only those women whose influence on society would be of the most valuable kind are likely to seek their education at the men's university.[14]

In response to this letter, the Registrar, on behalf of the Board of Trinity College, noted that the Board had 'already taken steps for directing the higher education of women' and that they did 'not think it desirable that the education of young men and young women should be considered in the manner proposed, which appears to involve very serious practical difficulties'.[15] Later in the month, the Board of Trinity College received a supporting petition from the committee of the National Union for Improving the Education of Women in London. It stated that, although great advantages had been conferred by the system of separate examinations for women, 'small practical value' was attached to the certificates. Women destined to be teachers needed the opportunity to study in a university and to show that their education and attainments were equal to those of men:

> The Committee of the National Union trusting to the enlightened spirit of the Irish Universities and to the sympathy they have long shewn for the efforts by women to obtain higher education, earnestly hope that they will take this petition into serious consideration.[16]

However, both the petitions to Queen's University and to Trinity College were refused, and the defeat of Gladstone's University Bill in the House of Commons put an end to the debate in the short term.[17]

FOUNDING OF THE ROYAL UNIVERSITY OF IRELAND (RUI), 1879

A turning point in the campaign for higher education for Irish women was the founding of the Royal University of Ireland (RUI) in 1879, as a compromise measure to provide acceptable higher education for Catholics. Under the terms of the University Education (Ireland) Act, the Queen's University was to be abolished and students attending the existing Queen's Colleges and the Catholic University College would henceforth take Royal University degrees. No residency was required for courses except in the medical school. However, although the degrees of the Royal University were open to women, the University had serious drawbacks for women students. Women were not appointed to the Senate of the University, nor were they admitted to Convocation. Moreover, the twenty-six Royal University fellowships were to be divided between the

Queen's Colleges and the Catholic University College, none of which admitted women. Nor were women allowed to attend lectures given by RUI Fellows at these colleges. There was no alternative university college for women and no state funding available for such an institution. Women thus had to organise their own university classes to study for the Royal University degrees.

The new leading girls' high schools took up the challenge and set up senior classes in their schools, offering teaching for the Royal University matriculation and arts degree examinations. Protestant academic schools and colleges for women drove the movement in the early stages, in particular Alexandra College, Dublin, and Victoria College, Belfast. Catholic schools for girls were slow to enter the public examination arena. The Catholic hierarchy was opposed to the new departure in the education of Irish women and made its stance on the issue very clear. Its opposition was based on the alleged impropriety of girls competing with boys in public examinations, on the anticipated opposition of parents and on the transformation of the curriculum.[18] The hierarchy's opposition ensured that few convent schools participated.

Despite the obstacles facing them, many young women were keen to enter for the degree examinations of the Royal University and in 1884 the first RUI degrees were awarded to a group of women graduates popularly known as 'The Nine Graces'. Six of these women had been educated at Alexandra College and three had studied privately. The students of Alexandra included Isabella Mulvany, who became head of Alexandra School, and Alice Oldham, who was to become one of the main advocates for women's higher education.[19] Of the nine graduates, five were already on the staff of Alexandra College, and these women became role models for others to follow. The graduation ceremony was a historic occasion when the nine women walked up the Royal University Great Hall in Earlsfort Terrace to receive their degrees. As a new graduate, Charlotte Taylor was invited to play her B. Mus. Composition on the organ while the Chancellor of the University made a speech about the 'sweet girl graduates'. Mary Hayden, who was then still a student, recorded the scene in her diary, noting how well the women looked in their gowns and white hoods:[20]

> Then the conferring of degrees began, the schools of Law and Medicine being first: the girls walked up with great dignity and composure amidst loud applause: the five Honour BA's separately, the four Pass, together: Jessie Twemlow, Marion Kelly, Miss Sands and 'the chief' looked especially well: not a

1. Linen production by girls at the Mercy Convent, Queenstown, County Cork, 1900. Source: Lawrence Collection, National Library, Dublin (permission pending).

2. A National School classroom, Clash, County Limerick, c.1910. Source: Folklore Department, University College Dublin.

3. National School girls, Roscommon, c.1890. Source: D. Raftery, Irish Education Visual History Collection, UCD.

4. Directions for measurement, in the *Manual for Needlework*, CNEI, 1869. Source:
D. Raftery, Personal Collection.

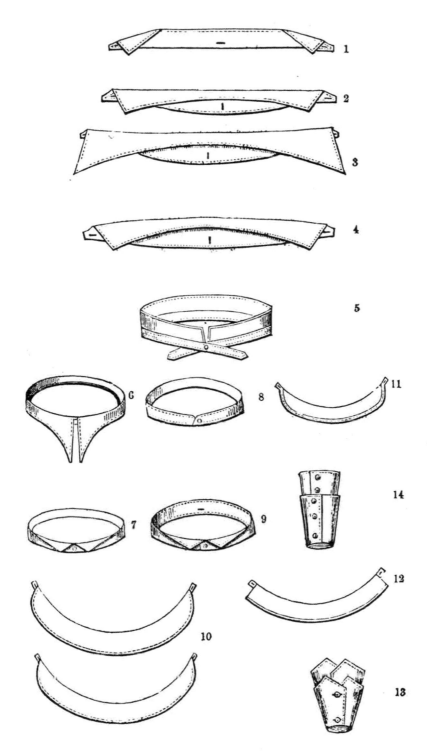

5. Directions for making wrist-bands and collars, in the *Manual for Needlework,*
CNEI, 1869. Source: D. Raftery, Personal Collection.

From Report of a Results Examination of *Grange*
National School, District *44* Visited on *12th November* 1890.
by Mr. *Macdonnell* District Inspector.

Mr Mallen discharges his duties in a very satisfactory manner. The general proficiency of his classes, is good. Order and discipline are properly maintained, the accounts are well kept, and the house is in good order. Needlework is well taught, by Miss Mallen. Taken as a whole, the school is doing its work well. I would suggest, that the garden attached to the school, should be cultivated, as a school garden. It is in a very untidy state at present.

6. Inspector's Report on Grange National School, County Wicklow, commenting on the teaching of needlework to girls. Source: Mary Munro, Personal Papers, Dublin.

7. Gymnastics lesson at the Ursuline Convent, Waterford, 1908. Source: National Library, Dublin (permission pending).

8. The Nine Graces: the first women graduates of the Royal University of Ireland,
1884. Source: Susan M. Parkes, Personal Collection, Dublin.

bit the typical 'blue stocking', which I was glad to see, since Chief Justice Morris, having only seen Alice Oldham, pronounced them 'an ugly lot'.[21]

ADMISSION OF WOMEN TO THE QUEEN'S COLLEGES

The type of higher education offered at the girls' schools was limited, and the campaign to obtain entry to the main university colleges continued. In 1882, the Belfast Ladies' Institute again petitioned Queen's College, Belfast, to allow women students to attend arts lectures. The memorial stressed the fact that, since women were now eligible to take RUI degrees, a different relationship had been established:

> There are now a number of ladies who have passed the Matriculation Examination, of the Royal University, for whom instruction of the nature of that imparted in your Honours classes is in the highest degree desirable. We, therefore, very respectfully, beg you to take into your early consideration whether you might not be able to make arrangements by which these matriculated students might be admitted to the Honours classes of the Belfast Queen's College.[22]

Attitudes had changed in the ten years since the 1873 petition, and this time the Queen's College Council agreed to admit women to lectures in arts. The following year they were admitted to science lectures and in 1889 they were admitted into the medical faculty. Among the first women students was Alice Everett, daughter of Joseph David Everett (1831–1904), distinguished Professor of Natural Philosophy at Queen's College, Belfast. She was the first woman to obtain first place in the first-year scholarship examination in science, and later she went to Girton College, Cambridge, where she was awarded the Mathematical Tripos in 1889. She went on to have a distinguished career in astronomy. She was followed at Queen's, Belfast, by Florence Hamilton (later mother of the author C.S. Lewis), who gained fourth place in the second-year examinations.[23] As women students they were not eligible for college scholarships, the college statutes had to be amended, and by 1895 this process had been completed.[24]

In Cork, women were first admitted to the Queen's College in 1885, although numbers were small. A group called The Ladies' Association for the Promotion of Higher Education of Women in

Cork had been founded to organise lectures and seminars, and by 1878 the association was permitted to use the Aula Maxima in the college. In 1883 the association petitioned the College Council to be allowed to attend full lectures in the college and this was granted. The president of the college at the end of the first year commented favourably on the high standards obtained by the girls and added that 'the presence of ladies in the classrooms and the library greatly contributes to the preservation of order . . . their example will stimulate the men to a more regular and attentive work'.[25] The majority of students who entered were Protestant. Between 1885 and 1896, there were thirty women students and of these only one-fifth was Catholic. Among the first cohort of women students who entered was Mary Tierney Downes, who proved to be a forceful personality and may indeed have caused the college to regret the entry of women.[26]

In Galway, the Queen's College admitted women in 1888. Few female students attended, but the most outstanding was Alice Perry, who qualified as the first woman graduate in engineering in 1906. Her father, James Perry, was County Surveyor for Galway West, and on his death she was appointed as Temporary County Surveyor in his place. Her appointment later was made permanent, and she was the only woman county surveyor in Ireland. She subsequently emigrated to England and had a career in industrial safety.[27] Another distinguished early woman graduate was Dr Rosalind Clarke, daughter of the Presbyterian minister in Galway, who graduated in 1904 with an honours degree in chemistry and experimental physics. In 1910 she was appointed assistant to Alfred Senier, Professor of Chemistry in Queen's College, Galway, and she served on the academic staff in Galway until 1942.[28]

THE CATHOLIC WOMEN'S COLLEGES

It was not until the late 1880s that the Catholic hierarchy changed its policy on higher education for Catholic women. Concerns were expressed over the fact that Catholic women had been left with no alternative but to attend Protestant institutions such as Alexandra College, Dublin, to pursue their studies. The perceived threat of proselytism galvanised a previously apathetic hierarchy, under the direction of Archbishop William Walsh, into formulating a comprehensive strategy *vis-à-vis* the higher education of Catholic women.[29] Walsh was an important ally for those at the centre of the higher education campaign, and, although not hugely committed to the reform of higher education for Irish women, he was driven by a desire to provide for equality of provision for Catholics. Walsh was also in a powerful position to effect reform as a member both of the Intermediate Board of Education and of the Senate of the RUI. Religious women cultivated his support, keenly aware of the importance of his collaboration and patronage.

The Dominican order was the first to engage in the provision of higher education. The Dominican College, Eccles Street, was founded in 1882, originally as an orphanage for the maintenance and education of orphan daughters of the middle and upper classes who could be trained in the profession of governessing.[30] Eccles Street, however, soon began preparing women for public examinations and by 1886 the first Catholic women, Mary Joe McGrath, Agnes O'Sullivan, Gertrude Cahill and Katherine Roche, successfully presented for matriculation. Mother Antonia Hanley, Prioress, and Mother Patrick Shiel, Sub-Prioress, were key agents in the Dominican involvement in higher education. Hanley was described as 'a remarkable and valiant woman' whose 'rare talent and administrative and organising power' were essential to the success of the Eccles Street initiative.[31] Shiel was considered 'a woman of wide culture and great teaching ability [who] would advance Irish Catholic womanhood to the forefront in the intellectual world'.[32]

A second Catholic women's college, St Mary's University College and High School, was established in 1893, also under the auspices of the Dominican order. St Mary's was to act as the 'common centre' for Catholic teaching and was based at 28 Merrion Square, formerly the town residence of Lord Howth.[33] Mother Patrick Shiel became Prefect of Studies at the new college and proved a powerful force in negotiating the rights of Catholic women to higher educational provision during this crucial period. From the outset, the college was positioned to compete with Alexandra College and to provide Catholic women with 'an equal share in those educational advantages which [had] been the monopoly of other denominations'.[34] Among those women who played a key role in the college in the early stages were Mother M. Augustine Clinchy, Prioress; Mother M. Patrick Sheil, Prefect of Studies; Sister M. Aloysius Keighron; Sister M. Reginald Mulcahy; and Sister M. Martha Roche. Mother M. Stanislaus McCarthy subsequently joined the community from Sion Hill as Sub-Prioress.[35]

The Loreto order also began their involvement in university provision in 1893 and Loreto College, 53 St Stephen's Green, became the centre of university teaching. Mother Michael Corcoran, Fourth Superior-General IBVM, 1888–1918, was the vision behind the

Loreto initiative in higher education. Corcoran succeeded Mother Xaveria Fallon as Superior General in July 1888 at the age of forty-two, and remained in office until 1918. She was a committed educationist, her first objective being to promote the cause of higher education for Irish women. She was deeply committed to the provision of higher education for Catholic women and particularly for women religious.[36] Students at Loreto College were prepared for the examinations of the Royal University of Ireland; the Intermediate Board; the Department of Science and Art, South Kensington; the Incorporated Society of Musicians, London; and the Royal College and Royal Academy of Music, London. Loreto College's close proximity to the Catholic University meant that arrangements could be made for some of the professors to assist the nuns in giving lectures.

The Ursuline order was, by this stage, also involved in the provision of higher education. St Angela's College and High School was established in 1887 with the direct aim of counteracting 'the great evil of the day, the pursuit of learning unaccompanied by religious training'.[37] Among those most actively involved in the Ursuline initiative in higher education were Rev. Mother M. Louisa, Foundress; Mother M. Leonardo Barry, First Head of the House; Mother M. Liguori Keating, First Headmistress; M. Elizabeth Dunlea; M. Stanislaus Coppinger; Sister Patricia Spillane; Sister Philip McCartan and Sister Benedicta Daly. Of these sisters, Mother M. Louisa Hoey was particularly instrumental in the development of the Ursuline strategy in higher education. Deeply committed to the importance of higher education, the Ursuline Convent Annals record that 'her zeal and knowledge of the needs of the Institute showed themselves by her introduction of a new arrangement of the educational programme and the appointment of a mistress of studies whose duty it would be to superintend and examine the classes in concert with the M[other] General'.[38]

CAMPAIGN FOR ADMISSION TO THE CATHOLIC UNIVERSITY COLLEGE

Although access to the Queen's Colleges was now open to women, the prohibition on attendance by Catholic students, both men and women, prevented many from entering. The only publicly funded Catholic college which Catholic women would have been able to attend was University College, St Stephen's Green, Dublin, but this college remained firmly closed to women students. Established in

1854, as the Catholic University of Ireland, University College had no endowment or charter, although Gladstone's Bill in 1873 had offered it the possibility of becoming part of a single university of Ireland. With the setting up of the Royal University in 1879 the opportunity of offering degrees became a reality, and a number of RUI fellowships were allocated to the Catholic University. In 1883 University College was placed under the management of the Jesuit order, and Fr. William Delany S.J. was appointed president.[39] With the growth of Catholic secondary schools and of the Intermediate Board examinations, the number of students entering the college steadily increased and a lively collegiate life developed around Newman House, 86 St Stephen's Green. The women students who were attending Loreto College, St Stephen's Green, and St Mary's University College, Merrion Square, were anxious to be allowed to attend the lectures that were given by the RUI Fellows at University College. However, Delany was strongly opposed to women attending the college, though eventually he did allow the RUI Fellows to give lectures to women students in their own colleges.

The inadequate state of provision for Catholic women prompted one student, Margaret Downes, to organise a memorial signed by thirteen 'Catholic Lady Graduates and Undergraduates' calling attention to the 'serious disability' under which they laboured because of their exclusion from lectures given by the University Fellows. The memorial presented to the Standing Committee of the RUI requested the Senate to take some steps to remedy this 'hardship'.[40] The Committee noted that, while they sympathised with the request of the memorial, 'the Senate had neither the right nor the power to attempt to interfere with the arrangements made in any of the Colleges in which the Fellows teach'.[41] They suggested that, if any of the women could arrange with any of the Fellows to deliver courses of lectures specifically for women students, a room would be provided in the RUI buildings. A minority of Fellows belonging to University College availed of the Standing Committee's suggestion to deliver courses of lectures specifically for women.

Disappointed with the outcome of the memorial, Margaret Downes published the grievances of Catholic women students in *The Case of the Catholic Lady Students of the Royal University Stated* (1888).[42] She observed that, if Catholic women were not put on an equal footing with Catholic men, the liberal professions of the founders of the university would be falsified and the reform which it was intended to usher in would become a mockery.[43] Delany, in his second term as President of University College, agreed to hold 'public lectures' for students from the second year of their BA degree. These lectures were held in the Aula Maxima beside University House, emphasising the marginal status of women in the College. Eighteen women attended lectures in the session 1901–02.[44] Most of these women came from St Mary's University College and Loreto College, St Stephen's Green.

EARLY WOMEN GRADUATES IN MEDICINE

The one area of higher education where women were making good progress was in the field of medicine. Following the decision of the Royal College of Physicians in Ireland in 1876 to allow women to register as doctors, the first Irish women to qualify in medicine were either licentiates of the Royal College of Surgeons, which admitted women to its examinations from 1885, or graduates of the Royal University. Those who studied medicine at one of the Queen's Colleges or at the Catholic University Medical School were eligible for RUI degrees. The Medical School at Queen's College, Belfast, was opened to women in 1889 and that of Queen's College, Cork, in 1893. The Catholic University Medical School was opened to women from 1896. In the 1890s, thirty-nine women doctors qualified as medical practitioners.[45] However, employment was difficult for them to find. Some became missionaries and served abroad, while others served in local district asylums, in gynaecology or private practice. There was strong opposition, particularly in Catholic households, to women taking up such a career because of the apparent impropriety of such work for females. The majority of the early women doctors were from Protestant families and among the early women medical graduates of the Royal University were three daughters of Church of Ireland clergy – Katherine Maguire (1891), Amelia Grogan (1895) and Kathleen Lynn (1899). Lynn was to become well known for her strong support for the nationalist cause and for her work among the poor of Dublin and the founding of St Ultan's Hospital for Sick Children in Dublin.[46] Another early medical graduate, Eleonora Fleury (1890), had studied at the London School of Medicine for Women and was the first woman to obtain a Doctor of Medicine (MD) degree (with gold medal) in 1896 from the RUI. She was later appointed assistant medical officer at the Richmond District Asylum, Grangegorman. Emily Winifred Dickson, who had studied at the Royal College of Surgeons, obtained the MB (1893) and MD (1896) of the Royal University and later became the first woman Fellow of the RCSI. She became the first woman gynaecologist in Ireland, working first at the Richmond Hospital and later at the Coombe Lying-in-Hospital, where she was assistant master and responsible for many of the improvements in the care of patients. Adeline English, one of the first women graduates of the Catholic University Medical School when it opened to women in 1896, became medical superintendent of Ballinasloe Mental Hospital. Of those who went abroad, Anna Church (1891) and Hester Russell (1891) served in India, as did Eva Jellett, the first woman medical graduate of Trinity College, Dublin (1905).

Another institution where women were admitted was the Royal College of Science, founded in 1866. From the outset women had been admitted to lectures, and the college offered a Diploma Associate while the RUI recognised some of its courses as part of a degree. Among the first women associates (ARCScI) was Mary Thompson (*née* Robertson), who later graduated at the RUI and taught science at Alexandra College for many years.

ROBERTSON COMMISSION ON UNIVERSITY EDUCATION (IRELAND) 1901–03

Another turning point in the struggle for higher education for women came with the setting up of the Robertson Commission on University Education in 1901.[47] There was growing dissatisfaction with the fact that the Royal University was operating as an examining university only. In addition, because of the inadequate funding available to the Catholic University, the 'university question' had become a major political issue. Pioneering women used the opportunity of the Robertson Commission to publicise and highlight their grievances, and to emphasise the lack of facilities for women, both Catholic and Protestant. As with the Palles Commission on Intermediate Education (1898), no women were appointed to the Robertson Commission, despite a request from the Central Association of Irish Schoolmistresses that one or two distinguished English women in higher education should be invited to serve. The CAISM noted that three women had served on the Bryce Commission on Secondary Education in England in 1895.[48]

Irish women graduates therefore had to rely on their own resources and submit their case to the Commission as best they could. This effort was made all the more difficult in that women pioneers could not agree among themselves as to whether co-educational higher education was the best approach for women students, or whether they should have 'women's colleges', modelled on the Oxbridge style. The group which favoured co-education and 'mixed' colleges was led by recent graduates of the Royal University. Three women academics played prominent roles. These were Mary T. Hayden of St Mary's Dominican College, Agnes M. O'Farrelly of Loreto College and Alice Oldham of Alexandra College. After 1908, Hayden and Farrelly were to be appointed members of staff at the newly constituted University College Dublin, and Hayden was to be the first woman to serve on the Governing Body of the College. The opposing faction which supported the development of separate women's university colleges was led by Henrietta White, the long-standing principal of Alexandra College, and by Margaret Byers, principal of Victoria College, Belfast.

FOUNDING OF THE IRISH ASSOCIATION OF WOMEN GRADUATES, 1902

In 1902, the Irish Association of Women Graduates (IAWG) was founded in order to present a cogent case to the Robertson Commission. The Central Association of Irish Schoolmistresses sent out a questionnaire in December 1901 to all women graduates of the RUI to ascertain their views. The majority of them supported the proposal to establish an organisation that would protect and publicise their interests. On March 14, 1902, Alice Oldham was elected first president with Mary Hayden as vice-president at the opening meeting of the association in the Gresham Hotel. The organisation's first major task was to prepare the women's case to present to the commission, and two members were nominated to give evidence, Annie McElderry, principal of Rutland High School, Dublin and Agnes M. O'Farrelly, lecturer in Irish at Alexandra College and Loreto College. In addition, Mary Hayden was invited by the Dominicans to give evidence on behalf of St Mary's College. Loreto College appointed James Macken, Professor of English at St Patrick's Training College, Drumcondra, to give evidence on their behalf. Earlier in September 1901, both Henrietta White of Alexandra College and Alice Oldham of the CAISM had already given their evidence to the commission. Therefore, the women's demand for equality in higher education was well represented and it became a major issue for discussion by the Commission.

The IAWG presented a strong case in support of co-education in higher education in June 1902.[49] The two witnesses, Agnes O'Farrelly and Annie McElderry, stated that the association was representative of both Catholic and Protestant women graduates.

O'Farrelly was a distinguished Irish scholar and a strong supporter of Gaelic games. She was later to become Professor of Irish at University College Dublin. McElderry, on the other hand, was from Co. Antrim and had taught at Victoria College, Belfast, prior to being appointed to Rutland School in Dublin, which had a strong academic record. McElderry suggested to the Commission that lectures should be compulsory and that women should be entitled to attend 'general colleges', not just women's colleges. Arguing that the IAWG didn't 'want the women to be shut up in Women's Colleges alone',[50] she continued:

> In the first place, we simply want to claim equality for women, that exactly the same advantages which are open to men should be open to them. We want all the advantages of Colleges and Universities to be open to women in respect of Convocation and Senate, as well as all other appointments, taking London University as our model.[51]

She noted the difficulties that the women's colleges had in providing adequate facilities, and argued that Irishwomen's higher education was currently taking place in what were, in effect, secondary schools. These schools could not supply a full collegiate education such as was being offered at colleges such as Girton and Newnham. On the other hand, in a co-educational setting women academics could expect to be appointed to university staff, and women lecturers could prove themselves capable of lecturing to both male and female students.

In support of their case, the IAWG presented a number of documents including a letter from W.B. Harris, the US Commissioner of Education. Harris supported the development of co-education in higher education. The IAWG listed eight key recommendations that stressed the need for equality of provision for women and the importance and value of a full collegiate life. The first four recommendations dealt with rights of women to higher education. First, they stated that, whatever scheme of university education was adopted, there must be full equality for women. Second, they recommended that all lectures, laboratories and professional schools should be open to women. The third recommendation was that attendance at lectures should be a 'necessary preliminary' to graduation, and the fourth was that 'lectures by fellows and professors in the general college only, and not those lectures delivered exclusively for women, be recognized'.[52] The final four recommendations stated that bursaries should be established for university students of limited means; that extern students who did not attend lectures should receive a distinct degree; that endowed halls of residence for women should be provided where they could 'enjoy the full advantage of collegiate life'; and, finally, that the university fellowships should be awarded by examination or by examination with combined original work. The Robertson Commission was so impressed by the submission of the IAWG that the list of eight recommendations was included *verbatim* in the section of the Commission's final report relating to the higher education of women.[53]

EVIDENCE OF WOMEN PIONEERS BEFORE THE ROBERTSON COMMISSION

One of the key witnesses to give evidence on female education to the Robertson Commission was Mary Hayden, who represented St Mary's Dominican College. For Hayden, the occasion of giving evidence to the Commission was very important and in her diary she recorded the excitement:

> Put on my extra best clothes and was at the RU at 12 sharp but had to wait over an hour. At length I was called. Justice Madden began about the Fellowship and myself. I let myself go rather regarding Dr Delany, which was both wrong and foolish. In the other part I got on better. It lasted only twenty minutes and I was free and ran over to the Chief's – I found her at lunch and stayed for it . . .[54]

Hayden's evidence to the Robertson Commission made a strong case for mixed-sex higher education, and for the general value to society of the education of women:

> It is of the greatest importance for the interests of society, and of the community at large, that opportunities for higher education should be open to women; not only those who intend to earn their livelihood by teaching, or in other more or less similar ways, but also, and even especially, to those who will marry, and in whose hands will be the training and the early education of future generations.[55]

She disagreed with the common view that women who had received a university education were 'rendered less fit for the discharge of domestic duties', and she emphasised the value of university education in obtaining employment in teaching and in secretarial work. She argued that the existing women's colleges (such as St Mary's, where she taught) had inadequate facilities and that to provide them with 'efficient teaching, laboratories, libraries etc' would be very expensive, as would be the provision of duplicate lectures by the RUI Fellows. She noted that there was an insufficient number of women to create an adequately sized female college and that the graduates of such a college would not have equal status with men. She submitted to the Commission a list of all the distinctions achieved by the students of St Mary's since the 1880s.

Alice Oldham also gave evidence before the Robertson Commission. She strongly argued for equality of provision for women and, as one of the earliest graduates of the Royal University, she recounted how much that university had contributed to the development of women's higher education.[56] She considered it was a serious disadvantage that women did not have access to the lectures given by the Fellows of the RUI, and she presented the Commission with copies of memorials which the CAISM had submitted over the years to the government and the university on this matter. In 1892 a memorial had been addressed to the Irish Chief Secretary, A.J. Balfour, which stated that, at a time when government funds were being directed to national and Intermediate education, a portion of it on a 'payment-by-results' basis should be awarded to those girls' schools who were preparing students for university degrees. In 1896, another memorial, signed by a group of distinguished men of the peerage and the professions, as well as women academics and teachers, had been submitted to Gerald Balfour, the Irish Chief Secretary. It requested that in any consideration of the future of Irish higher education the women's case should be given attention:

> We are convinced that to no better purpose could educational funds be devoted, not only because of the great value to the whole community of good education for women, but also because of the necessity which exists at present in Ireland for giving to women of the upper and middle classes educational advantages that will enable them to gain a livelihood.[57]

The memorial stated that 1,461 women had matriculated and 269 had obtained BA degrees at the RUI between 1882 and 1895. In two further memorials addressed to the Standing Committee of the RUI, the CAISM had made a number of complaints. First, they were critical of the standards in examining, particularly in history, which was not yet examined as a separate subject. Second, they raised the issue of the appointment of women to Senior Fellowships. From the outset, RUI Junior Fellowships had been open to women and were appointed by open competition. In 1899, there were three women Junior Fellows (Mary Hayden in English and history, Katherine Murphy in modern languages and Mary Ryan in modern languages). Their duties were largely concerned with university examining. The Senior Fellows were appointed from among the Junior Fellows but no women had attained the position of Senior Fellow.[58] The CAISM noted that:

> The high mental power and learning shown by the women who have won the posts of Junior Fellowships is a proof that they possess the qualifications (which should be the first consideration), for the position of Senior Fellows equally with the men students in competition with whom they have won their present distinctions.[59]

Alice Oldham, like many of her fellow members of the CAISM who taught in girls' schools, favoured the continuation of separate women's colleges, but she emphasised the essential need for endowment for these colleges to assist them in establishing residential women's colleges. She considered that the RUI should be retained and that colleges such as Alexandra College, where she taught, should be given public funding to support its university classes. She later submitted on behalf of the CAISM the results of the questionnaire which had been sent out to all RUI women graduates in December 1901. The majority of the respondents favoured the restructuring of the RUI to form a teaching university that would be fully open to women. They also suggested that an endowment should be given to two colleges for women, one Protestant and one Catholic, to provide residential accommodation and tutorial teaching for women students.

WOMEN'S COLLEGES VS. CO-EDUCATION

The CAISM questionnaire of 1901 had created some disquiet among those women graduates who were opposed to co-education.[60] In April 1902, in an article in the *New Ireland Review* entitled 'Women and the University Question', Lilian Daly, a RUI graduate of 1900, criticised the questionnaire, arguing that higher education was not always good for women and that women belonged in a sphere separate from that of men. She claimed that too much study could lead to exhaustion, that the employment of women in competition with men lowered wages, and that home life would suffer if women were allowed to participate in higher education. She concluded the exclusion of women from higher education, the franchise and the professions should be a matter for women alone. They should be able to decide for themselves as to whether they wished to 'abandon their special domestic sphere' and not allow the decisions to be made for them by the male sex.[61]

The case for the retention of the separate women's colleges was strongly supported by other women witnesses to the Robertson Commission, in particular by Henrietta White (Principal of Alexandra College) and Margaret Byers (Principal of Victoria College, Belfast). Byers stressed the success of Victoria College and the high standards achieved by her staff and students in the university classes. She requested that Victoria College should be recognised as an Arts faculty of a university, that its students should be eligible for all university prizes and exhibitions, and that attendance at the college should be fully recognised. She also suggested that women's colleges *per se* could offer specific advantages to women students, such as a full degree in domestic economy, in music and in teacher training, both for the Froebel kindergarten and for secondary schools.[62] Henrietta White (Alexandra College), who strongly supported separate education for women, also stressed the need for endowment for the women's colleges. She noted that Bedford College for Women, London, received a state endowment of £1,200. She argued that the women's colleges had been very successful in the Royal University degree results and that the girls' convent schools would support this view too. She stated that she saw little hope of Trinity College, University of Dublin, recognising Alexandra College as a women's university college, and that therefore in any reorganisation of the structure of higher education in Ireland, the Protestant girls would have to be accommodated. She considered that Dublin women would be reluctant to travel to Queen's College, Belfast, for their education. She concluded that she had received 'no encouragement' regarding the entry of women to Trinity College, and she recalled how, after five Alexandra students had successfully sat the Trinity College matriculation examination, she had enquired with little satisfaction as to what provision for them was now available:

> I sent to the Registrar to know what provision was made for the five girls to go on with their courses in the University of Dublin,

and the answer, was 'No provision has been made.' That is how
the matter stands. I think it would be rash on our part to decide
that Trinity College would be likely to do anything for us.[63]

In fact in this matter Henrietta White was unduly pessimistic, as
Trinity College was to admit women to degrees three years later. On
the other hand, the two leading girls' schools in Derry which had
been preparing senior girls for university education both supported
the development of co-educational colleges. Margaret MacKillip,
headmistress of Victoria High School, stressed that twenty students
had matriculated to the RUI from Victoria College. Both the
Honorable Irish Society of London and the Drapers' Company of
London had established university scholarships for girls from the
city and county of Londonderry. These were awarded on the results
of the RUI matriculation examinations. The most valuable of the
scholarships was held at Girton College, Cambridge, where women
students were able to study for the Cambridge University tripos
examinations. MacKillip stressed that continuous attendance at
university lectures should be required from both men and women.
She argued that 'women's interests can only be safeguarded by
giving them their share in this provision, without any restriction
whatever on the score of sex, and without arranging teaching for
them exclusively in women's Colleges'.[64] Margaret Deane, headmistress of Strand House School, Derry, similarly argued that
women should be given equality of treatment and admitted on
equal footing to men. Although she had attended a residential
women's college in London (Royal Holloway), she considered that
residence at women's colleges such as was offered in Cambridge,
Oxford and London was 'desirable, but not of the first importance'.[65]
The other main support for separate women's colleges came
from the Loreto order, which had opened its own university college
in 1893. Evidence on behalf of the Order was presented to the
Commission by James Macken, Professor of English at St Patrick's
Training College, Drumcondra. He highlighted the achievements to
date of Loreto College, St Stephen's Green, from which 104 students
had matriculated and twenty-seven had obtained RUI degrees. He
stressed how the college suffered from a lack of facilities and
resources:

> A College thus endeavouring to supply a University course for
> its students out of its own resources, labours under great and
> obvious disadvantage. Its staff has no official connection in any
> way with either the governing body or the professional staff of

the University . . . Their pupils, moreover, must compete with the pupils of the Colleges in which the Fellows of the University deliver their regular courses of lectures.[66]

Macken stressed the great work that had been achieved by the Catholic religious orders in the education of Catholic women. He stated that it was 'of supreme importance that the teachers of these Orders should themselves have received a broad and liberal education, which would enable them to take up the important duty of education, prepared to fill it with greater advantage to the nation at large'.[67] As regards a possible solution, the Loreto order recognised that 'the question of the higher education of Catholic women is essentially a part of the general question of provision for the higher education of the Catholic body' and would keep an open mind.[68] However, one outcome would be to retain the women's colleges and provide financial support to them for staff and resources, and to give recognition to the lectures provided. Another was to allow Catholic women to be admitted to the university laboratories and attend the regular lectures of the professors and fellows. Finally, if there were to be one new single university college acceptable to Catholics, then the Loreto order would ask for their institution to be recognised as a hall of residence which would provide tutorials.

Unexpected support for the admission of women into a co-educational college came from the Right Rev. Monsignor Molloy, Rector of the Catholic University and a member of the Senate of the RUI. He argued that the experience to date of the Catholic University Medical School, which had opened to women in 1896, showed that co-education could work successfully and in any case the numbers of women students would not be large:

> I would open all degrees quite freely to them, and I think that the number coming in would not be inconveniently great. As long as you keep them out by iron bars, they imagine they have a great grievance, and that an immense number are being deprived of the advantages of getting degrees. There is one point I should like to mention in this connection. I have taken pains to ascertain whether any practical inconvenience has arisen from having women in our Medical School, and I am informed that there has been none whatever, although the difficulty with us has been specially great, on account of the limitation of our space in relation to the number of our students.[69]

Further support for co-education was given to the Commission by two outside witnesses, Dr H.R. Reichel, Principal of University College of North Wales at Bangor, founded in 1884, and Professor Gonner of University College, Liverpool, founded in 1881. Reichel argued that, given the small numbers involved in university education, it made better economic sense to have one single college and, moreover, the presence of women students had a 'civilizing' influence:

> Firstly, a dual College can be worked far more economically than two Colleges, and, in a poor country like Wales, if the women are not admitted to the University Colleges, their total exclusion from higher education would be the almost inevitable consequence. That is the first point. The second is that, as far as my experience goes, the dual system, if rightly managed, is productive of advantage to both sexes, having a civilizing influence on the men, and promoting a more healthy tone in certain respects amongst the women.[70]

When asked about the disadvantages of co-education Reichel agreed that such a college was more difficult to manage and that there was danger of the women 'overtaxing their physical strength in competition with the men'.[71] There was also less open discussion in the student societies when the two sexes were present. However, overall, he concluded that he was in favour of the dual system, and believed that some of the difficulties could be overcome by, first, providing supervised halls of residence for women where they could be advised not to over-work, and, second, by allowing freedom of choice in courses which were more suitable for women. Professor Gonner of University College, Liverpool, which was part of the Victoria University, stated that all degrees were open to women in his college (except medicine) and that the women who attended were of a high calibre and most of them were destined to become teachers.[72]

FINAL REPORT OF THE ROBERTSON COMMISSION, 1903

When the final report of the Robertson Commission on University Education was published in 1903 it showed that the women's case for equality in higher education had been accepted and that the evidence of women witnesses had significantly influenced the outcomes of the commission. The case for co-education had won the day. The report recommended 'that women and men should attend lectures and pass examinations in the same Colleges and obtain Degrees on the same conditions'.[73] It also recommended 'that all Degrees and other privileges of the University should be open, without distinction of sex'.[74] The report summarised the achievement that the women graduates of the RUI had gained and acknowledged the contribution of the women's schools and colleges. Alexandra College, St Mary's University College and Loreto College in Dublin, Victoria College, Belfast and Victoria High School, Londonderry, were singled out for their high standard of work. The report regretted that the University of Dublin was still closed to women but commented favourably on the achievements of the women students (though small) at the Queen's Colleges and particularly at Magee College, Londonderry, the Presbyterian college founded in 1865 which offered courses for RUI degrees. In the decade 1890–1900, out of a total of 216 RUI women graduates, Victoria College, Belfast had ninety-five, Alexandra College had eighty-four, St Mary's College had seventeen, and Loreto College had twenty. In contrast, Queen's College, Belfast had only nineteen, Queen's College, Cork, had one, Queen's College, Galway, had two, while Magee College had seventeen. In considering the alternative of either supporting separate women's colleges or co-educational colleges open to both sexes, the Commission had been most impressed by the submission of the Irish Association of Women Graduates and chose to quote in full the association's eight recommendations in the final report. It concluded that these recommendations had convinced the members to decide in favour of co-education in any future development of higher education.[75]

However, the Robertson Commission failed to agree on a future structure for Irish higher education in general. The report itself was indecisive, and, while all members save one had signed it, all members had reservations. The report favoured the retention of the RUI, but as a teaching federal university which would include the Queen's Colleges and a new Catholic college in Dublin. The exclusion of Trinity College from the terms of the Commission had made the finding of a solution more difficult, and the Catholic hierarchy was still seeking a full Catholic University. As a result, it was to be a further five years before it proved possible to find an acceptable solution and, in the meantime, women had to continue their efforts to present their case. This was made all the more difficult as the division between those who wished to see the women's colleges recognised as university colleges and those who favoured co-educational colleges grew wider, and threatened to split the women's cause. The CAISM continued to lobby for the entry of women to the men's colleges, while Henrietta White of Alexandra College continued to lobby for recognition of the women's colleges. The Catholic women graduates continued to seek entry to University College Dublin and the lectures of the RUI Fellows, while others chose to support the Dominican and Loreto women's colleges, both of which were gaining a good reputation for scholarship.

CAMPAIGN FOR ADMISSION OF WOMEN TO TRINITY COLLEGE, DUBLIN: 1895–1904

During the next five years a number of key events influenced the outcome of the university question as regards the position of women. The first of these was the decision by Trinity College in 1904 to admit women to the university campus.[76] The struggle for the admission of women to Trinity had intensified since the Tercentenary celebrations of the College in 1892. In that year the CAISM, led by their able secretary, Alice Oldham, had sent a petition signed by over ten thousand Irish women to the Board of the College requesting the admission of women:

> The time has now come when the throwing open of the Curriculum and Degrees of Trinity College would be a most important service to the higher education of Irish women, and would be widely taken advantage of. We venture to ask for this boon now, when the Tercentenary of the University is being celebrated, feeling that no greater commemoration of such an event could be made than by extending the benefits of Trinity College to a large portion of the community, who, while earnestly desiring culture and knowledge, are at present debarred from obtaining it in the best way in their own country.[77]

Three further petitions had been presented in 1892, one from professional men, one from a majority of the Fellows and Professors of the College, and one from the Medical Professors. Despite these, the Board refused to take any action. However, the CAISM tried again the following year, this time addressing the University Council, which was responsible for academic affairs. Under increasing pressure from the women's lobby, the Board invited the CAISM to present a proposal which would be less radical than that of admitting women to full rights on the university campus. The association, seizing the opportunity, suggested that, as an initial step, degrees, examinations and lectures should be open to women. This time the Board agreed to receive a deputation of three men to speak on behalf of the women. The Board sought legal opinion and were relieved when counsel advised them that the admission of women would be contrary to the College's Statutes and Charter. The Board's 1895 statement declared that it could not agree to the request to admit women. It emphasised the dangers of admitting women students to a male residential campus such as Trinity: 'The Board are of the opinion that [the education of women] cannot be suitably conducted within the walls of an Institution intended for the residence of young men. Parents who place their sons in residence in Trinity College, Dublin, do so in the persuasion that their morals will be subject to some supervision . . . On the whole the Board consider that the introduction of female students into our classes would be attended with risks, which they are in no way called to incur and which they do not choose to run . . .'[78]

However, in the next few years the composition of the Board of the College changed and the younger Fellows, such as Dr Anthony Traill, Mr. E.P. Culverwell and Dr J.P. Mahaffy, who supported the admission of women, became influential.[79] Moreover, after 1902, the College was very aware of the work of the Robertson Commission and of the imminent reorganisation of Irish higher education, as well as the growing support for women's rights. There was increasing pressure to give recognition to Alexandra College as a college of the University of Dublin. The Board, therefore, determined to maintain the position of Trinity as the sole college of the University of Dublin, agreed to admit women students to the university campus. This decision was a major step forward in the movement towards the acceptance of co-education in higher education and had a significant influence on the whole campaign. In December 1902 the Board wrote to the government to request that a King's Letter Patent be issued to allow the College legally to admit women. There were legal doubts expressed as to whether the term 'Studiosi' as used in the Statutes could apply to students of both sexes. The Provost, Dr George Salmon, was still implacably opposed to the admission of women, but as an old man he could see that the tide of College opinion had turned against him.[80] He is reported to have said, 'Over my dead body will women enter this College': that was how it was to be. Salmon died in January 1904 and the first women students entered Trinity College, Dublin, in Hilary Term 1904.

EARLY WOMEN STUDENTS IN TRINITY COLLEGE
AND THE 'STEAMBOAT LADIES': 1904–07

The first women students, Marion Johnston, Averina Shegog and Ellen Tuckey, entered in Hilary Term, 1904. 'The real beginning' came in Michaelmas Term, when forty-seven women entered.[81] Women were initially admitted to degrees in arts and medicine in Trinity College, and later in 1920 to degrees in engineering. They were not allowed to reside in the College and had to leave the campus by six o'clock. A Lady Registrar, Lucy Gywnn, was appointed to supervise the women, who were required to wear cap and gown and to be chaperoned if visiting in College rooms. By 1914 women formed around fifteen per cent of the student cohort. They were mostly the daughters of Protestant middle-class and professional families. One of the distinguished early woman graduates was Constantia Maxwell, the Irish historian, who gained a degree in history in 1908 and was to become the first woman professor in Trinity College. Another outstanding student was Olive Purser, daughter of Alfred Purser, chief inspector with the Board of National Education. She was the first woman to be awarded a university scholarship and gained a double first-class degree in 1908. She later succeeded Lucy Gwynn as Lady Registrar in 1918. The College marked the occasion of the admission of women by awarding honorary degrees to six distinguished Irishwomen. In 1904, an honorary LLD was awarded to Isabella Mulvany, headmistress of Alexandra School, and an honorary LittD was awarded to Sophie Bryant, headmistress of North London Collegiate School and Jane Barlow, poet and novelist. The following year, honorary degrees were awarded to Henrietta White, Margaret Byers and Emily Lawless, author and poet. However, no honorary degree was offered to Alice Oldham, who had been the leading campaigner in the struggle for admission. As secretary of the CAISM, she had worked tirelessly from 1892 to sustain pressure on the university, but her severe and direct manner seems to have alienated those in authority in the College. She died in 1907 and Alexandra College in particular mourned her death, which was a great loss to women's higher education. As one of the first group of graduates of the RUI she had led the way and had been a selfless example to the next generation of women students. An Alice Oldham Memorial Prize was set up at Trinity College to mark her achievements and it was awarded biennially to the student judged to be most distinguished in the Junior Sophister year and who had attended Alexandra College for at least one session.[82] An obituary in the *Journal of Education* stated:

It is a pleasing thought that she [Alice] lived to see the complete realization of her great object of getting Trinity College and the University of Dublin opened to women on the same terms as men. These are achievements, which will not die. It was all done so quietly, so tactfully and unostentatiously, that the women of the present day who now enjoy these privileges hardly realize what they owe to this fragile, gentle, unobtrusive, but most gifted woman.[83]

One unexpected outcome of the admission of women to Trinity College, Dublin, was the appearance between 1904 and 1907 of the so-called 'Steamboat Ladies', who were Oxbridge graduates in all but title. They had taken their degree examinations at one of the women's colleges such as Girton, Newnham or Somerville, but at Cambridge and Oxford they were still not eligible for university degrees. Despite a strong campaign, these two ancient universities had refused to admit women to degrees, although from the 1880s they had allowed women to sit for the degree examinations. Under an old *ad eundem gradum* privilege between the 'ancient universities', Oxbridge graduates could take University of Dublin degrees. In June 1904 the Board of Trinity College passed a grace to allow Oxbridge women to apply for degrees in the three-year period 1904–1907, after which time Trinity College would have its own women graduates. In all, over seven hundred women availed of the privilege, crowding into the commencement ceremonies in Trinity College and taking out BA and MA degrees on the same day. Many of them were distinguished English headmistresses who came to Dublin for one night by sea, hence the term 'Steamboat Ladies'. These women set an example to the younger women students of Trinity College of what could be achieved by academic women. Trinity College was somewhat embarrassed by the numbers of 'Steamboat Ladies' each year, but the new provost, Traill, shrewdly decided to use the Oxbridge women's commencements' fees to fund the setting up of Trinity Hall, a university residence for women students. In 1908, Trinity Hall opened in Dartry, a suburb of Dublin. The first warden, Margaret Cunningham, herself a 'Steamboat Lady', organised Trinity Hall on the lines of Girton College, and thus attempted to provide a residential collegiate life for the women students even though they were attending a co-educational university.[84]

The entry of women to Trinity College in 1904 was a major disappointment to Henrietta White and to Alexandra College, as it put an end to its hopes of gaining university status. The majority of women students who had been pupils at Alexandra chose to enter Trinity

College for their university degrees, and Alexandra College had to be content with becoming a superior second-level school.[85] White continued to advocate the advantages of single-sex education and in 1904 she tried unsuccessfully to have the lectures offered at Alexandra College recognised as suitable preparation for Dublin University degrees. In 1905, Alexandra College offered to provide a residential hall for women students, but the success of Trinity Hall made this offer redundant. Instead, Alexandra College set up three professional 'extra departments': housecraft, secretarial training and teacher training, in order to retain a higher education presence in the college.

FRY COMMISSION ON TRINITY COLLEGE, DUBLIN, 1907

In 1906, in a further attempt to try to 'solve' the university question, the government established another royal commission (under the chairmanship of Sir Edward Fry) to examine the position of Trinity College and the University of Dublin and its place in higher education in Ireland.[86] Women graduates used the occasion to further their cause. Henrietta White once again presented a case for the recognition of Alexandra College by the university, making a very strong argument for the merits of single-sex higher education and its importance to women.[87] She stressed the valuable links which had existed between Alexandra and Trinity College and noted that, of the eighty-eight women students attending Trinity College in 1907, sixty-six per cent were former students of Alexandra. She argued:

> if the degree is to have the same value in the case of women as of men, that women should have the opportunity of sharing in the corporate life of a women's college. This corporate life can never be fully developed for women in a men's college, and it is deemed on all hands an indispensable preparation for filling the highest educational posts. A University degree that does not include it is therefore of considerably less value.[88]

Meanwhile the campaign to gain admission for women to University College continued, led by the IAWG and by those who favoured the entry of women to the male colleges. The IAWG was somewhat alarmed by Henrietta White's submission to the Fry Commission in support of single-sex colleges. It therefore appointed two of its members, Agnes O'Farrelly of Loreto College and Ethel Hanan, a recent graduate of Trinity College, to present evidence to the Fry Commission. Despite the fact that the Commission had no direct concern with the Royal University, the two women made a strong case for co-education and for the inclusion of women in all future Irish university structures. They pointed out that one-third of Royal University graduates were women and that it was a grave injustice that fifteen RUI Fellows were attached to University College, which no women could attend.[89] In addition, the IAWG submitted a statement drawing attention to their evidence before the Robertson Commission and to the decision of Trinity College to admit women. They also noted the great performance of the women students who had entered. The statement concluded with a request that in Trinity College all professional schools and fellowships should be opened to women, and that any new scheme for university education in Ireland should offer full equality to women:

> We earnestly hope that the principle advocated by our asso-
> ciation – the giving to women students in Universities the same
> educational advantages, in every possible respect, as men
> students enjoy – may be supported by your Commission in
> regard not only to Trinity College, but also to the Royal
> University and the colleges connected with it, or any other
> institution that may be established in Ireland.[90]

The report of the Fry Commission (1907) included the recommen-dation that 'watchful care' was needed for women students in a mixed college in Dublin. To ensure that women at Trinity College were as safe as possible, the report recommended that the position of the Lady Registrar in Trinity College should be made permanent and that students should be at least seventeen before commencing their courses. It also recommended that the university could recog-nise 'any public College for women in Dublin or within thirty miles of Trinity College' for teaching purposes, provided the staff and facilities were satisfactory. While this clause theoretically left the way open for Alexandra to become a college of the university, Trinity College was not prepared to agree to such a proposal.[91] The women students were now accepted within Trinity College and were becoming integrated into a co-educational institution.

STRUGGLE FOR ADMISSION TO UNIVERSITY COLLEGE DUBLIN, 1903–08

Thus encouraged by the experience of women in Trinity, the Catholic women continued their campaign to gain entrance to the

RUI lectures at University College. Fr William Delany, SJ, who had returned as President of the College in 1897, found himself in sharp conflict with his students and staff regarding the matter. The Catholic University Medical School was opened to women in 1896 and the number of women attending St Mary's Dominican College and Loreto College was steadily increasing. The founding of the Irish Association of Women Graduates and the opening of Trinity College to women further increased the pressure on Delany. In 1904 the IAWG sent a letter to the President requesting full entry for all students to the arts lectures given by the RUI Fellows. The Council of the College refused the request, saying that no more could be done than to provide lectures in the Great Hall. A further letter was sent to the Senate of the Royal University regarding the matter. Delany discovered to his great annoyance that his own Registrar, Francis Sheehy Skeffington, had been instrumental in organising the drafting of the letter and in gathering signatures. Skeffington, a graduate of the college, was a staunch supporter of women's rights and had married Hanna Sheehy, the political and social activist, who was an early graduate of St Mary's Dominican College.[92] Skeffington resigned his position as Registrar due to his differences with the president and the president was placed in an even more difficult position. Delany defended his policy of only admitting women (excepting first years) to the public lectures in the Great Hall, and he did not approve of co-education as he believed that it was harmful for women. In 1907 Delany faced another conflict within University College – namely that of allowing women to attend meetings of the College debating society, the renowned Literary and Historical Society. He vetoed the admission of women students to the society on the basis of 'the great dangers which would result from the ladies being out late at night and having to cross the city on their return home' as well as of 'the gravity of the situation for the male students, whose morality would be or might be jeopardized through intercourse with the lady students in the Literary and Historical society.'[93]

FOUNDING OF THE NATIONAL UNIVERSITY OF IRELAND, 1908

The 'university question' continued to prove problematical and in 1908 Augustine Birrell, who had been appointed Irish Chief Secretary in 1907, was determined to find a solution. His plan was to create two new universities, one in the north in Belfast, and one in the south. Both universities would be non-denominational, but the

governing body of each would reflect the dominant religious tradition of the majority of its student body. He gained the support of
the Catholic hierarchy for such a solution, which, while not establishing a Catholic university, was designed to establish a 'university
for Catholics'. By accepting the need for two new universities, one
north and one south, Birrell was recognising the reality of 'religious
partition' within the country. The Royal University was abolished
and Queen's College, Belfast was accorded full university status.
Magee College in Derry, founded in 1908 without university
accreditation, chose to negotiate with Trinity College rather than
with Queen's Belfast. Magee students, male and female, then began
to come to Dublin for the two final years of their degree course.
Alexandra College had reason to be annoyed by this arrangement,
as it was the kind of privilege that it sought in vain from Trinity.

Throughout 1907, and when the university Bill was being drafted,
the women's higher education campaign continued and the
protracted debate between the women themselves regarding the
preference of single-sex colleges over mixed colleges became more
public. In January 1908, Norah Meade, a scholar of the RUI and a
student at St Mary's College, wrote an article in the *Irish Educational
Review* on 'Women in Universities' in which she argued strongly the
case in support of women's colleges. Quoting Tennyson's poem 'The
Princess', she advocated that women benefited from a distinct and
separate collegiate atmosphere, while competing on equal terms
with men in all other aspects of university life. Women's colleges
could offer lectureships to women academics who could hold
fellowships of the university, as well as offer specific courses for
women. Girton College, Cambridge, offered such a model, where
women students, while not necessarily seeking a full university
degree, benefited from the social intercourse and interchange of
ideas with women of high intellectual standing. Meade argued that:

> these colleges are the training-ground for women, to prepare
> them for their after-life. It is here that they learn self-confidence
> and a feeling of pride in their own sex. A college-trained girl
> always bears the stamp of dignity without haughtiness, and
> self-reliance without arrogance. This is the age in which women
> have to compete with men in earning their livelihood, and that
> they may do so satisfactorily a feeling of independence and self-
> confidence in the battle of life is absolutely necessary.[94]

Meade's article drew a strong rebuff in the next month's edition
of the *Irish Educational Review*. Mary Hayden and Hanna Sheehy

Skeffington, in a joint article, replied, arguing the case for co-education and its value to both women and men. Their article argued that the experience of other universities showed that co-education was advantageous to women and that it was what the majority of Irish women preferred. The evidence of the Robertson Commission and of the CAISM questionnaire of 1902 had confirmed this. They contradicted Meade's arguments, stating that there were insufficient women academics to staff separate colleges, that specific courses for women such as domestic science were out of place in a university and, in any case, women students should aspire to professions other than teaching. They suggested that residential university halls could provide sufficient collegiate life while allowing women to participate in the full academic life of the university.[95]

Norah Meade replied the next month, defending her arguments that collegiate life was of the essence of university life and that it could only be provided in a residential college which by its nature had to be single sex. In her opinion, women should be 'educated in separate colleges in order that they might derive the highest advantages from their University courses, namely that they should become highly cultured, refined, and self-reliant women'. She concluded that 'Miss Hayden's and Mrs Sheehy Skeffington's educational ideas were too much affected by the intercompetition of the sexes, and that they lay too little stress on the culture and refinement to be derived for women from a properly thought out system of collegiate education'.[96] A further reply came from Hayden and Sheehy Skeffington, countering her arguments and emphasising that women's colleges such as Girton and Newnham were the exception, as they had been pioneer colleges. All modern universities such as those in Scotland, England and Wales were providing residential halls for women but admitting them as full members of the university and, contrary to expectations, the admission of women to Trinity College, Dublin, in 1904 had created few difficulties.[97] Norah Meade in the end lost the argument, but she herself went on to graduate with a first-class honours degree in Modern Literature from University College Dublin, in 1909.

POSITION OF WOMEN IN THE NATIONAL UNIVERSITY OF IRELAND

The 1908 Universities' Act marked the end of the campaign of women for equal access to higher education. Women were admitted to all degrees and offices in the two new universities of Queen's

University, Belfast and the National University of Ireland. The Senate of the National University was required to have at least one woman member nominated by the Crown, and Mary Hayden was appointed to this office as a mark of her achievements on behalf of her fellow women. She and Agnes O'Farrelly were appointed to the Governing Body of the new University College Dublin, which, along with University College, Cork and University College, Galway, became constituent colleges of the NUI. Hayden was appointed Professor of Irish History at UCD, a post she held until 1932. O'Farrelly was appointed as Lecturer in Irish at UCD and later, in 1932, Professor of Irish Poetry. Both women gave leadership to their colleagues and students in the early years of the new college. Hayden also served as first president of the National University Women Graduates' Association that was set up in 1913, and she was to hold this office until 1942.[98] The other two universities, Queen's Belfast and the University of Dublin, also set up their own women graduate associations in 1923, and in 1925 the three associations joined together to form the Irish Federation of University Women. Thus the work of the pioneer Irish Association of Women Graduates, which had done so much to promote the cause of women's higher education, was to be continued by this association.

At the new University College Dublin, there were two other women professors appointed in 1908, as well as Mary Hayden. These were Mary Macken, Professor of German and Maria Degani, Professor of Italian and Spanish. Macken had been a student of Loreto College and had taught at St Mary's College. In her account of the history of women in the university, written in 1954, which she subtitled 'A Struggle within a Struggle', she paid tribute to the achievements of the early women's colleges and to the pioneer work of the religious orders.[99] In the other colleges of the National University of Ireland women were also to gain senior posts. At University College, Cork, Mary Ryan was appointed Professor of Romance Languages in 1910. The first three professors of education at University College, Cork were also to be women – Elizabeth O'Sullivan (1910–35), Frances Vaughan (1936–48) and Lucy Duggan (1949–62). At University College Galway, two of its own women, graduates were appointed to university chairs. M.J. Donovan O'Sullivan became Professor of History in 1914, and Emily Anderson was appointed Professor of German in 1917.[100]

The establishment of the co-educational National University of Ireland in 1908 brought with it considerable difficulties for the Dominican and Loreto orders, which made several attempts to obtain recognition for their courses by the National University. First, both orders were concerned about the viability of their colleges, now that women could avail of full privileges in the NUI. A further concern was the higher education of their own nuns. Without the presence of single-sex women's colleges, these women would be left with no alternative but to attend lectures in a co-educational setting. The matter was referred to the Governing Body of University College Dublin, but there was strong opposition from the groups who had favoured co-education. The IAWG itself argued that to give recognition to the women's colleges would undermine the three constituent colleges of the NUI, which were now all open to women. Neither of the women's colleges had sufficient resources or specialist qualified staff, and both had been engaged in the provision of intermediate education. One of the conditions laid down by the Universities Act for recognition as a university college was that such a college would not 'prepare students for Intermediate, or other school examinations or . . . give education of an Intermediate or Secondary kind'.[101] There might have been a case for recognising a single Catholic women's college, but unfortunately the two religious orders were unable to co-operate and after 1912 the matter was dropped.[102] Instead, the two orders established university halls of residence for women students attending University College Dublin, both of which were situated nearby in St Stephen's Green.[103] In 1915, the university hall of residence model was similarly followed by Queen's University, Belfast, when it established a women's residence, Riddel Hall. At University College, Cork, La Retraite Hall was opened for women in 1923. These halls of residence were to provide a collegiate and supportive environment for young women, many of whom were first-generation university students.

The progress which the women had achieved in the thirty years since 1879 was remarkable. From their exclusion from all university colleges in the 1870s to their inclusion, on an equal footing, to all the male colleges by 1908, the women's movement for higher education had won a great victory. Irish university education had been restructured by the beginning of the twentieth century and all the universities were co-educational. The founding of the Royal University in 1879, while seen at the time as only a 'stop-gap' measure, had served women well. It had given them the opportunity to show that their academic ability equalled that of male students, a situation which the early separate university examinations for women had not allowed. The leadership of the first cohort of graduate women and the founding of the Irish Association of Women Graduates had proved invaluable in presenting the women's cause in public. The women's 'struggle within a struggle' had benefited from being part of the political 'university question' and had taken advantage of the major university campaign for the rights of Catholic higher education in Ireland. The opportunities offered by the Robertson and Fry Commissions to demand the reform and reorganisation of higher education were used well by the women's campaigners.

On the other hand, the cause of the separate women's university colleges was lost, and with it some of the high ideals which women had hoped for. In the co-educational colleges there were to be fewer opportunities for women academic staff and, for most of the twentieth century, the senior management of the universities was to lie in the hands of men. Careers for graduate women remained limited to teaching, the civil service and administration. In Catholic girls' schools, where the majority of staff was religious, the openings for lay teachers remained few. In the universities the number of appointments of women to academic posts remained small, even at a time when women were beginning to hold senior posts at universities in England and North America.

In Ireland, however, given the small student population, the decision to establish co-educational colleges was to prove a wise one. These colleges offered women the opportunity for high quality teaching and research, and they offered a lively student social life. For young women who had been educated in single-sex secondary schools, this was the beginning of a new and important educational and social experience.

NOTES

1 See Joan Burstyn, 'Education and Sex: The Medical Case against Higher Education for Women in England, 1870–1900', *Proceedings of the American Philosophical Society*, Vol. 117, 1973, pp. 79–89 and Raftery, *Women and Learning in English Writing, 1600–1900*, Chapter 4.

2 At this time, there was a widely held belief that men and women should occupy separate spheres, men the public and women the private. The ideology of the separate sphere promoted man's sphere as the public world of work and commerce and woman's sphere as the private world of the home, in her natural role as wife and mother. This dominant ideology was reinforced through medical and religious arguments.

3 Carol Dyhouse, *No Distinction of Sex? Women in British Universities, 1870–1939* (London: UCL Press, 1995); Rita McWilliams Tullberg, *Women at Cambridge* (Cambridge: Cambridge University Press, revised edition, 1998); Vera Brittain, *Women at Oxford: A Fragment of History* (London: Harrap, 1960).

4 James C. Albisetti, 'Unlearned Lessons from the New World? English Views of American Co-education and Women's Colleges, c.1865–1910', *History of Education*, Vol. 29, No. 5, 2000, pp. 473–89.

5 See *An act to enable Her Majesty to endow new colleges for the advancement of learning in Ireland*, 8 & 9 Vict., c. 66, 31 July 1845.

6   Fergal McGrath, *Newman's University: Idea and Reality* (Dublin: Browne and Nolan, 1951).
7   *Bill for the extension of university education in Ireland*, 1873 (55.) vi. 329.
8   Isabella M.S. Tod, 'The Education of Women', *Journal of the Women's Education Union*, 1, 1873.
9   Ibid.
10 Minute Book of the Ladies' Institute Belfast, 22 September, 1873, Victoria College Archives, Belfast.
11 Ibid.
12 See Patricia Philips, 'The Queen's Institute, Dublin (1861–1881)', in McMillan (ed.), *Prometheus's Fire*, pp. 466–73.
13 Trinity College, Dublin Library, College Muniments, P/1/2153.
14 Ibid.
15 Trinity College, Dublin Library, College Muniments, P/1/2154.
16 Trinity College, Dublin Library, College Muniments, P/1/2184.
17 Gladstone's 1873 Bill was defeated by three votes in the House of Commons at Westminster and Gladstone subsequently resigned. See Susan M. Parkes, 'The Irish University Question', in W.E. Vaughan (ed.), *A New History of Ireland*, Vol. VI: *Ireland under the Union, II, 1870–1921* (Oxford: Clarendon Press, 1996) pp. 539–70.
18 See Judith Harford, 'The Movement for the Higher Education of Women in Ireland: Gender Equality or Denominational Rivalry?', *History of Education*, Vol. 34, No. 5, September 2005, pp. 497–516.
19 Alice Oldham (1850–1907), the daughter of Eldred Oldham, a linen draper, was born in Dublin. One of the first women graduates of the RUI, she became Honorary Secretary of the Central Association of Irish Schoolmistresses (1882) and President of the Irish Association of Women Graduates (1902). She was actively involved in the campaign for the admission of women to Trinity College, Dublin.
20 Hayden was the daughter of Dr Thomas Hayden, a distinguished Dublin doctor who had been a professor at the Catholic Medical School and had served on the first Senate of the Royal University. Educated at the Ursuline convent in Thurles and at Alexandra College, Hayden was the first woman to gain a scholarship at the Royal University and she graduated with a BA in 1885 and a first-class honours MA in 1887. A historian of marked ability, Hayden was appointed to a Junior Fellowship of the RUI from 1895 to 1899, but was rejected on grounds of her sex for a senior fellowship in 1900. She became a member of the teaching staff of St Mary's Dominican College, and as such was in a key position to argue the women's case. A forceful and capable person, she impressed all who worked with her and she was to become the first Professor of modern Irish history at University College Dublin and a leading academic.
21 MS Mary Hayden Diaries, 22 October 1884; MS 16, 641, National Library of Ireland.
22 Minute Book of the Ladies' Institute Belfast, 29 September 1882.
23 Ronald W. Bresland, *The Backward Glance – C.S. Lewis and Ireland* (Belfast: Institute of Irish Studies, 1999).
24 Moody and Beckett, *Queen's Belfast, 1845–1949*, pp. 317–18; Brian Walker and Alf McCreay, *Degrees of Excellence – The Story of Queen's, Belfast, 1845 – 1995* (Belfast: Institute of Irish Studies, 1994), pp. 23–4.
25 Murphy, *University College, Cork, 1845–1995* (Cork: Cork University Press, 1995).
26 See Margaret Tierney Downes, *The Case of the Catholic Lady Students of the Royal University Stated* (Dublin: E. Ponsonby, 1888).
27 Tadhg Foley and Thomas Boylan (eds), *From Queen's College to National University: Essays Towards an Academic History of QUG/UCG/NUI*, Galway (Dublin: Four Courts Press, 1999) p. 139.
28 Ibid., p. 225.

29 See Harford, 'The Movement for the Higher Education of Women in Ireland: Gender Equality or Denominational Rivalry?'

30 Eccles Street Convent Annals, 1883–1911, Dominican Archives, Griffith Avenue, Dublin.

31 *The Freeman's Journal*, 5 December 1888.

32 *The Lanthorn, Year Book of the Dominican College Eccles Street Dublin, Golden Jubilee, 1882–1932*, p. 183.

33 ALS William Walsh to Mother Prioress, 5 August 1893, Dominican Generalate Archives, Dublin.

34 *First Report, St Mary's University College and High School, Session, 1893–4*, Dominican Generalate Archives, Dublin.

35 *The Lanthorn, Year Book of the Dominican College Eccles Street Dublin, Golden Jubilee, 1882–1932*, p. 186.

36 ALS Mother Michael Corcoran to M.M. Antonia, 4 December 1902, Loreto Convent Archives, Saint Stephen's Green Dublin.

37 *Ursuline Convent Annals, 1886–1929*, Vol. III. Ursuline Convent Archives, Blackrock, Co. Cork.

38 Ibid., p. 90

39 William Delany, SJ, was President of University College from 1883 to 1888. He subsequently pursued missionary work for nine years before returning to the position in 1897. He was also a Senator of the RUI from 1885.

40 *Royal University of Ireland, Minutes of the Proceedings at the Meetings of the Senate, Volume II*, 1887–1896, p. 207, National University of Ireland Archives, Dublin.

41 Ibid.

42 Downes, *The Case of the Catholic Lady Students*.

43 Ibid.

44 *Royal Commission on University Education in Ireland; Appendix to the Third Report, Minutes of Evidence*, 1902, p. 558.

45 Irene Finn, 'Women in the Medical Profession in Ireland, 1876–1919', in Whelan (ed.), *Women and Paid Work in Ireland, 1500–1930*, pp. 102–19.

46 Medb Ruane, 'Kathleen Lynn (1874–1955)', in Mary Cullen & Maria Luddy (eds,) *Female Activists: Irish Women and Change, 1900–1960* (Dublin: Woodfield Press, 2001), pp. 68–88.

47 *Royal Commission on University Education (Ireland)* (Robertson); *First Report*, 1902 [Cd. 825–6.] xxxi. 21; *Second Report*, 1902 [Cd. 899–900.] xxxi. 459; *Third Report*, 1902 [Cd. 1228–9.] xxxii.i; *Final Report*, 1903 [Cd. 1483–4.] xxxii.i.

48 Sophia Bryant, head of the North London Collegiate School, Lady Frederick Cavendish and Eleanor Sidgwick, head of Newnham College, Cambridge. Three women had also been appointed to the reconstructed London University Senate: Bryant, Sidgwick and Emily Penrose, then principal of Royal Holloway College, London.

49 *Robertson Commission, Third Report, Minutes of Evidence*, pp. 318–22.

50 *Robertson Commission, Appendix to the Third Report, Minutes of Evidence*, p. 319.

51 Ibid.

52 *Robertson Commission Third Report, Minutes of Evidence*, pp. 564–5.

53 *Robertson Commission, Final Report*, p. 49.

54 MS Mary Hayden Diaries, 11 June 1902, MS 16,682, National Library of Ireland. ('The Chief' was Isabella Mulvany, Principal of Alexandra School, which was in Earlsfort Terrace, across the road from the Royal University).

55 *Robertson Commission, Third Report, Minutes of Evidence*, pp. 357–9.

56 *Robertson Commission, First Report, Minutes of Evidence*, pp. 218–21.

57 Ibid., p. 391.

58 The issue of Senior Fellowship had been publicly raised when Mary Hayden, who had been a successful Junior Fellow since 1895, had not been awarded a senior fellowship in 1899.

59   See *Memorial addressed to the Standing Committee of the Royal University of Ireland in the year 1899,* by the Central Association of Irish Schoolmistresses and other Ladies Interested in Education, *Robertson Commission, First Report, Minutes of Evidence,* p. 395.

60   *Robertson Commission, Appendix to the Third Report, Minutes of Evidence,* pp. 565–70.

61   Lilian Daly, 'Women and the University Question', *New Ireland Review,* 17, April 1902.

62   *Robertson Commission, Third Report, Minutes of Evidence,* pp. 60–4.

63   *Robertson Commission, First Report, Minutes of Evidence,* p. 211.

64   *Robertson Commission, Third report, Minutes of Evidence,* p. 64.

65   Ibid., p. 65.

66   Ibid., p. 317.

67   Ibid., p. 318.

68   Ibid.

69   *Robertson Commission, Second Report, Minutes of Evidence,* p. 156.

70   Ibid., p. 204.

71   Ibid.

72   Ibid., p. 79.

73   *Robertson Commission, Final Report,* pp. 49–50.

74   Ibid., p. 50.

75   Ibid., pp. 46–50.

76   Parkes (ed.), *A Danger to the Men?*

77   Trinity College, Dublin Library, College Muniments P/I/244I [2].

78   Trinity College, Dublin Library, College Muniments P/I/2526[3].

79   Traill was Provost of Trinity College, Dublin, 1904–14; Mahaffy was Provost of Trinity College, Dublin, 1914–19; Culverwell was appointed Professor of Education in 1905.

80   George Salmon (1819–1904) was Provost of Trinity College, Dublin, from 1888 to 1904. He was opposed to the admission of women to the college and his opposition had to be formally withdrawn before women could be admitted.

81   Olive Purser, *Women in Dublin University, 1904–1954* (Dublin: Dublin University Press, 1954), p. 5.

82   M.S. Joynt, 'Alice Oldham', *Alexandra College Guild Magazine,* December 1907, Alexandra College Archives, Dublin.

83   *Journal of Education,* February 1907, pp. 126–7.

84   Susan M. Parkes, 'Trinity College and the "Steamboat Ladies", 1904–07', in Mary R. Mason and Deborah Simonton (eds), *Women and Higher Education, Past, Present and Future* (Aberdeen: Aberdeen University Press, 1996), pp. 244–50.

85   O'Connor and Parkes, *Gladly Learn and Gladly Teach,* pp. 66–7.

86   *Royal Commission on Trinity College and the University of Dublin* (Fry): 1906 (Cd.3174, 3176.) lvi, 1907 (Cd.3311–12.) xli.

87   *Fry Commission, Statements and Returns, Appendix to the First Report,* pp. 134–9.

88   Ibid., p. 134.

89   *Fry Commission, Appendix to the Final Report, Minutes of Evidence,* pp. 266–8.

90   *Fry Commission, Appendix to the First Report,* p. 133.

91   Ibid. *Final Report,* pp. 27–8.

92   Ward, *Hanna Sheehy Skeffington;* F.J.C. Skeffington, *A Forgotten Aspect of the University Question* (Dublin: n.p., 1901).

93   Ibid., p. 284.

94   Norah Meade, 'Women in Universities', *Irish Educational Review,* Vol. 1, No. 3, January 1908, pp. 236–72.

95   Mary Hayden and Hanna Sheehy Skeffington, 'Women in Universities: A Reply', *Irish Educational Review,* Vol. 1, No. 5, February 1908, pp. 272–83.

96 Norah Meade, 'Women in Universities: A Rejoinder', *Irish Educational Review*, Vol. 1, No. 6, March 1908, pp. 355–61.

97 Mary Hayden and Hanna Sheehy Skeffington, 'Women in Universities: A Further Reply', *Irish Educational Review*, Vol. 1, No. 7 April 1908, pp. 410–18.

98 Anne Macdona (ed.), *Newman to New Woman, UCD Women Remember* (Dublin: New Island, 2002).

99 Mary Macken, 'Women in the University and the College: A Struggle within a Struggle,' in Michael Tierney (ed.), *Struggle with Fortune* (Dublin: Browne and Nolan, 1954), pp. 142–56.

100 Murphy, *University College Cork*, p. 131; Foley, *University College Galway*, pp. 375–6, p. 410.

101 *An Act to make further provision with respect to university education in Ireland*, 1908. [8 Edward VII, c. 38].

102 See ALS William Walsh to Mother Patrick Shiel, 19 October 1909, Dominican Generalate Archives, Dublin; ALS Mother Peter McGrath to William Walsh, 30 October 1909, Walsh Papers, Dublin Diocesan Archives; ALS Mother Peter McGrath to William Walsh, 9 November 1909, Walsh Papers, Dublin Diocesan Archives.

103 Dominican Hall was located at 48–49 St Stephen's Green and Loreto Hall was located at 73 St Stephen's Green.

Appendix

REPORT FROM A REFORMATORY SCHOOL
FOR FEMALE JUVENILE OFFENDERS

SPARK'S LAKE, MONAGHAN.
MANAGER'S REPORT FOR 1861

The year now closing has been marked by a vast improvement in our building arrangements. This circumstance has had the most beneficial results in the working of the Establishment, and in the conduct and general progress of the children. Our warmest thanks are due to those friends who, by their untiring exertions, have thus co-operated with us in one of the charitable objects to which we have devoted our lives and energies. We have now the facility of classifying the inmates of the Institute, and can thus apply to the various phases of moral disease the remedies which, under God, we hope to be the means of restoring these former little outcasts to their place in the human family, as Christians and useful working members of society.

The present accommodation is for forty girls; but the entire Reformatory buildings, if suitably fitted up, could contain 100 children.

There are at present 30 juveniles in our charge, 26 of whom are under sentence; the remaining four are with us voluntarily, and are supported by private charity – one had already completed, before admission, a *short* sentence in another Reformatory – much too short to prepare her for a situation – and was received here in the hope that her reformation might be completed; the second was, at the time of conviction, above the age specified by the act, and could not be sentenced to a Reformatory; but being an orphan, and as it was her first conviction, she was admitted here after the expiration of her sentence of imprisonment in the gaol, on the recommendation of a benevolent judge; the two others were placed here by charitable persons, who pay a small pension for their support; one after having undergone three years penal servitude for arson; the other, fourteen months' imprisonment for being privy to a robbery committed by her two sisters. These four girls, all from eighteen to twenty years of age, would be fit subjects for emigration; but not having been committed here under the Act 21st and 22nd Victoria, chap, 103, and not paid for by Government, are consequently not entitled to aid for emigration from the funds of the Institution. The donations received in the two first cases, and the pension paid for the two latter, are entered in our account as 'Donations and Subscriptions'; and the maintenance of these girls are reckoned in the general 'Expenditure'.

Nine girls have been received here since the publication of our first report. Each of these poor fallen creatures have reason, justly and fervently, to thank Divine Providence – and will, we trust, do so – for having chosen them to benefit by the advantages of the charitable 'Reformatory System', by which they may re-establish their lost characters, and 'cease to do evil, and learn to do good'. The following details of particular cases will not be devoid of interest fort those benevolent persons who co-operate directly or indirectly in this 'labour of love'.

The friends of M. are in indigent circumstances, but bear an excellent character. The depravity of this girl was considered so great a disgrace, that the real name of the family has never been allowed to transpire. M., notwithstanding her vice and criminality, has carefully guarded her parents' secret; and is known here only by the alias adopted at the time of her conviction. She was sentenced to a Dublin Reformatory, where she gave considerable trouble to those in charge, and serious scandal to the other girls. After a short stay, she was removed to an hospital, and remained there two months. When a cure was effected, she was transferred here by order of the Chief Secretary. For several weeks after her reception M. feigned insanity, acts of violence were of constant occurrence; her language and songs were worse than had previously been heard from the most degraded of our poor children. The case appeared hopeless, until at length we perceived in her nature a certain susceptibility of attachment, which we cultivated – an oasis in a desert. In proportion as these better feelings were developed, she became less violent; and longer intervals of calm permitted us to allow her to associate with a few of the other girls. During the last two months, there has been no outbreak of blasphemy, obscenity, or passion; and M. is now an example to her companions in the Probationary Class by her industry and self-control.

T. is the daughter of a poor widow, who labours hard to support herself and her younger children. This girl was employed as a furniture-polisher. Going to and from her work she met with bad company, was led through the different phases of vice, left her mother's dwelling to reside with her immoral associates, became an expert thief, and was finally convicted and sentenced to a Reformatory. One of her companions, convicted at the same time, was sent to a Reformatory in Dublin; and the magistrates, to ensure separation, sent T. here. This arrangement did not coincide with her wishes, and she came with a fixed determination to make her escape. The new buildings were not then completed, and we were badly prepared to counteract so large an amount of dexterity, cunning, and *ruse*; a few days' experience, however, proved that a *cell* with barred windows and prison locks was of temporary necessity. Forks, spoons, slates, snuffers, etc, became implements to effect the *one* end – her escape; ordinary locks were repeatedly slipped with skill and expertness. On one occasion, T. was placed in a room separated by a wooden partition: a small plank was cleverly removed; she jumped from the window of the adjoining apartment (a distance of 14 feet from the ground) and was in the act of scaling the garden wall when the rustling of the shrubs attracted attention. Three times, during the first month, T. succeeded in absconding, notwithstanding the utmost vigilance; and would have made her way back to Dublin but for the constant watch which was kept over her. In her last excursion, she so far disguised the form and colour of her garments that they could no longer be distinguished as the Reformatory costume. The singular and scandalous stories related by this girl of her mother caused us to make inquiries relative to the woman; but the result was most favourable to her character; and her letters to her daughter confirmed all previous statements. Whether these tales were the insane wanderings of a diseased imagination, or the inventions of a singularly depraved heart, He alone 'who knows the secret of hearts' can decide. A short interval of better conduct afforded us the opportunity of a relaxation of discipline; and T. was allowed to associate all day with some of the other children. By degrees she showed a slight desire to improve herself in reading and writing. The winter months are an unpropitious time for travelling on foot, and we were then enabled to give her a certain amount of liberty, and so to work more successfully on her better qualities. From these small beginnings this girl has so far progressed that she is now giving satisfaction in the Probationary Class, and is on the list for promotion to the Class of Honour.

F., fifteen and a-half years of age, was convicted of larceny. Although on her first conviction, it would be impossible to imagine a more pitiable object of ignorance, misery, and ill-health – but still a human soul, created to the image of God himself, and redeemed by the precious blood of his Divine Son, was contained within that loathsome being, reduced below the level of the brute creation. No reliable information has been obtained of this poor creature's family or parentage; her whole life appears to have been passed as a vagrant and mendicant, exposed to the degrading influence of those unfortunate beings who crowd the lanes and by-ways of a large commercial town. She had not the most simple notions of religion, or of the distinction between right and wrong; and was ignorant of every kind of useful occupation – even the humblest household duty. During the nine months which this girl has spent with us, she has learned an elementary catechism, committed to memory portions of Holy Writ, can read and write a little, knits, and is beginning to sew and mark; she can now manage to perform household duties. The foul cutaneous disease which covered her emaciated form is nearly eradicated from the system; and her physical appearance is rapidly improving.

D. has the misfortune to have a bad mother! Can we wonder that the poor child is depraved and vicious? She has seen the hard earnings of an honest and industrious father expended by her mother on intoxicating liquors; has been initiated into all the tricks and dissimulation to be practised in order to receive clandestinely the frequent visits of the profligate and the criminal; has had her youthful ears profaned under the parental roof, by the curses and obscene language of her mother's daily visitors; has witnessed the degradation of the being who should, above all others, have commanded her love and respect. Where could she have learned to serve God? to possess honesty, industry, sobriety, and truthfulness? to cherish purity and modesty as the brightest ornaments of her sex – the only dowry of the poor man's daughter? Years of untiring efforts and patience are necessary to obliterate *first* impressions. Human nature, in its fallen state, clings tenaciously to vicious habits and inclinations. In the present case, the poor girl is, happily, *young*, and eager for instruction.

G. is the only child of a widowed mother, too infirm for labour. Her early education appears to have been attended to, and she has good natural qualities; but mendicancy, habits of idleness, and bad associates, have seriously deteriorated the work commenced. The charge against her was a serious one – housebreaking and robbery. She was tried at the Quarter Sessions, found guilty, and sentenced to a Reformatory. It is to be regretted that her sentence is a *short* one, as it will require much time and a strong sense of religion to overcome her strong and marked propensity for stealing. Although improved in many ways, she still continues to pilfer articles of small value, as if from instinct.

F. is also the daughter of an honest widow. She was sent to a good school, can read and write well, and was for many years surrounded by healthy moral influences. However, she fell into bad company; and at a time when strong passions would have required a skilful and experienced hand to guide, forcibly withdrew from her mother's care, rushed madly into vice of the most degrading kind, and in a very short career, reaped the worst results. She was then convicted of larceny, sentenced to a Dublin Reformatory, absconded, was imprisoned for the offence, and ultimately transferred to our care by an order of the Chief Secretary. A foul disease obliges us to keep her from the other children; but in this partial solitude the pious lessons of her childhood will, we trust, return to her mind, and He, who, in His almighty power, can 'draw good from evil', may mercifully lead her to a sincere detestation of, and profound sorrow for, the past. In the meantime, she is usefully employing her time in learning different kinds of needlework; and is grateful for all that is being done to improve her physical state.

E. is an orphan, without friends or relatives, except one brother, who belongs to a regiment stationed in India. It is unnecessary to say that she has been sadly neglected. A natural propensity for stealing has 'grown with her growth, and strengthened with her strength'. She has been employed from year to year as a little drudge in the humble families of her native town. Her employers over-looked much in consideration of her friendless position, and fearing worse consequences if they ceased to protect her. At length she stole a quantity of wearing apparel, was prosecuted, and sentenced to three months' imprisonment in a jail – her age, 18 years, not permitting her to be sentenced under the Reformatory Act. Her character was then irretrievably lost, and a career of infamy alone was open to the poor creature. These facts were brought under our notice by charitable persons, and a situation was found in a town where the poor girl was not known; her antecedents were confided only to the benevolent family who engaged her, and who hoped the lesson she had received might suffice. However, she again indulged in her propensity for pilfering, and, as a last resource, we admitted her gratuitously into our Reformatory School. Her conduct here is satisfactory in many respects. She is much less depraved than were the greater number of our poor children, and is earnestly endeavouring to overcome the *one* great evil propensity.

At present the average age of the inmates of our Institution, calcu-lated from official documents is 15 and three-quarter years; but it would be impossible to ascertain the true ages of girls whose con-stitutions have suffered so much neglect and disease.

Thirteen of the juveniles are from the city of Dublin, two of whom are not under sentence, and consequently are dependent on the charity of the Institution; ten are from Belfast; the others from Longford, Fermanagh, Tyrone, Roscommon, Kildare, and Londonderry.

Twenty are sentenced for five years, four for four years, one for three years, and one for two years.

The parents of five who were convicted in Dublin and one in Belfast pay towards the support of their children.

Nineteen have lost one or both parents – i.e. fourteen their fathers, two their mothers, and three both parents.

None of our juveniles have as yet completed their sentence, but that of the girl committed here for two years will expire on the 19th April, 1862. Three left the Reformatory under circumstances detailed in our first Report, pages 4, 5, and 6. One who had undergone penal servitude, and who remained twelve months here, not under sentence, has been recently received as children's maid in an excellent family, and is giving satisfaction.

We have one girl who, it is to be feared, is incorrigible. She has entered upon the third year of her sentence, and, though a few days' improvement sometimes permits us to hope for the best, her general conduct would lead to suppose that a change of heart has not been effected in her. We consider that removal from the Reformatory to the Convict Prison at Mountjoy, Dublin, where harsher measures could be employed, might, if it could legally be effected, prove efficacious in those few but melancholy cases in which instruction, religion, emulation, kindness, and even the slight punishments applicable to *children*, fail in ensuring satisfactory results . . .

. . . Of our thirty children, *three* only could return to their family with any reasonable degree of security; doubtless the percentage is at the same low figure in the other Reformatories. Our position in a rural district, removed from the baneful influences of large cities, has immense advantages for the training process; but the future resources are lessened in proportion; and it will require years of patience to smooth down and reason away old prepossessions, founded, here more than elsewhere, on religious prejudices.

As far as the *Ulster* Reformatory is concerned, it would be necessary, for the complete success of the system, to have –

1st – A *Patronage Society*, formed of influential ladies, who would procure situations in their own localities for such of the discharged juveniles who have distinguished themselves as to conduct, and can be *well* recommended as servants for good families. Care to be taken that each girl be far removed from her parents, if vicious, and from all previous evil associations.

2nd – An *Extern Industrial* Establishment attached to the Reformatory, where very young girls – those of inferior capacity and those of delicate health – could remain voluntarily after the expiration of their sentence, under the guidance of those persons who had been chosen as the instruments of their reformation. Each girl to earn her support in an independent manner, to be the mistress of her little earnings, and to enjoy, in every way, the privileges of liberty. Such girls to lodge with respectable, though struggling, families in the town. This little establishment to be also a resource for the first class of girls waiting for a situation.

3rd – A *System of Emigration* for such cases as it may be desirable or necessary to enable to emigrate, ensuring aid and protection for the voyage, providing an industrial home until permanent employment can be procured, and exercising a careful supervision during the first few years of residence in the new country. . . .

We have at present in this Reformatory twenty juveniles under sentence, and paid for by Government. We have also one whose sentence has expired, and consequently is not paid for, but who has obtained a refuge amongst us until some provision can be made for her. She had completed a short sentence in a Dublin Reformatory, but too short to make an impression sufficiently permanent. She is now going on well, and we hope the care bestowed on her may not be in vain.

A benevolent judge has also induced us to receive, on her discharge from prison, a girl sentenced by him at the late assizes, who was above the age, to be committed under the act, to a Reformatory School, but who must inevitably perish if there were no home to receive her.

The maintenance of these two girls, and similar cases, will press heavily on the benevolence of private individuals, but they come within the scope of the objects for which we have devoted our lives.

SR GENEVIEVE BEALE

Manager
Spark's Lake Reformatory,
Monaghan.
25th March, 1861.

ANON., 'ST JOSEPH'S INDUSTRIAL INSTITUTE AND THE WORKHOUSE ORPHANS'

At first it had been contemplated to train them for domestic service; but a little experience showed that no more unsuitable destination could be devised for them. Girls of this class are stupid to the last degree, from the want of having their natural faculties called into exercise; and they are so totally devoid of knowledge of the common things of life, that they make the effect at first of being completely deprived of ordinary intelligence. Most of them have never seen the interior of a dwelling-house, have never handled a breakable article, or used a knife and fork; consequently they are so awkward, that they destroy a considerable amount of property, 'buying experience at famine prices', and often seriously injuring themselves; one can imagine it would take a considerable time to train a cook who never saw a pot put on the fire, or beheld a whole joint of meat in its integrity, or vegetables in their natural form; or a housemaid who could not go up or down stairs without falling; or a nursery maid who perhaps had never laid eyes on an infant in her life. It was soon discovered that a course of rudimental object-lessons should be gone through, before one of them could be trusted to execute the most trifling order or commission. What could be expected from a girl, who, never having seen a railway train in her life, could not contain her terror and surprise at being put into one? Or from another who had indeed seen snow on the roof and flagways of the Union Mansion, yet innocently asking on finding the whole country white after a fall, 'How will the dust be got off the trees?' or again from a third, who, accustomed only to the workhouse style of serving repast – the dry portion in nets, and the liquid in tin porringers, being desired to bring up potatoes to the dining-room, made her appearance carrying saucepan and all?

Very difficult too it is to teach these girls the value of property. Naturally they know nothing of the use of money. As long as they can recollect, everything has been supplied to them, they know not how – food, clothing, and so on. The want of the half-penny, which want sharpens the wit of every scapegrace about the streets, never tempted or troubled them; consequently their utter indifference, no matter what amount of mischief they may achieve, is equally perplexing and tantalising to those in charge of them.

Their notion of dependence and independence are curiously awry. One of the most sensible of the set thought proper to boast one day of her brothers being well off in the world. It was remarked that if that were the case, it was wonder they would leave their mother in the workhouse. 'Oh, indeed', said the girl, with the most conceited air imaginable, 'my mother would never go to them; she's a great deal too independent for that!'

Stupidity and awkwardness, confirmed into habit, are not peculiarities likely to be long endured by masters or mistresses even of the fairest temper; but the list of objections is not completed until violent passion and obstinate sulk are added. This, perhaps, is the most difficult thing to get over, and requires a particular study of individual character which, many persons are not competent, or patient enough to exercise. Those who have experience of children are fully aware, that while boys may be governed *en masse*, influenced by a general appeal, and led on by the public opinion of the school-room, girls cannot be so taken. They require to be trained separately and singly; nature will have it so; and any attempt to ignore that law, stops the machinery at once. Now, in the workhouse, where girls, to the number of some hundreds, are shut up, with no higher order of influence brought to bear upon them than the strong hand of the salaried overseers, no gentler sway exercised than the scant word of approval now and then accorded to the least troublesome of the lot; where they are driven to the hall, or turned out to the yard, or ordered to this or that ward like a flock of sheep – it is plain assuredly, that whatever may have been the innate difference of temper and disposition, the outer character must inevitably tend to conform to a certain type, and that not of the best.

The rule is so cut out that there is little choice left. The girl has only to choose whether she will obey orders at once without a word or be made to do so with sharp pin and howling. She may let what gall she likes fester the inner life, under the pressure of what is dimly perceived to be injustice and tyranny; she may choke with despair when she would fain escape but finds no outlet. Sooner or later, that doggedness and darkness which distinguishes the class, over-crusts the whole character.

Coming thus before the mistress of a household, amidst the hurry and preoccupation of daily life, the girl can turn out no otherwise than incomprehensible and unmanageable. Coming into an institution, the business of which is to deal with difficult cases, and overcome with patience and hourly Christian influence the spirit of evil, the obstinate, surly creatures have a better chance. The only way is to believe firmly that the girl was born with a heart and feelings like other people; and seek out these buried treasures at any cost. One gets into deep soundings, but the search is seldom altogether in vain.

Source: Irish Quarterly Review, 9 January 1859.

TWELVE PRACTICAL RULES FOR THE TEACHERS
OF NATIONAL SCHOOLS

1. The Teachers of National Schools are required – To keep at least one copy of the *general lesson* suspended conspicuously in the School-room, and to inculcate the principles contained in it on the minds of their Pupils.

2. To exclude from the School, except at the hours set apart for Religious Instruction, all Catechisms and Books inculcating peculiar religious opinions.

3. To avoid fairs, markets, and meetings – but, above all, *political* meetings of every kind; to abstain from controversy; and to do nothing either in or out of School which might have a tendency to confine it to any one denomination of Children.

4. To keep the Register, Report Book, and Class Lists accurately and neatly, and according to the precise form prescribed by the Board.

5. To classify the Children according to the National School Books; to study those Books themselves; and to teach according to the improved method, as pointed out in their several prefaces.

6. To observe themselves, and to impress upon the minds of their Pupils, the great role of regularity and order – *a time and a place for every thing and every thing in its proper time and place*.

7. To promote both by precept and example, *cleanliness, neatness,* and decency. To effect this, the Teachers should set an example of cleanliness and neatness in their own persons, and in the state and general appearance of their Schools. They should also satisfy themselves, by personal inspection every morning, that the Children have had their hands and faces washed, their hair combed, and clothes cleaned, and, when necessary, mended. The School apartments, too, should be swept and dusted every *evening*; and white-washed at least once a year.

8. To pay strictest attention to the morals and general conduct of their pupils, and to omit no opportunity of inculcating the principles of *truth* and *honesty*: the duties of respect to superiors, and obedience to all persons placed in authority over them.

9. To evince a regard for the improvement and general welfare of their Pupils, to treat them with kindness, combined with firmness, and to aim at governing them by their affections and reason, rather than by harshness and severity.

10. To cultivate kindly and affectionate feelings among their Pupils; to discountenance quarrelling, cruelty to animals, and every approach to vice.
11. To record in the School Report Book the amount of all grants made by the Board, and the purposes for which they were made.
12. To take strict care of the *Free Stock* of Books granted by the Board; and to endeavour to keep the School constantly supplied with National School Books and Requisites, for sale to the Children, at the reduced price charged by the Commissioners.

Source: *Thirteenth Report of the Commissioners of National Education in Ireland*, 1846, pp. 132–3.

CONVENT NATIONAL SCHOOLS AND FEMALE EDUCATION: COMMENTS OF AN INSPECTOR

Mr Nixon, Tralee District, says, in reference to reading, including oral spelling and explanation:

In many schools the reading was unsatisfactory, owing principally to a bad accent and incorrect pronunciation; and I have constantly endeavoured, in the course of my inspection, to impress upon the teachers that the highest importance is attached to good reading, and that, therefore, they should give the reading their most careful attention. After finishing the reading lesson, the pupils of each class are exercised in oral spelling and in explanation of words. In oral spelling the answer is usually respectable, but in the meaning of words, great deficiency is frequently shown.

Penmanship – Writing is taught with much care in this part of the country, and with few exceptions, both teachers and pupils write well; in the convent schools particularly, the writing of the senior classes is excellent, both as regards execution and style. It would, in my opinion, be a very great improvement, and would also economise much time, if the copy books were so prepared as to have the precedent or copy line at the top of each page, and similar to those now in use in many respectable schools in large towns, but which are not in connection with the National Board.

Arithmetic – In too many cases this branch is not taught with that degree of care that the subject requires. It is made a dry exercise of the memory, and pupils are not infrequently found unable to account for the several steps of the process in some of the simplest questions in the compound rules and proportion, much less to give anything like the reason of the rule by which such questions are solved. It has always been my object, in examining upon this most necessary branch of knowledge, to see that the pupils are well grounded in the elementary principles, and are made to possess a correct notion of notation and numeration, as well as to have been made acquainted with the more useful tables; and this much once acquired, the study of arithmetic, under a judicious teacher, becomes to the youthful mind a profitable and a pleasing intellectual exercise.

Mr O'Loughlin, Mallow District, says, in reference to reading, including oral spelling and explanation:

Generally speaking, the reading is coarse, monotonous, and mechanical. Many of the teachers pronounce incorrectly – still more do the pupils. This, however, is only a secondary defect, though still an important one. What I mainly find fault with is, that the pupils repeat the words without understanding either the individual or collective sense of them. Hence, it is, that as reading is the source of most of their knowledge, the latter is the same half-understood thing as the former.

Penmanship – As writing is a purely mechanical operation, the main things essential to success in it are proper appliances, taste, and practice. The last is amply provided for by the every-day arrangements of the schools. Taste, in a matter where there is room for so little variety, is but another name for attention, and is, there-fore, always at command; proper appliances are still, I regret to say, by no means so common in the schools as they ought to be. Paper is seldom superabundant; and notwithstanding the advantages offered by the Board, generally shows a large proportion of the rubbish purchased in the shops; the ink is invariably scarce, and so curdled and gritty as to be almost unfit for use; the pens are, in a word, abominable – mere rusty bits of iron, which, scraping, sticking, and spattering, make writing a physical impossibility. In order not to disfigure my note-book with them and the ink, I have always been obliged to carry about with me some for my own use . . .

Source: *Special Report of Convent Schools in Connection with the Board of National Education* HC 1864 (405), p. xivi.

'THE EDUCATION OF WOMEN' BY ISABELLA M.S. TOD

Why should women be left out of account? Whatever the reasons may be, all friends of education, all who care more for the education of the people than for carrying out any particular theory as to the mode, should make a united effort to obtain consideration of the claims of women now, while the whole question is under discussion. If we neglect this opportunity, no other may occur for fifty years to come. The indifferentism will get hardened in new grooves, and we shall soon find ourselves worse off than English women, who are claiming and getting some share of school endowments, if not of college endowments. I am exceedingly thankful for the university examinations which have lately been instituted. They are the first really efficient help that has been offered to women and, though only in their infancy, have already done great good. But, after all, they only test teaching – they do not give it. Considering that there are not, I suppose, above half-a-dozen schools or institutions in the country that are capable of preparing girls well, for the senior examinations at least, and that those who are working privately with friends or tutors are at a disadvantage in many ways, my wonder is that the average attainments of the candidates at these examinations has been so high. Of course, there have been exceptionally brilliant candidates, but these would have done well under any system. We must draw the attention of the government and the legislature to the facts of the case, and claim from them that in arranging for the higher education of one half of the nation they shall not shut out the other half from its advantages. Having been only this moment asked to bring the matter before you, I have no detailed scheme to suggest; but all the friends of education should take it into immediate consideration, to see what is the most practicable plan. No body in Ireland has a better right to take the lead in such a movement than the Queen's Institute; and it would be well that those who feel the importance of the subject should communicate with Miss Corlett or the committee, and indicate their willingness to co-operate in any feasible plan for opening at least some of the advantages of collegiate education to women.

Source: *Journal of the Women's Education Union*, 1 (1873).

'THE INTERMEDIATE ACT AND THE EDUCATION OF GIRLS' BY ISABELLA MULVANY

Prior to the passing of the Act [Intermediate Act] the curriculum in the majority of girls' schools was limited to English, history and geography, French and the elementary arithmetic with music and drawing. Instruction in classics and mathematics was available in certainly not more than half a dozen schools located in large centres of population, such as Dublin or Belfast, and working on the lines of the not long established English high schools for girls. Such were the sources from which were to come the first intermediate candidates. The requirements of the Board were at the outset wisely arranged to be of a moderate nature, their policy being to encourage scholars to come into the system freely . . .

What do we note has taken place? Marked increase not alone in the numbers taking the more solid educational subjects such as Latin, German, geometry, and algebra, but also in the percentage of successes all round. Further, in the subjects which formed the old curriculum for girls, the work is more thorough; for example, the percentage of passes in English rises from 53.8 to 91.1; in French from 69 to 81; in music, from 71 in theoretical work alone to 98.8 in practical and theoretical work combined; and in drawing from 40 to 96.

Is further proof of the potency and success of the Intermediate Education Act in uplifting the educational level for girls necessary? Yet, to judge from the comparative numbers of boys and girls entering, there must be larger numbers of girls remaining outside the scheme than of those taking part in it. In 1905, 7,018 boys entered, 2,659 girls, a disparity which can only take origin in either the indifference or prejudice of the parent or guardian. It is difficult to overcome prejudice . . . but can we not try to remove indifference?

The programme now introduced contains the essential subjects of study for a sound secondary education and approaches more nearly to the satisfactory substructure for university work than any yet tried. Is this, then, not a fitting time for the parent to determine to get for his child the full benefit of any state measure of education, and also to co-operate with educationists in the effort to secure that the measure shall be adequate and stable. So long as the intermediate system is not backed up by the public support which should be accorded to it, so long will the secondary schools of Ireland be without adequate measure of state aid, aid which is now so liberally bestowed in the sister countries.

Source: *Irish Educational Review*, Vol. 1, No. 1, October 1907.

Bibliography

MANUSCRIPT MATERIAL

Archival Collections and Convent Annals

Dominican Archives, Cabra, Dublin
MS Immaculata Boarding School, Roll Book, 1889–92.
Prospectus of the Immaculata Boarding School (1835) in *Annals of the Dominican Convent, Saint Mary's Cabra 1647–1711.*

Dominican Archives, Griffith Avenue, Dublin
Eccles Street Convent Annals, 1883–1911.

Dominican Generalate Archives, Dublin
ALS William Walsh to Mother Prioress, 5 August 1893.
ALS William Walsh to Mother Patrick Shiel, 19 October 1909.
ALS Sister Mary Perpetual Succour to Mother Patrick, 25 July 1911.

Dublin Diocesan Archives
ALS Mother Peter McGrath to William Walsh, 30 October 1909, Walsh Papers.
ALS Mother Peter McGrath to William Walsh, 9 November 1909, Walsh Papers.

National Library of Ireland
MS Mary Hayden Diaries, 22 October 1884, MS 16,641.
MS Mary Hayden Diaries, 11 June 1902, MS 16,682.

National University of Ireland Archives, Dublin
Royal University of Ireland, Minutes of the Proceedings at the Meetings of the Senate, Vol. II, 1887–1896.

Saint Angela's College Archives, Cork
Ursuline Convent, Souvenir Book, 1952.

Trinity College, Dublin Library
TCD Library, College Muniments, Mun.Women/9.
TCD Library, College Muniments, P/1/2153.
TCD Library, College Muniments, P/1/2154.
TCD Library, College Muniments, P/1/2184.
TCD Library, College Muniments, P/1/2441[2].
TCD Library, College Muniments, P/1/2526[3].

Ursuline Convent Archives, Blackrock, Cork
MS Blackrock Convent Female National School, form no. 197, roll
  no. 5940.
MS Important Contracts, 1771.
ALS Sister M Charles Molony to Mother M Joseph McLoughlin, 18
  August 1836.
Ursuline Convent Annals, 1886–1929, Vol. III.

Victoria College Archives, Belfast
MS Minute Book of the Ladies' Institute Belfast, 22 September 1873.
MS Minute Book of the Ladies' Institute Belfast, 29 September 1882.
Margaret Byers, 'Girls' Education in Ireland: Its Progress, Hopes and
  Fears'. Paper read at the Annual Meeting of the Schoolmasters'
  Association, Dublin, 28 December 1888.

PARLIAMENTARY PAPERS

Reports of Commissions, Committees, and Parliamentary Debates

Select Committee on Foundation Schools and Education in Ireland (Wyse);
  1835 (630.) xxiii.
First Report of the Commissioners of Irish Education Inquiry, 1825 (400.)
  xii.
Second Report of the Commission of Inquiry (*Abstract of Returns in 1824,
  from the Protestant and Roman Catholic Clergy in Ireland, of the State
  of Education in their respective Parishes*), 1826–7 (12.) xii.
Report from the Select Committee on Criminal and Destitute Juveniles,
  1852 (515.) vii.
*Report of Her Majesty's Commissioners appointed to inquire into the
  Endowments, Funds and actual condition of Schools endowed for the
  purpose of education in Ireland* (Kildare) 1857–58; (2336 i–iv.) xxii.
  Parts i–iv.
*Special Reports to Commissioners of National Education in Ireland on
  Convent Schools, 1864*, [405] xlvi. 63.

Royal Commission on Nature and Extent of Instruction by Institutions in Ireland for Elementary or Primary Education, and Working of System of National Education (Powis); Vol. i., pt. i. Rep., App. 1870 [C.6] xxxviii pt. i. 1; Vol. i. pt. ii. App., *Special Reps. on Model Schools, Central Training Institution and Agricultural Schools* 1870 [C. 6a] xxviii pt. ii. 1; Vol. ii. *Reps. of Assistant Coms.* 1870 [C. 6–i] xxviii pt. ii. 381; Vol iii. *Mins. of Ev.* 1870 [C.6–II] xxviii pt. iii. 1; Vol. iv. *Mins. of Ev.* 1870 [C. 6–iii] xxxviii pt. iv. 1; Vol. v. *Analysis of Ev., Index* 1870 [C.6–iv] xxviii pt. iv. 547; Vol. vi. *Educational Census* 1870 [C. 6–v] xxviii pt. v.1; Vol. vii. *Returns from National Bd. of Education* 1870 [C. 6–vi] xxviii pt. v. 361; Vol. viii *Miscellaneous Papers* 1870 [C.6–vii] xxviii pt. v. 917.

Census of Ireland 1871, *General Report* 1876 (c.1377.) lxxxi.

Hansard Parliamentary Debates, 3, Vol. ccxli, 8, 21 June 1878.

Report of the Intermediate Education Board for Ireland for 1879, 1880 (c.2600.) xxiii.

Report of the Intermediate Education Board for Ireland for 1885, 1886 (c.4688.) xxvi.

Report of the Intermediate Education Board for Ireland for 1900, 1901 (c.588.) xxi.

Report of the Intermediate Education Board for Ireland for 1910, 1911 (c. 5768.) xxi.

Report of the Commissioners appointed by the Lord Lieutenant of Ireland to inquire into the endowments, and condition of all schools endowed for the purpose of education in Ireland (Rosse) 1881 (c.2831.) xxv.

Royal Commission on Manual and Practical Instruction in Primary Schools under the Board of National Education in Ireland; First Report, Minutes of Evidence 1897 [C. 8383] [C. 8384] xliii.1 . . . *Final Report, Minutes of Evidence*, Apps. 1898 [C. 8923] [C. 8924] [C. 8925] xliv.1, 77, 531 (Belmore Commission). *Final Report of the Commissioners*; 1898.

First Report of the Commission on Intermediate Education (Ireland) with Appendix (Palles); 1899 (c.9116., c.9117.) xxii; *Final Report*, 1899 (c.9511.) xxii. 629; *Minutes of Evidence*; (c.9512.) xxiii.i; *Part II of Appendix to the Final Report*; 1899 (c. 9513.) xxiv.i.

Royal Commission on University Education (Ireland) (Robertson); First Report 1902 [C. 825–6.] xxxi. 21; *Second Report*; 1902 [C. 899–900.] xxxi. 459; *Third Report*; 1902 [C. 1228–9.] xxxii.i; *Final Report*; 1903 [C.1483–4.] xxxii.i.

Report of Mr F.H. Dale, His Majesty's Inspector of Schools, Board of Education, on Primary Education in Ireland, 1904 [Cd. 1981.] xx.

Report of Messrs F.H. Dale & T.A. Stephens, His Majesty's Inspectors of Schools, Board of Education, on Intermediate Education in Ireland, 1905 (C. 2546.) xxviii.

Royal Commission on Trinity College and the University of Dublin (Fry): 1906 (C. 3174, 3176.) lvi, 1907 (C. 3311–12.) xli.

Proposed Scheme for the Application of the Teachers' Salaries Grant, 1914 (C. 7368) lxiv.

Report of the Vice-Regal Committee on the conditions of Service and Remuneration of Teachers in Intermediate schools and on the distribution of grants from Public Funds for Intermediate Education in Ireland (Molony), 1919 (C. 66) xxi.

Vice-Regal Committee of Inquiry into Primary Education (Ireland) (Killanin), 1918; *Final Report of the Committee, Vol. I, Report*, 1919 (C. 60.) xxi; *Report of Committee, Vol. II, Summaries of Evidence, Memoranda and Returns*, 1919 (C. 178.) xxi.

Acts of Parliament

An Act to restrain foreign education (7 Will. c.4 (1695)).

An Act to prevent the further growth of popery (2 Anne c.6 (1703)).

An Act to enable Her Majesty to endow new colleges for the advancement of learning in Ireland (8 & 9 Vict. c. 66.)1845.

Bill to extend the Industrial Schools Act to Ireland, 1867 (17) iii; (102) ii; 1867–68 (6) ii.

Bill for the extension of university education in Ireland, 1873 (55) vi.

Bill, intituled, an Act to promote Intermediate Education 1878 (275) iii, and *Bill, intituled, an Act to amend the Intermediate Education (Ireland) Act, 1878* 1882 (258) ii.

The Intermediate Education (Ireland) Act, 1878 (41 & 42 Vict. c. 66).

Bill to improve national education in Ireland,1892 (c. 234) iv.

Bill to amend Law relating to Intermediate Education in Ireland, 1900 (c.210.) ii. {as amended in Cttee.} 1900 (315.) ii.

An Act to make further provision with respect to university education in Ireland, 1908 (8 Edw.VII.c.38).

The Intermediate Education (Ireland) Act, 1914 (4 & 5 Geo.V.c.29).

Government Reports

Third Report of the Commissioners of the Board of Education in Ireland (1809).

Fourteenth Report of the Commissioners of the Board of Education in Ireland (1812).

Reports of the Inspector of Charitable Institutions (1842).

First Report of the Commissioners of National Education in Ireland (1834).

Third Report of the Commissioners of National Education in Ireland (1836).

Eighteenth Report of the Commissioners of National Education in Ireland (1851).

Twentieth Report of the Commissioners of National Education in Ireland (1853).

Twenty-first Report of the Commissioners of National Education in Ireland (1854).

Twenty-seventh Report of the Commissioners of National Education in Ireland (1860).

Thirty-seventh Report of the Commissioners of National Education in Ireland (1870).

Eighteenth Report of the Inspector of Reformatory and Industrial Schools in Ireland (1880).

Nineteenth Report of the Inspector of Reformatory and Industrial Schools of Ireland (1881).

Forty-eighth Report of the Inspector of Reformatory and Industrial Schools of Ireland (1910).

Report of the Intermediate Education Board for Ireland for 1879 (1880).

Report of the Intermediate Education Board for Ireland for 1885 (1886).

Report of the Intermediate Education Board for Ireland for 1900 (1901).

Report of the Intermediate Education Board for Ireland for 1910 (1911).

Report of the Intermediate Education Board for Ireland for 1915 (1916).

Annual Report of the Commissioners of National Education (1902).

NON-FICTION PRINT SOURCES PUBLISHED BEFORE 1910

Textbooks and Manuals of Instruction

Reading Book for the Use of Female Schools (Dublin: Commissioners of National Education, 1850).

Girls' Reading Book for the Use of Schools (Dublin: Commissioners of National Education, 1864).

Fifth Reading Book for the Use of Schools (Dublin: Commissioners of National Education, 1869).

Manual for Needlework for Use in National Schools (Dublin: Commissioners of National Education, 1869).

Short Lessons in Domestic Science (Dublin: Commissioners of National Education, 1885).

Articles, Memorials and Reports

Annual Report of the House of Refuge, Baggot Street (1803).

An Old Convent Girl, 'A Word for the Convent Boarding Schools', *Fraser's Magazine*, Vol. x (1874).

(n.n.), 'Convent Boarding Schools for Young Ladies', *Fraser's Magazine*, Vol. ix (1874).

Daly, L., 'Women and the University Question', *New Ireland Review*, Vol. 17 (April 1902).

Fraser, W., 'The State of our Educational Enterprises: A Report of an Examination of the Working, Results, and Tendencies of the Chief Public Educational Experiments in Great Britain and Ireland' (Glasgow: Blackie and Son, 1858).

Hayden, M. and Sheehy Skeffington, H., 'Women in Universities: A Reply', *Irish Educational Review*, Vol. 1, No. 5 (February 1908).

Hayden, M. and Sheehy Skeffington, H., 'Women in Universities: A Further Reply', *Irish Educational Review*, Vol. 1, No. 7 (April 1908).

Joynt, M.S., 'Alice Oldham', *Alexandra College Guild Magazine*, (December 1907).

'Letters from Ireland, vi', *New Ireland Review*, Vol. (December 1901).

Meade, N., 'Women in Universities', *Irish Educational Review*, Vol. 1, No. 3 (January 1908).

Meade, N., 'Women in Universities: A Rejoinder', *Irish Educational Review*, Vol. 1, No. 6 (March 1908).

Memorial addressed to the Standing Committee of the Royal University of Ireland in the year 1899, by the Central Association of Irish Schoolmistresses and other Ladies Interested in Education, in *Robertson Commission, First Report, Minutes of Evidence, p. 395.*

Mulvany, I., 'The Intermediate Act and the Education of Girls', *Irish Educational Review*, Vol. 1, No. (October 1907).

Oldham, A., 'A Sketch of the Work of the Association of Irish Schoolmistresses and Other Ladies Interested in Education, from its Foundation in 1882 to the Year 1890', *Annual Report of the Association of Irish Schoolmistresses and Other Ladies Interested in Education* (Dublin: 1890).

Quin, Rev. T., 'Convent Schools, Correspondence' (Belfast: 'Morning News' Office, 1883).

Rolleston, T.W., 'National Ideals of Education', *New Ireland Review*, Vol. 17 (1902).

Russell, M., 'St Brigid's Orphans', *Irish Monthly*, 4 (1876).

(n.n.)'The Cultivation of Female Industry in Ireland', *Englishwoman's Journal*, Vol. ix (August 1862).

Tierney, M., 'The Revised Programme in National Schools', *New Ireland Review*, Vol. 15 (1901).

Tod, I.M.S., 'The Education of Women', *Journal of the Women's Education Union*, Vol. 1, (1873).

CONTEMPORARY NEWSPAPERS, PERIODICALS AND JOURNALS

Alexandra College Guild Magazine, (December 1907).
Englishwoman's Journal, Vol. ix (August 1862).
Fraser's Magazine, Vol. ix (1874).
Fraser's Magazine, Vol. x (1874).
Freeman's Journal (2 September 1886).
Freeman's Journal (1 July 1889).
Irish Educational Review, Vol. 1, No. 1 (October 1907).
Irish Educational Review, Vol. 1, No. 3 (January 1908).
Irish Educational Review, Vol. 1, No. 5 (February 1908).
Irish Educational Review, Vol. 1, No. 6 (March 1908).
Irish Educational Review, Vol. 1, No. 7 (April 1908).
Irish Quarterly Review, 9 (January 1859).
Journal of Education, (February 1907).
Journal of the Women's Education Union, Vol. 1, (1873).
Lady of the House (Christmas, 1903).
New Ireland Review, Vol. 15 (1901).
New Ireland Review, Vol. (December 1901).
New Ireland Review, Vol. 17 (April 1902).
The Irish Monthly, 4 (1876).
The Irish Times (8 October 1883).
The Nation (19 December 1898).

OTHER CONTEMPORARY PUBLICATIONS

Bremner, C.S., *Education of Girls and Women in Great Britain* (London: Swan Sonnenschein and Co., 1897).
Carleton, W., *Traits and Stories of the Irish Peasantry* (London: n.p., 1843).
Downes, Margaret Tierney, *The Case of the Catholic Lady Students of the Royal University Stated* (Dublin: E. Ponsonby, 1888).
Nulty, T., *The Relations Existing between Convent Schools and the Systems of Intermediate and Primary National Education* (Dublin: Browne and Nolan, 1884).
Register of Intermediate Teachers in Ireland (Dublin: Alex Thom, 1919).
Renault, J., *Les idées pédagogiques de Fénelon* (Paris: P. Lethielleux, 1879).
Skeffington, F.J.C., *A Forgotten Aspect of the University Question* (Dublin, n.p., 1901).

SECONDARY SOURCES

Books

Akenson, D., *The Irish Education Experiment* (London: Routledge and Kegan Paul, 1970).

Atkinson, N., *Irish Education: A History of Educational Institutions* (Dublin: Allen Figgis, 1969).

Barnes, J., *Irish Industrial Schools* (Dublin: Irish Academic Press, 1989).

Bowen, D., *The Protestant Crusade in Ireland, 1800–1870* (Dublin: Gill and Macmillan, 1988).

Brenan, M., *The Schools of Kildare and Leighlin, 1775–1835* (Dublin: M.H. Gill & Son, 1935).

Bresland, R.W., *The Backward Glance: C.S. Lewis and Ireland* (Belfast: Institute of Irish Studies, 1999).

Brittain, V., *Women at Oxford: A Fragment of History* (London: Harrap, 1960).

Clarke, Sr Ursula, *The Ursulines in Cork, 1771–1996* (Cork: Ursuline Convent, 1996).

Clear, C., *Nuns in Nineteenth-Century Ireland* (Dublin: Gill & Macmillan, 1987).

Colum, M., *Life and the Dream* (London: Macmillan, 1947).

Coolahan, J., *Irish Education: History and Structure* (Dublin: Institute of Public Administration, 1981).

— *The ASTI and Post-Primary Education in Ireland, 1909–1984* (Dublin: Cumann na Meánmhúinteoirí, Eire, 1984).

Corcoran, T., *Selected Texts on Education Systems in Ireland from the Close of the Middle Ages* (Dublin: Education Department, University College Dublin, 1928).

Cosgrove, A. and McCartney, D. (eds), *Studies in Irish History* (Dublin: University College Dublin, 1979).

Cullen, M. (ed.), *Girls Don't Do Honours: Irish Women in Education in the 19th and 20th Centuries* (Dublin: WEB, 1987).

Cullen, M. and Luddy, M. (eds), *Women, Power and Consciousness in 19th Century Ireland* (Dublin: Attic Press, 1995).

Cullen, M. and Luddy, M. (eds), *Female Activists: Irish Women and Change, 1900–1960* (Dublin: Woodfield Press, 2001).

Cullen, R. Owens, *A Social History of Women in Ireland, 1870–1970* (Dublin: Gill & Macmillan, 2005).

Curtin, C., Jackson, P. and O'Connor, B. (eds), *Gender in Irish Society* (Galway: Galway University Press, 1987).

Daly, M. and Dickson, D. (eds), *The Origins of Popular Literacy in Ireland: Language Change and Educational Development 1700–1920* (Dublin: Department of Modern History, Trinity College, Dublin, 1990).

Daly, M., *The Famine in Ireland* (Dublin: Historical Association, 1986).

Davin, A., *Growing Up Poor: Home, School and Street in London, 1870–1914* (London: Rivers Oram, 1997).

Dowling, P.J., *The Hedge Schools of Ireland* (Cork: Mercier Press, 1968).

Dyhouse, C., *Girls Growing Up in Late Victorian and Edwardian England* (London: Routledge and Kegan Paul, 1981).

—, *No Distinction of Sex? Women in British Universities, 1870–1939* (London: UCL Press, 1995).

Fealy, G. (ed.), *Care to Remember: Nursing and Midwifery in Ireland* (Cork: Mercier Press, 2005).

Fletcher, S., *Feminists and Bureaucrats: A Study in the Development of Girls' Education in the Nineteenth Century* (Cambridge: Cambridge University Press, 1980).

Foley, T. and Boylan, T. (eds), *From Queen's College to National University: Essays Towards an Academic History of QUG/UCG/NUI-Galway* (Dublin: Four Courts Press, 1999).

Goldstrom, J.M., *The Social Content of Education 1808–1870: A Study of the Working Class School Reader in England and Ireland* (Shannon: Irish University Press, 1972).

Hirsch, P. and McBeth, M., *Teacher Training in Cambridge: The Initiatives of Oscar Browning and Elizabeth Hughes* (London: Woburn Press, 2004).

Hunt, F. (ed.), *Lessons for Life, The Schooling of Girls and Women, 1850–1950* (London: Blackwell, 1987).

Hyland, A. and Milne, K. (eds), *Irish Educational Documents*, Vol. I (Dublin: CICE, 1987).

Jones, M.G., *The Charity School Movement* (Cambridge: Cambridge University Press, 1938).

Kamm, J., *Hope Deferred: Girls' Education in English History* (London: Methuen, 1965).

Kelleher, M. and Murphy, J. (eds), *Gender Perspectives in Nineteenth-Century Ireland* (Dublin: Irish Academic Press, 1997).

Larkin, E., *The Making of the Roman Catholic Church in Ireland, 1850–1860* (Chapel Hill: University of North Carolina Press, 1980).

—, *The Catholic Church and the Emergence of the Modern Irish Political System, 1874–1879* (Dublin: Four Courts Press and Catholic University of America Press, 1996).

Luddy, M., *Women and Philanthropy in Nineteenth-Century Ireland* (Cambridge: Cambridge University Press, 1995).

—, *Women in Ireland, 1800–1918: A Documentary History* (Cork University Press, 1995).

MacAonghusa, P. and Ó Réagáin, L. (eds), *The Best of Pearse* (Cork: Mercier Press, 1967).

McCartney, D., *A National Idea: The History of University College Dublin* (Dublin: Gill & Macmillan, 1999).

MacCurtain, M. and O'Dowd, M. (eds), *Women in Early Modern Ireland* (Dublin: Wolfhound Press, 1991).

Macdona, A. (ed.), *Newman to New Woman: UCD Women Remember* (Dublin: New Ireland, 2002).

McElligott, T.J., *Secondary Education in Ireland, 1878–1922* (Dublin: Irish Academic Press, 1981).

McGrath, F., *Newman's University: Idea and Reality* (Dublin: Browne and Nolan, 1951).

McManus, A., *The Irish Hedge School and its Books, 1695–1831* (Dublin: Four Courts Press, 2002).

McMillan, N. (ed.), *Prometheus's Fire: A History of Scientific and Technological Education in Ireland* (Carlow: Tyndale Publications, 2000).

MacSuibhne, S., *Oblivious to the Dawn: Gender Themes in 19th Century National School Reading Books in Ireland, 1831–1900* (Sligo: FDR, 1996).

McWilliams Tullberg, R., *Women at Cambridge* (Cambridge: Cambridge University Press, revised edition, 1998).

Magray, M. Peckham, *The Transforming Power of the Nuns: Women, Religion and Cultural Change in Ireland, 1750–1900* (New York and Oxford: Oxford University Press, 1998).

Mason, M.R. and Simonton, D. (eds), *Women in Higher Education, Past, Present and Future* (Aberdeen: Aberdeen University Press, 1996).

Milne, K., *The Irish Charter Schools 1730–1830* (Dublin: Four Courts Press, 1997).

Moody, T.W. and Beckett, J.C., *Queen's Belfast, 1845–1949: The History of a University* (London: Faber & Faber, 1959).

Moore, Kingsmill H., *An Unwritten Chapter on the history of education being the history of the society for the education of the poor of Ireland generally known as the Kildare Place Society* (London: Macmillan, 1904).

Morrissey, T., *Towards a National University: William Delany S.J. (1835–1924)* (Dublin: Wolfhound Press, 1983).

Murphy, A.B. and Raftery, D. (eds), *Emily Davies: Collected Letters, 1861–1878* (Charlottesville and London: University of Virginia Press, 2004).

Murphy, J.A., *The College: A History of Queen's College/University College Cork, 1845–1995* (Cork: Cork University Press, 1995).

O'Connor, A.V. and Parkes, S.M. (eds), *Gladly Learn and Gladly Teach: A History of Alexandra College and School, 1866–1966* (Dublin: Blackwater Press, 1984).

O'Flanagan, P., Ferguson, P. and Whelan, K. (eds), *Rural Ireland, 1600–1900: Modernisation and Change* (Cork: Cork University Press, 1987).

Parkes, S.M. (ed.), *A Danger to the Men? A History of Women in Trinity College, Dublin, 1904–2004* (Dublin: Lilliput Press, 2004).

Paseta, S., *Before the Revolution: Nationalism, Social Change and Ireland's Catholic Elite* (Cork: Cork University Press, 1999).

Purser, O., *Women in Dublin University, 1904–1954* (Dublin: Dublin University Press, 1954).

Raftery, D., *Women and Learning in English Writing, 1600–1900* (Dublin: Four Courts Press, 1997).

Robins, J., *The Lost Children: A Study of Charity Children in Ireland, 1700–1900* (Dublin: Institute of Public Administration, 1980).

Spender, D. (ed.), *The Education Papers: Women's Quest for Equality in Britain, 1850–1912* (London: Routledge and Kegan Paul, 1981).

Tierney, M. (ed.), *Struggle with Fortune* (Dublin: Browne and Nolan, 1954).

Tuke, M., *A History of Bedford College for Women, 1849–1937* (Oxford: Oxford University Press, 1939).

Vaughan, W.E. (ed.), *A New History of Ireland*, Vol. VI: *Ireland under the Union, II, 1870–1921* (Oxford: Clarendon Press, 1996).

Walker, B. and McCreay, A., *Degrees of Excellence: The Story of Queen's Belfast, 1845–1995* (Belfast: Institute of Irish Studies, 1994).

Walsh, O., *Anglican Women in Dublin: Philanthropy, Politics and Education in the Early Twentieth Century* (Dublin: University College Dublin Press, 2005).

Ward, M., *Hanna Sheehy Skeffington: A Life* (Dublin: Attic Press, 1970).

Whelan, B. (ed.), *Women and Paid Work in Ireland, 1500–1930* (Dublin: Four Courts Press, 2000).

Articles, Chapters and Papers

Albisetti, J.C., 'Unlearned Lessons from the New World: English Views of American Co-education and Women's Colleges, c.1865–1910', *History of Education*, Vol. 29, No. 5 (2000).

Burstyn, J., 'Education and Sex: The Medical Case against Higher Education for Women in England, 1870–1900', *Proceedings of the American Philosophical Society*, Vol. 117 (1973).

Clear, C., 'Walls within Walls: Nuns in Nineteenth-Century Ireland', in C. Curtin, P. Jackson and B. O'Connor (eds), *Gender in Irish Society* (Galway: Galway University Press, 1987).

Corish, P., 'The Catholic Community in the Nineteenth Century', *Archivium Hibernicum*, 38 (1983).

—, 'The Development of the National School System, 1831–40', in A. Cosgrove and D. McCartney (eds), *Studies in Irish History* (Dublin: University College Dublin, 1979).

Daly, M., 'Literacy and Language Change in the Late Nineteenth and Early Twentieth Centuries', in M. Daly and D. Dickson (eds), *The Origins of Popular Literacy in Ireland: Language Change and Educational Development 1700–1920* (Dublin: Department of Modern History, Trinity College, Dublin, 1990).

Dyhouse, C., 'Good Wives and Little Mothers: Social Anxieties and the Schoolgirl's Curriculum, 1890–1920', *Oxford Review of Education*, Vol. 3, No. 3 (1977).

Fahey, T., 'Nuns in the Catholic Church in Ireland in the Nineteenth Century', in M. Cullen (ed.), *Girls Don't Do Honours: Irish Women in Education in the 19th and 20th Centuries* (Dublin: WEB, 1987).

Finn, I., 'Women in the Medical Profession in Ireland, 1876–1919', in B. Whelan (ed.), *Women and Paid Work in Ireland, 1500–1930* (Dublin: Four Courts Press, 1992).

Fitzpatrick, D., '"A Share of the Honeycomb": Education, Emigration and Irishwomen', in M. Daly and D. Dickson (eds), *The Origins of Popular Literacy in Ireland: Language Change and Educational Development 1700–1920* (Dublin: Department of Modern History, Trinity College, Dublin, 1990).

—, 'The Modernisation of the Irish Female', in P. O'Flanagan, P. Ferguson and K. Whelan (eds), *Rural Ireland, 1600–1900: Modernisation and Change* (Cork: Cork University Press, 1987).

Harford, J., 'The Movement for the Higher Education of Women in Ireland: Gender Equality or Denominational Rivalry?', *History of Education*, Vol. 34, No. 5 (2005).

—, 'The Movement for the Higher Education of Women in Ireland: The Role of Margaret Byers and Victoria College Belfast', *History of Education Researcher*, 75 (May 2005).

Logan, J., 'The Dimensions of Gender in Nineteenth Century Schooling', in M. Kelleher and J. Murphy (eds), *Gender Perspectives in Nineteenth-Century Ireland* (Dublin: Irish Academic Press, 1997).

—, 'Sufficient to their Needs: Literacy and Elementary Schooling in the Nineteenth Century', in M. Daly and D. Dickson (eds), *The Origins of Popular Literacy in Ireland: Language Change and Education Development 1700–1920* (Dublin: Department of Modern History, Trinity College, Dublin, 1990).

Luddy, M., 'An Agenda for Women's History, 1800–1900', *Irish Historical Studies*, Vol. 28, No. 109 (1992).

Luddy, M., 'Isabella M.S.Tod', in M. Cullen and M. Luddy (eds), *Women, Power and Consciousness in 19th Century Ireland* (Dublin: Attic Press, 1995).

Macken, M., 'Women in the University and the College: A Struggle within a Struggle' in Tierney, M. (ed.), *Struggle with Fortune* (Dublin: Browne and Nolan, 1954).

O'Connor, A.V., 'Anne Jellicoe (1823–1880)', in M. Cullen and M. Luddy (eds), *Women, Power and Consciousness in 19th Century Ireland* (Dublin: Attic Press, 1995).

—, 'The Revolution in Girls' Secondary Education in Ireland 1860–1910', in M. Cullen (ed.), *Girls Don't Do Honours: Irish Women in Education in the 19th and 20th Centuries* (Dublin: WEB, 1987).

Parkes, S.M., 'The Irish University Question', in W.E. Vaughan (ed.), *A New History of Ireland*, Vol. 6, *Ireland under the Union, II, 1870–1921* (Oxford: Clarendon Press, 1996).

—, 'Trinity College and the "Steamboat Ladies", 1904–07', in M.R. Mason and D. Simonton (eds), *Women and Higher Education, Past, Present and Future* (Aberdeen: Aberdeen University Press, 1996).

Pearse, P., 'The Murder Machine', in P. MacAonghusa and L. Ó Réagáin (eds), *The Best of Pearse* (Cork: Mercier Press, 1967).

Phillips, P., 'The Queen's Institute, Dublin (1861–1881), the First Technical College for Women in the British Isles', in N. McMillan (ed.), *Prometheus's Fire: A History of Scientific and Technological Education in Ireland* (Carlow: Tyndale Publications, 2000).

Raftery, D., 'Ideological Differences in the First Formal Programmes of Education for Roman Catholic and Protestant Women in Ireland', *Proceedings of the International Standing Conference of the History of Education* (Montreal: ISCHE, 1995).

—, 'The Nineteenth-Century Governess: Image and Reality', in B. Whelan (ed.), *Women and Paid Work in Ireland, 1500–1930* (Dublin: Four Courts Press, 2000).

— 'The Higher Education of Women in Ireland, 1860–1904', in S.M. Parkes (ed.), *A Danger to the Men? A History of Women in Trinity College, 1904–2004* (Dublin: Lilliput Press, 2004).

Ruane, M., 'Kathleen Lynn (1874–1955)', in M. Cullen and M. Luddy (eds), *Female Activists: Irish Women and Change 1900–1960* (Dublin: Woodfield Press, 2001).

Tod, I., 'On the Education of Girls of the Middle Classes', in D. Spender (ed.), *The Education Papers: Women's Quest for Equality in Britain 1850–1912* (London: Routledge and Kegan Paul, 1981).

Trimingham, Jack C., 'The Lay Sister in Educational History and Memory', *History of Education* Vol. 29, No. 3 (2000).

Walsh, L., 'Images of Women in Nineteenth-Century Textbooks', *Irish Educational Studies*, Vol. 4, No. 1 (1984).

JOURNALS

Archivium Hibernicum, 38 (1983).
History of Education, Vol. 29, No. 3 (2000).
History of Education, Vol. 34, No. 5 (2005).
History of Education Researcher No. 75 (May 2005).
Irish Educational Studies, Vol. 4, No. 1 (1984).
Oxford Review of Education, Vol. 3, No. 3 (1977).
Proceedings of the American Philosophical Society, Vol. 117 (1973).

UNPUBLISHED PAPERS, DISSERTATIONS AND THESES

Fahey, T., 'Female Asceticism in the Catholic Church: A Case Study of Nuns in Ireland in the Nineteenth Century', unpublished PhD thesis, University of Illinois (1981).

Hislop, H., 'The Kildare Place Society: An Irish Experiment in Popular Education', unpublished PhD Thesis, University of Dublin, Trinity College (1990).

Raftery, D. and Harford, J., 'Reading for Maidens and Maids: The Use of Eighteenth-Century Englishwomen's Writing in the Education of Irish Girls', University of Southampton Conference, 'Women's Writing in Britain, 1660–1830', July 2003.

Index

Page numbers in *italics* refer to illustrations, figures and tables

Alexandra College, Dublin
  background 69, 72, 73
  examinations 75, 76, 84, 110
  and higher education 89, 110, 127, 132
  objectives 73
  and Trinity College, Dublin 75
  university status 129, 131, 132, 133, 135
Alexandra School, Dublin 73, 84, 90
Anderson, Emily 137
Association of Irish Schoolmistresses and
  other Ladies Interested in Education
  (AISLIE) 85–6 *see also* Central
  Association of Irish Schoolmistresses
Association of Secondary Teachers, Ireland
  (ASTI) 97, 98, 100
Aylward, Margaret 19, 20

Barbauld, Hannah Letitia 17
Barlow, Jane 130
Beale, Dorothea 70–1, 74
Belfast Ladies' Institute 71, 74, 75, 78, 107,
  108, 111
Belmore Commission (1898) 57, *58*, 59–60, 61
Bible societies 20
Bird's Nest orphanages 20
Birrell, Augustine 97, 134–5
Blackrock Convent Female National School,
  Cork 34–5
'bluestockings' 105, 110
Boulter, Hugh 10
Boyd, Eliza 88, 91–2
Bryant, Sophie 130
Burney, Fanny 16
Buss, Frances 70–1, 74
Byers, Margaret
  background 72
  on examinations 84, 107
  on female education 38, 70, 71, 72
  on higher education 107, 118, 123
  honorary degree, Trinity College, Dublin
    130
  on intermediate education 78, 84, 88–9
  as Palles Commission witness 88–9
  on women's colleges 118, 123

Cairns, Lord 78
Carleton, William 14
Carrickmacross Female Industrial School 25
Carthy, Catherine 13

Casey, Judith 13
Castledermot Charter School, Kildare 11
Catholic Church
  concerns about Protestant education 19,
    20, 33, 83, 87, 112
  on female education 1–2, 36, 42, 56–7, 76,
    82–3, 92–3
  Hedge Schools 6, 10, 14
  and higher education 76, 106, 109,
    112–16, 124–5, 128, 135, 137–8
  industrial schools 19, 21, 24–6
  and intermediate education 71, 76, 79,
    82–3, 84, 87, 92–3
  on National System 34, 35–6, 37, 56–7
  orphanages 19, 20
  reformatories 19, 21, 22, 23
  voluntary agencies 6
Catholic University of Ireland, Dublin (later
  University College) 106, 110
Central Association of Irish
  Schoolmistresses (CAISM) 86, 89, 91,
  101, 117, 118, 121–2, 128–9
charitable institutions *see* voluntary agencies
Charter Schools
  background 6, 10–11
  conditions 12
  daily schedule 11, 12–13
  diseases 12
  funding 11
  government support 11
  ill-treatment 12
  labour *vs.* education 11, 12–13
  laundrywork 11
  literacy and numeracy skills 11, 12–13
  needlework 11
  objectives 10
  uniforms 11, 12
Cheap Book Society 16
Cheap Repository Tracts (More, 1795) 16
Chenevix Trench, Dr Richard 73
Christian Brothers 35, 37, 51
Church, Anna 117
Church Mission Society 20
Clarke, Dr Rosalind 112
Clash National School, Limerick *178*
co-educational schools 69–70
Cobwebs to Catch Flies (Fenn, 1783) 17
Colum, Mary 86–7
Commissioners for National Education in
  Ireland (CNEI) 19, 25, 26–7, 35, 46, 57, 59

Commissioners of the Board of Education 11–13, 33
compulsory education 39
Connaught *39*
Convent of Mercy, Killarney 38
convent schools
  background 50
  class distinctions 51, 53–5, 78
  curriculum 40, 41, 50–1, 52, 54–5, 86–7, 92–3
  domestic science 41–3, 54
  employment prospects 55–6
  examinations 78, 82–3, 84, 92
  female attendance 51
  gymnastics *183*
  literacy skills 158–9
  middle-class girls 53, 54, 55, 76, 78
  moral training 50, 51, 52–3, 54, 56
  in National System 34–5, 40, 41, 50–6, 158–9
  needlework 41, 54–5, *177*
  on 'non-denominational' education 34–5
  numeracy skills 41, 52, 158
  nuns as teachers 41, 51, 98
  for the poor 53–4, 55
  'struck off' register of national schools 35
cookery 23, 44–5, 56, 57, 59, 60–1
Corcoran, Mother Michael 113–14
Cork Street Reformatory for Protestant Girls 23
Corlett, Ada B. 73, 108, 161
Corry, James 78, 79, 80
Coyle, Frances 13
Crolly, William 35
Cullen, Paul 20, 22, 77, 78
Cunningham, Margaret 131

Dale and Stephens' Report on Intermediate Education (1905) 94–5
Daly, Lilian 122–3
Davies, Emily 74, 105
Deane, Margaret 124
Degani, Maria 137
Delany, Father William 115–16, 134
Dickson, Emily Winifred 116–17
Diocesan Free Schools 6, 69
diseases 12, 46
domestic science 41–3, 47, 54, 57, *58*, 59, 61
Dominican College, Dublin 113, 128
Dominican order 1, 70, 76, 84, 87, 113, 137–8
Downes, Margaret Tierney 112, 115
Doyle, James 35
Dublin Catholic Reformatory Committee 22
Dublin Foundling Hospital and Workhouse 6–8
Dublin Parochial Association 22
The Dublin Reading Book (1822) 17, 18
The Dublin Spelling Book (1819) 17–18
Duggan, Lucy 137

Edgeworth, Maria 17, 18
'The Education of Women' (Tod) 160

Endowed Schools' Commission (Kildare) (1857–58) 69
English, Adeline 117
Erasmus Smith Schools 6, 69
Everett, Alice 111
examinations
  as cause of stress 82–3, 87–8, 89, 91, 92
  in convent schools 78, 82–3, 84, 92
  higher education 74–5, 106–9, 110
  inequality issues 74–5, 83–4, 86, 106
  intermediate education
    background 1, 73–6, 77–8, 79–85, 87–93, 94, 100–1
    debated 74, 77–8, 82–3, 85–6, 87–93, 94
    defended 74, 78, 84, 85–6, 96–7, 100–1, 161
  and middle-classes 78

Female Orphan House, Dublin 19
Fenn, Lady Eleanor 17
Fleury, Eleonora 116
Foster, John Leslie 33
The Friendly Gift for Servants (1817) 17
Fry Commission (1907) 132–3, 139

Gallaher, Fannie 80
gendered education 36, 40–5, 59–62
Girls Reading Book for Use of Schools (1864) 44–5
Gladstone, W.E. 79, 107
Gonner, Professor 126
Governesses' Association of Ireland (GAI) 75, 76
government
  on Catholic population 33
  and Charter Schools 11
  on higher education 117–22, 123–8, 132–3, 136, 139
  on intermediate education 76–80, 88–93, 94
  and Kildare Place Society Schools 19
  on National System 29, 33–4, 36–8, 51, 52, 57–60, 61
  and voluntary agencies 5, 34
  and workhouses 6, 9
Grange National School, Wicklow *182*
Granville, Earl 78
Great Famine (1845-49) 8, 9, 20, 24, 39
Grey, Maria 72
Gwynn, Lucy 130

Hamilton, Florence 111
Hanan, Ethel 132–3
Hanley, Mother Antonia 113
Harris, W.B. 119
Hayden, Mary 91, 110–11, 118, 120–1, 122, 135–6, 137
Haywood, Eliza 16
Hedge Schools
  background 14
  Catholic involvement 6, 10, 14
  curriculum 13, 14, 16
  literacy skills 14, 15–16

Hibernian Military School 20
Hicks-Beach, Sir Michael 76, 77
higher education
    campaigns for admission
        Queen's Colleges 108, 111–12
        Trinity College, Dublin 108, 109–10,
            128–33
        University College, Dublin 109–10,
            114–16, 128, 133–4
        see also Fry Commission; Robertson
            Commission
    Catholic involvement 76, 106, 109,
        112–16, 124–5, 128, 135, 137–8
    degrees 74–5, 106, 108, 109–11, 116, 125,
        127, 131
    detrimental effects? 105, 120–1, 122–3
    development 105–9, 112–14, 134–9 *see also*
        medicine below; Royal University
    employment prospects 105, 116, 120, 139
    in England 70, 74, 105–6, 131
    examinations 74–5, 106–9, 110
    fellowships 109–10, 120, 122
    government involvement 117–22, 123–8,
        132–3, 136, 139
    inequality issues 74–5, 106, 108, 109–10
    management positions 109, 118, 130, 131,
        133, 137, 139
    medicine 109, 111, 116–17, 125, 134
    opposition to 105, 109, 110, 115, 116
    Protestant involvement 123
    in USA 106
    women's colleges *vs.* co-education 117–18,
        119, 120, 121, 122–8, 132–3, 135–6, 139
History of the robins (Trimmer, 1819) 17
Hoey, Mother M. Louisa 114

Incorporated Society for Promoting English
    Protestant Schools in Ireland *see*
    Charter Schools
industrial schools
    background 21, 24
    case studies 153–5
    Catholic involvement 19, 21, 24–6
    curriculum 24–5, 26, 27, 28
    daily schedule 26, 27
    diet 26
    expansion 28, 29
    funding 25–6, 28, 29
    labour *vs.* education 24–5, 26, 27
    literacy skills 24, 25, 26, 27, 28
    needlework 24–5, 26, 28
    objectives 24, 153
    reform 29
Industrial Schools Act (1857) 29
inequality issues
    and the Catholic Church 42
    education management issues 80, 109
    examinations 74–5, 83–4, 86, 106
    higher education 74–5, 106, 108, 109–10
    teachers' salaries 38, 95

Infant's Friend (Fenn, 1800) 17
'The Intermediate Act and the Education of
    Girls' (Mulvany) 96–7, 161
intermediate education
    Catholic involvement 71, 76, 79, 82–3, 84,
        87, 92–3
    curriculum 75–6, 80–1, 83, 86–7, 88–9,
        92–3, 94, 100
    denominational problems 69, 76, 77
    development 69–72, 76–81
    in England 70–1
    examinations
        background 1, 73–6, 77–8, 79–85,
            87–93, 94, 100–1
        debated 74, 77–8, 82–3, 85–6, 87–93, 94
        defended 74, 78, 84, 85–6, 96–7,
            100–1, 161
        supposed stress factor 82–3, 87–8, 89,
            91, 92
    government involvement 76–80, 88–93, 94
    payment-by-results scheme 76, 82, 84–5,
        89–90, 101
    Protestant involvement 69–70, 71, 76, 77,
        79, 82, 93–4, 98
    state inspectorate schemes 88, 90, 91, 93,
        94, 99
Intermediate Education Board 80, 87
Intermediate Education (Ireland) Act (1878)
    1, 2, 39, 73, 76–9, 81, 87
Intermediate Education (Ireland) Act (1900) 93
Irish Association of Women Graduates
    (IAWG) 118–20, 127, 132, 133, 134, 137,
    138
Irish Education Act (1892) 39
Irish Federation of University Women 137
Irish language 18, 39, 79
Irish Poor Relief Act (1838) 8
Irish Sisters of Charity 20
Irish University Bill (1873) 107, 109, 115

Jellett, Eva 117
Jellicoe, Anne 70, 71, 72–3, 108
juvenile delinquency 21, 22

Keenan, Sir Patrick 76–7
Kildare Commission *see* Endowed Schools'
    Commission (1857–58)
Kildare Place Society Schools 5
    Catholic opposition 19, 33
    government support 19
    inappropriateness of materials 18
    language problems 18
    Protestant involvement 16–19
    reading and reading materials 16–18, 33
    teacher training 16, 33
Killanin Report (1919) 100
Kinsale Female Industrial School 26

Ladies' Association of Charity of St Vincent
    de Paul 20

Ladies' Collegiate School, Belfast (later
    Victoria College) 69, 72, 74, 75, 84, 107
Lancasterian Industrial National School for
    Females, Belfast 27–8
laundrywork 11, 23, 57, 59, 61
Lawless, Emily 130
Leinster *39*
Lessons for children from two to three years old
    (Barbauld, 1778) 17
literacy skills
    Charter Schools 11, 12–13
    convent schools 158–9
    Hedge Schools 14, 15–16
    industrial schools 24, 25, 26, 27, 28
    National System 36, 39–40, 46–7, 48, 49,
        158–9
    reformatories 24
    workhouses 46–7, 48, 49
Literary and Historical Society, University
    College 134
Literary and Historical Society, University
    College Dublin 134
Local Government Board for Ireland 50
Loreto College, Dublin 113–14, 115, 116, 118,
    124–5, 127, 128, 134
Loreto Convent National School, Bray 61
Loreto order 1, 70, 76, 84, 92, 113–14, 124–5,
    137–8
Lowther, James 77, 79
Lucas, Lizzy 20
Lynn, Kathleen 116

Macken, James 118, 124–5
Macken, Mary 137
Magee College, Londonderry 127, 135
Manual for Needlework (1869) 44, 45, *180–1*
Marshal, Ida 99
Maule, Bishop 10
Maurice, F.D. 70, 73
Maxwell, Constantia 130
McCabe, Dr 78
McElderry, Annie 118, 119
McHugh, Annie 99
McKillip, Margaret 88, 90, 124
Meade, Norah 135, 136
Mercy Convent, Queenstown *177*
Methodist Orphan Society 19
middle-class females
    convent schools 53, 54, 55, 76, 78
    educational opportunities 1, 2, 70, 71–2,
        76, 89
    employment prospects 55, 70, 71–2, 73
    examinations 78
Millstreet Industrial National School 26
Molloy, Right Rev. Monsignor 125
Molony Vice-Regal Committee on
    conditions of Service and
    Remuneration (1918) 98–100
Moran, D.P. 96
More, Hannah 16, 17

Mulvany, Isabella 73, 84, 88, 90, 96–7, 110,
    130, 161
Munster *39*
Murphy, Katherine 122
Murray, Daniel 35
Murray, Lindley 17, 18

National Board of Education 5, 25, 27, 37, 57
National System *178, 179, 182*
    absenteeism 36–7, 38–9, 40
    after Powis Commission 37–8
    'alternative' scheme (1889) *58*, 59–62
    Catholic involvement 34, 35–6, 37, 56–7
    convent schools 34–5, 40, 41, 50–6, 158–9
    cookery 44–5, 56, 57, 59, 60–1
    curriculum 36, 40–5, 50–1, 52, 54–5, 56–7,
        59 *see also* 'alternative' scheme above
    denominational problems 35–6
    development 33–4, 36
    educational standards 36, 37, 41
    employment prospects 55–7, 59
    female attendance 38–9, 40, 51, 60–1
    gendered education 36, 40–5, 59–62
    government involvement 29, 33–4, 36–8,
        51, 52, 57–60, 61
    labour *vs.* education 46–8
    laundrywork 57, 59, 61
    literacy skills 36, 39–40, 49, 158–9
    needlework 40, 41, 45, 47–8, 54–5, 57, *58*,
        59–60
    'non-denominational' character 34–5
    numeracy skills 40–1, 81, 158
    objectives 34, 35
    payment-by-results scheme 37–8, 57, 76
    practical *vs.* literary education 56–7,
        59–62
    reform 36–8
    Revised Programme of Instruction (1900)
        57, 59
    rules for teachers 156–7
    Special Industrial Departments 60
    teachers' salaries 38, 49, 51
    textbooks 42–5
    workhouse schools 45–50
National University of Ireland 98, 134–5,
    136–8
needlework
    Charter Schools 11
    convent schools 41, 54–5, *177*
    industrial schools 24–5, 26, 28
    National System 40, 41, 45, 47–8, 54–5,
        57, *58*, 59–60
    reformatories 23
    workhouses 47–8
'The Nine Graces' 110, *184*
numeracy skills
    Charter Schools 11, 12–13
    convent schools 41, 52, 158
    National System 40–1, 46, 52, 81, 158
    workhouses 46, 48

O'Connell, Daniel 33
O'Farrelly, Agnes M. 118–19, 132–3, 137
Oldham, Alice 86, 88, 91, 110, 118, 121–2, 128, 130–1
orphanages 6, 19–21, 50
O'Sullivan, Elizabeth 137
O'Sullivan, M.J. Donovan 137

Palles Commission on Intermediate Education (1898) 87–94
Pauper Children Act (1898) 50
pay schools *see* hedge schools
Pearse, Patrick 96
Perry, Alice 112
poor females
    Charter Schools 11, 13
    convent schools 53–4, 55
    employment prospects 10, 13, 20–1, 24–8, 55
    Hedge Schools 13, 14–15, 16
    industrial schools 23, 24–9
    Kildare Place Society Schools 16, 18
    orphanages 19, 20–1
    reformatories 22–4
    voluntary agencies 9
    in workhouses 6–9, 46–8
Poor Law Commission 48, 50
Powis Commission (1870) 9, 29, 36–8, 51, 52
Presbyterian Orphan Society 19
primary education 5, 29, 37, 56–7 *see also* National System; voluntary agencies
proselytism in education 10, 18–19, 20, 33, 34, 35
Protestants
    Charter Schools 10–13
    concerns about Catholic education 8, 10, 19
    educational involvement 1, 5–6
    higher education 123
    intermediate education 69–70, 71, 76, 77, 79, 82, 93–4, 98
    Kildare Place Society Schools 16–19
    orphanages 19–20, 50
    reading materials influenced 18–19
    reformatories 22, 23
    voluntary agencies 5–6, 17, 34
    workhouses 6–7, 8
Purser, Olive 130

Queen's Colleges 71, 106, 110, 111–12, 114, 116 *see also* Queen's University of Ireland
Queen's Institute, Dublin 73, 108, 161
Queen's University, Belfast (previously Queen's College, Belfast) 98, 135, 136–7
Queen's University of Ireland 74–5, 106, 107, 108

reading and reading materials 15, 16–18, 33
The Reading Book for Use of Female Schools (1854) 42–4

reformatories
    background 21–2
    case studies 146–52
    Catholic involvement 19, 21, 22, 23
    cookery 23
    daily schedule 23–4
    labour *vs.* education 24
    laundrywork 23
    literacy skills 24
    needlework 23
    objectives 21, 22, 24, 147
    Protestant involvement 22, 23
Reformatory Schools Act for Ireland (1858) 22
refuges 19, 21
Reichel, Dr H.R, 126
Reid, Elizabeth 70
Religious Tract Society 16
Reports of the Commissioners of Irish Education Inquiry 5, 8, 11–12, 16
Reports of the Commissioners of National Instruction 26
Reports of the Commissioners of the Board of Education in Ireland 11–13
Reports of the Inspector appointed to visit Reformatory and Industrial Schools in Ireland 29
Robertson Commission on University Education (1901–1903) 117–22, 123–8, 136, 139
Roscommon National School 179
Rowlette, Charlotte 99
Royal College of Science, Dublin 117
Royal Commission of Inquiry into Primary Education *see* Powis Commission
Royal Commission on Manual and Practical Instruction in Primary Schools *see* Belmore Commission
Royal Irish Association for Promoting the Training and Employment of Women 60
Royal Schools, Ulster 6, 69
Royal University of Ireland (RUI) 138
    background 2, 73, 109–11
    Catholic involvement 109, 115
    degrees for women 2, 109–10, 115, 121
    Fellows' lectures closed to women 110, 115, 121, 133–4
    fellowships 122
    and Fry Commission 132–3
    medicine 116
    and Robertson Commission 121, 122, 127
    women graduates 98, 110, 121, 122, 127, 138, 184
Russell, Hester 117
Ryan, Mary 99, 122, 137

Salmon, Dr George 129
secondary education *see* intermediate education
Secondary Teachers' Registration Council 97–8
Select Committee on Foundation Schools *see* Wyse Report

Sherwood, Mrs 16
Shiel, Mother Patrick 113
Short Lessons in Domestic Science (1885) 44
Sisters of Mercy 21, 24, 25–6, 26, 53, 54
Skeffington, Francis Sheehy 134
Skeffington, Hanna Sheehy 87, 134, 135–6
Smyly, Ellen 20
Society for Promoting Christian Knowledge
    (SPCK) 16
Spark's Lake Reformatory, Monaghan 146–52
St Angela's College and High School, Cork
    114
St Brigid's Orphanage 20
St Joseph's Female Orphanage 20
St Joseph's Reformatory for Roman Catholic
    Girls, Limerick 23
St Joseph's Reformatory School, Ballinasloe
    23, 24
St Mary's Industrial National School,
    Limerick 25–6, 153–5
St Mary's University College and High School,
    Dublin 113, 115, 116, 118, 121, 127, 134
Stanley Letter 34
Stansfield, Mr (MP) 79
'Steamboat Ladies' 131
Steele, Elizabeth 97, 99
Synge, Edward 10

Taylor, Charlotte 110
TCD Examinations for Women 75–6, 106–7
teachers
    at Hedge Schools 15
    at National Schools 25
    nuns in convent schools 41, 51, 98
    payment-by-results scheme
        intermediate education 76, 82, 84–5,
            89–90, 101
        National System 37–8, 57, 76
    qualification 52, 90, 91, 94–5, 96, 97
    registration 90, 91, 95, 96, 97–8, 101
    rules (National System) 156–7
    salaries
        intermediate education 77, 87, 94, 95,
            98, 99, 100, 101
        National System 38, 49, 51
        see also payment-by-results scheme
            above
    security of tenure 99–100
    teacher training 16, 27, 33, 37, 49, 55, 60,
        95–6
    in workhouse schools 48–9
The Teacher's Assistant (Trimmer) 17
Teachers' Salaries Grant 97, 98
Tennison, Bishop 10
textbooks 37, 42–5
Thompson, Mary (née Robertson) 117
Thurles Industrial School 26
Tipperary Union Girls School 46–7
Tod, Isabella 70, 71–2, 78, 107, 160
Trimmer, Sarah 16, 17, 18

Trinity College, Dublin 73, 74, 75–6, 106,
    108–9, 123–4, 127, 128–33

Ulster *39*
Ulster Schoolmistresses' Association 86, 89
Universities' Act (1908) 134–5, 136
University College, Dublin (previously
    Catholic University of Ireland) 114–15,
    128, 132, 133–4, 137 *see also* National
    University of Ireland
University Education (Ireland) Act (1879) 2,
    39, 109
Ursuline Convent School, Waterford *183*
Ursuline order 1, 70, 76, 84, 114

vagrant females 6, 21
Vaughan, Frances 137
Victoria College, Belfast (previously Ladies'
    Collegiate School) 38, 110, 123, 127
voluntary agencies
    Catholic involvement 6
    educational involvement 5–6
    government support 5, 34
    Protestant involvement 5–6, 17, 34
    see also named agencies

Wakefield, Priscilla 17
Walsh, Dr William 83, 112–13
White, Henrietta
    on examinations 90
    on higher education 118, 123–4, 128
    honorary degree, Trinity College 130
    on improvement of teachers' conditions
        97, 99
    on intermediate education 89, 90
    as Palles Commission witness 88, 89, 90
    on university status for Alexandra
        College 89, 123, 131, 132
    on women's colleges 118, 123–4, 128,
        132
Woodlock, Dr 78
workhouses and workhouse schools
    background 6, 7, 8
    boarding out 50
    conditions 6, 7, 8–9, 46
    daily schedule 8
    diseases 46
    domestic science 47
    female inhabitants 9, 153–5
    foundlings 7, 8, 9
    government involvement 6, 9
    labour *vs.* education 46–8
    literacy skills 46–7, 48, 49
    mortality rates 7
    needlework 47–8
    numeracy skills 46, 48
    Protestant involvement 6–7, 8
    reform 7
    teachers (female) 48–9
    uniforms 46
Wyse Report (1835) 69